AF656088

Performance Evaluation of Integrated Child Development Services in Himachal Pradesh

Performance Evaluation of Integrated Child Development Services in Himachal Pradesh

Mrs Rajiya Sultan

CRESCENT
PUBLISHING CORPORATION

Performance Evaluation of Integrated Child Development Services in Himachal Pradesh

© Reserved

Edition 2026

ISBN 978-93-87537-78-1

Published by:
CRESCENT PUBLISHING CORPORATION
4806/24, Mathur Lane,
Ansari Road, Darya Ganj,
New Delhi - 110 002
Ph.: 011 - 23244131
Mob.: + 91 - 9711991838, 9999021668
E-mail: crescentbook@gmail.com
Website: www.crescentpublishingcorp.weebly.com

Printed at:
Balaji Digital
Delhi

PREFACE

Children are the future of the country and therefore, their growth and development have to be looked after by all the sections of community. However, it is noticed that a large proportion of children face problem of under-nutrition or malnutrition. India is in the curious position of having very high levels of malnutrition despite of large stocks of food-grains from increased agricultural productivity. By far the biggest nutrition supplementation programme is the Integrated Child Development Services (ICDS). The National Policy for Children (1974) lays down that the State should provide adequate services to children before and after birth and also during the period of growth to ensure their full physical, mental and social development. This was in response to a shift in focus from 'child welfare' to 'Child Development' during the Fifth Five Year Plan (1974-79) which emphasis on integration and coordination of a multitude of inter-related services within the ambit of a broad-based objective. In pursuance of this policy, Integrated Child Development Services (ICDS) Scheme was launched on 2 October, 1975 by the Government of India as a centrally sponsored scheme of the Ministry of Women and Child development (earlier a department under Ministry of Human Resource Development). It is one of the world's largest programmes for Early Childhood Care and Education and represents country's commitment to its children and nursing mothers, its response to the challenge of providing Pre-school non-formal education on one hand and breaking the vicious cycle of malnutrition, morbidity, reduced learning capacity and mortality on the other. The ICDS is a self-selecting scheme and is open to all children below six years of age for their holistic development and pregnant and lactating mothers, irrespective of their economic status.

Integrated Child Development Services (ICDS) programme is being implemented in Himachal Pradesh in all Developmental Blocks of the State through 78 ICDS projects. The department is providing supplementary nutrition, nutrition and health education, immunization, health check-ups referred services and non-formal pre-school education.

The programme approaches a holistic child health comprising health, nutrition, and education components for pregnant women, lactating mothers, and children less than six years of age. The programme is implemented through a network of community- level Anganwadi Centres. The range of services targeted at young children and their mothers for growth monitoring, immunization, health check-ups and supplementary feeding as well as nutrition and health education to improve the childcare and feeding practices that mothers adopt. Pre-school education is provided to children between three and six years of age. Present research is completed in eight chapters.

First chapter discusses in detail demographic profile of Children & throws light on the concept of Child welfare status & evolution of ICDS Programme in India & Himachal Pradesh. This chapter also discussed in detail the literature related to topic. Various books, magazine, article etc. were reviewed before study. It also discussed about the importance of study, objectives of study, hypothesis, research methodology & chapterization in the end of chapter.

Second chapter discusses in detail about Organizational set up. At the central level Ministry of women and Child development is responsible for the implementation of Integrated Child Development Services in the Country. In Himachal Pradesh Department of Social Justice and Empowerment has the overall responsibility of implementing Integrated Child Development Services. It works for the socio-economic development of the women, child and weaker sections of the society. Himachal Pradesh has shown its concern for the welfare of children through setting a new directorate of Women and Child Development.

Third chapter examined Constitutional provisions, legislative measures ,Policies & Programmes for Child welfare in India. Constitutional provisions has been made for child welfare ,various legislative provisions has been made & various policies, programmes has been started for child protection and welfare and various laws has been passed for child protection .All these initiatives are discussed in this chapter. Government of Himachal Pradesh has been implementing various child development, child welfare and child protection programmes and schemes in the state.

Fourth chapter throws light on working of ICDS in Himachal. ICDS approaches a holistic child health comprising health, nutrition, and education elements for pregnant ladies, wet mothers, and children upto six years. The programme is enforced through a network of community- level Anganwadi Centres. The variety of services targeted at young children and their mothers for growth observations, immunization, health check-ups, supplementary feeding, nutrition and health education. Pre-school education is provided to children between 3 and 6 years of age. In this Chapter working of ICDS in Himachal Pradesh & Kangra District is discussed in detail.

Fifth chapter assesses the impact and implementation of ICDS programme,a sample of 350 respondents were selected. The sample respondents for the present study were 250 ICDS beneficiaries,100 Anganwadi Workers .An attempt has been made in this chapter to analyse the socio-economic background of the sample respondents with the help of some indicators such as, gender, age, marital status, size of family, family status, educational attainment, social classification, income etc.

Sixth Chapter analyses the perception of officials of ICDS .Perception of 100 Anganwadi workers regarding the working of ICDS is discussed in detail in this chapter. Informal interview of officials were also taken in order to gather various information pertaining to ICDS in study area.

Seventh Chapter analyses the perception of beneficiaries of ICDS. Perception of 250 beneficiaries who were beneficiaries under ICDS programmes were discussed and analysed in present Chapter.

Eight Chapter discusses in detail about findings of study & concludes by giving concrete suggestions for the effective functioning of ICDS in Himachal Pradesh.

India has been ranked at the 103rd position among 119 countries on the Global Hunger Index Report 2018 thus working of ICDS can play instrumental role in lacking hunger problem in effective manner as nation most valuable assets are healthy children and mother of society.

ACKNOWLEDGEMENTS

First of all I am thankful to the Almighty for his showered blessings. It gives me great pleasure to express my sincere and heartfelt thanks to all those who helped me during the period of my research. First and foremost, I feel pride and pleasure in putting on record a deep sense of gratitude to Professor Mamta Mokta, Department of Public Administration, Himachal Pradesh University, Shimla, under whose supervision, I completed this research work. She gave me the liberty to encroach in her precious time as and when I approached her for discussing the matters pertaining to this research work research, I received enlightenment, inspiration and encouragement through her guidance. Without her critical insight and scholastic suggestions, it would have been impossible to bring this work to existence. I feel fortunate to work under her supervision. Her role as a motivator and inspirer has enabled me to pursue this research for which I have no words to express my gratitude.

I extend my gratitude and thanks to faculty members, Department of Public Administration, chairperson Prof. Simmi Agnihotri, Prof. Sewa Singh Chauhan, Chairperson, Prof. S.K. Mahajan for their co-operation and words of encouragement during the execution of this research work.

I am also thanks full to our official staff of Department of Public Administration Mr. Sawroop Sharma & Mr. Sanjay Kumar.

It gives me heartiest pleasure to express my gratitude to CDPO, ACDPO, Supervisors Of ICDS, Block and Anganwari workers of Selected Blocks for their constant encouragement and scholarly suggestions which I received from them during this study.

Thanks are also due to the staff of Himachal Pradesh University Library for their valuable time assistance in making available the required library resources for use during this research.

It is difficult to find words to express my heartiest feelings of indebtedness towards my family Mummy, papa, bhaiya, bhabi, sisters, jiju and all children for their inspiration and encouragement not only during the course of this study but throughout my academic career.

I express my gratitude to my beloved Husband Mr. Rameez Kimta and my sweet and lucky son Rahil Kimta for their constant cooperation. I am warmly thankful to my father-in-law and mother-in-law, Monu, Zoya & Samad for their support and encouragement.

I am indebted to many scholars and authors whose scholarly writings and viewpoints have been used at various stages in this study. I should be failing in my duty if I do not place on record my gratitude to the respondents for their cooperation and help in extracting the primary data.

I am also thankful to all My Friends Mrs. Anju Devi, Mrs Seema, Itika, Satya, Teena, Pavneet, Khushi, Pradeep, Tripathi, Suman, & Tarsaim who always kept me nudging to complete this research successfully.

I feel extremely privileged in expressing my deep sense of gratitude to Mr. Tikal Sharma who has typed this thesis and also Dr. Vinod Kumar, Tabbassum Prolta and Ajay for their help and assistance.

Lastly, I would like to express my sincere apologies to all those people who have contributed to this work but their names do not find a mention here. Deep in my heart I owe them sincere thanks as well.

(Rajiya Sultan)

CONTENTS

LIST OF FIGURES

LIST OF MAPS

LIST OF GRAPHS

LIST OF CHARTS

LIST OF TABLES

LIST OF PHOTOS PLATE

ACRONYMS AND ABBREVIATIONS

ACDPO	-	Assistant Child Development and Project Officer
AWC	-	Anganwadi Centre
AWW	-	Anganwadi Worker
BCC	-	Behaviour Change Communication
BCPC	-	Block Child Protection committee
CDPO	-	Child Development and Project Officer
CARA	-	Central Adoption Resource Authority
DCPC	-	District Child Protection committee
DLIC	-	District Level Inspection Committee
DWCRA	-	Development of Women and Child in Rural Area
GSDP	-	Gross State Domestic Product
ICDS	-	Integrated Child Development Services
IGMSY	-	Indira Gandhi Matritva Sahyg Yojana
LOW	-	Low Birth Weight
MHFW	-	Ministry Of Health and Family Welfare
MWCD	-	Ministry of Women and Child Development
MW	-	Mega Watt
NCC	-	National Charter for Children

NCPCR	-	National commission for health for protection of child right
NFHS	-	National Family Health Survey
NHED	-	Nutrition, Health and Education
NIPCCD	-	National Institute of public cooperation and Child development
NICP	-	National Initiative for Child Protection
NISD	-	National Initiative of Social Defence
NPA	-	National Plan of Action for Children
ORT	-	Oral Rehydration Therapy
PHC	-	Primary Health Centre
PSE	-	Pre-School Education
SC	-	Scheduled Caste
SCPC	-	State Child Protection committee
SLIC	-	State Level Inspection Committee
SNP	-	Supplementary Nutrition Programme
THR	-	Take Home Ration
UTs	-	Union Territories
VCPC	-	Village Child Protection committee

1

INTRODUCTION
A THEORETICAL FRAMEWORK

Children are living beings – more living than grown-up people who have built shells of habit around themselves. Therefore it is a necessary for all section of community to look after their growth and development.

Ravindera Nath Tagore

Life's early years have a profound impact on a child's future. When loved, nourished and cared for in safe and stimulating environment, children develop the skills they need to embrace opportunity and bounce back from adversity. But nearly 43 per cent of children under 5 in low and middle income countries are not getting the nutrition, protection and stimulation they need. This diminishes both the child's potential and sustainable growth for society at large.[1]

Early childhood is a crucial period in a child's life which determines the quality of learning, well-being, health and behaviour across the life span. It is a period of great opportunity, but also of great vulnerability to negative influences and constitutes a unique phase for capitalizing on developmental forces to prevent or minimize disabilities and potential secondary conditions. Development of each person depends on providing the quality of stimulation, support and nurturance that the child experiences in his or her family, neighborhood, and care environment. When these are deficient or unsupportive child development can be seriously malaffected.[2]

Disease and malnutrition have close relations in many ways, malnutrition is one of the largest single contributor to disease in the world, according to the UN's Standing Committee on Nutrition. In many cases, ill health or disease could be a direct consequence of malnutrition, while in others, it is a key contributor. Malnutrition effect the physical and mental development of the children. Stunting, for example, affects more than 147 million preschoolers in developing countries. Worldwide, mal-nutrition is responsible for 45 per cent of children death, directly or through diseases made more severe because of it. Even mildly under-weight children face twice the risk of death as compared to well-nourished children.[3]

Among micronutrients, Vitamin A deficiency compromises the immune system and leads to the death of approximately one million children each year. Globally, severe iron deficiency is the cause of more than 60,000 deaths per year of women during pregnancy. Similarly, maternal folate deficiency leads to 250,000 severe birth defects and iodine deficiency in pregnancy causes mental impairment of almost 18 million infants per year and a lowering of 0-15 IQ points in school children. Iron deficiency weakens the maternal body, impairs intrauterine growth and increases the risk of both maternal and foetal morbidity and mortality. Malnutrition also has widespread economic ramifications. Problems related to anemia, for example, including cognitive impairment in children and low productivity in adults, cost US$5 billion a year in South Asia alone.[4]

1.1 Reducing malnutrition: Women's health holds the key

In the first half of the new millennium, India's performance on health, especially maternal and child health, remains dismal. Good health is important not only as an end in itself, but also for allowing an individual to enjoy a high-quality life and contribute productively to a country's economic and social progress.[5]

Improving care for young children is fundamental to achieve the Millennium Development Goals as well as Sustainable Development Goal.[6]

Children are the future of the country and therefore, their growth and development have to be looked after by all the sections of community. However, it is noticed that many of the children face problem of under-nutrition or malnutrition. Globally, the malnutrition contributes to nearly 30 lakh (35%) deaths of children below five years of age which can only be prevented when policy, programme and budgetary actions are directed towards children during prenatal and their first few years of life. Any interference at later stage of their lives might not be very effective. Moreover, there is now evidence that rapid weight gain after first two years of age increases the risk of chronic diseases later. The National Family Health Survey (NFHS)-III revealed that 40.4% of children below the age of three years are underweight in India. In view of this, there is an urgent need to redress malnutrition in children[7].

It is now globally acknowledged that investment in human resource development is a pre-requisite for Development of any nation. Early childhood, that is the first six years constitutes the most crucial period in life, when the foundations are laid for cognitive, social and emotional language, physical/ motor development and cumulative lifelong learning. The young child under 3 years is most vulnerable to the vicious cycles of malnutrition, disease/ infection and resultant disability all of which influence the present condition of a child at micro level and the future human resource development of the nation at the macro level[8].

Feeding is a primary event in the life of an infant and young child. It is the focus of attention for parents and other caregivers, and a source of social interaction through verbal and non-verbal communication. The eating experience provides not only nourishment but also an opportunity for learning of child. It affects not only children's physical growth and health but also their psychosocial and emotional development. The feeding relationship is affected by culture, health status and temperament.[9]

India is in the curious position of having very high levels of malnutrition despite large stocks of food-grains resulting from increased agricultural productivity. Moreover, the country experienced rapid economic growth during the 1990s, but this was accompanied by very modest declines in child malnutrition. There are two factors responsible for this outcome. A significant proportion of the population remains unable to buy enough food and the whole population is vulnerable to becoming malnourished due to exposure to diseases in particular diarrheal diseases and parasitic infections resulting from poor sanitation and living conditions and malnutrition in turn increases future susceptibility to disease. These synergies take a heavy toll in labour productivity and outlays on health care, as well as mortality.[10]

To overcome the situation, the government of India has launched several major programs for increasing access to food. One approach is through price controls: for example, the Public Distribution System makes some staple foods such as food-grains and sugar available at controlled prices through "fair-price shops". Another thrust has been through income support: such as a range of food for work programs and employment guarantee programs, where people are paid (often in food grains) for working on building or maintaining public infrastructure. A third approach has been to directly feed children: this includes mid-day meal programs for school-going children, and nutrition supplementation programs. By far the biggest nutrition supplementation program is the Integrated Child Development Services (ICDS).[11]

The provision of 'basic needs' forms an integral part of development. Growth alone has not always let to equitable development, and governments feel the need for direct intervention, especially in the fields of nutrition, health and education[12]. The ICDS is such a scheme. It is a national level scheme of the government of India providing a package of services to children below six years and to pregnant and nursing mothers, such as supplementary nutrition, immunization, health check-ups, referral services and pre-primary education. The scheme now covers almost all districts in the country; however this does not mean that all children below six years from poorer sections of society are covered by the scheme.[13]

1.1.1 Children in India: Demographic Profile

India is the second most populous country in the world, with 1.21 billion people while China is on the top with over 1.35 billion people. The figures shows that India represents almost 17.31 per cent of the world's population, which means one out of six people on this planet, live in India. Every year, an estimated 26 millions of children are born in India which is nearly 4 million more than the population of Australia. It is significant that while an absolute increase of 181 million in the country's population has been recorded during the decade 2001-2011, there is a reduction of 5.05 millions in the population of children aged 0-6 years during this period. The decline in male children is 2.06 million and in female children is 2.99 millions. The share of Children (0-6 years) in the total population has showed a decline of 2.8 points in 2011, compared to Census 2001[14].

Table-1.1 Population (0-6 years) 2001-2011–India

Census	Children (0-6 yrs) (in millions)			Total population (in millions)			Share of children (0-6 yrs) to the corresponding		
	Male	Female	Total	Male	Female	Total	Male	Female	Total
2001	163.84	85.01	78.83	1028.74	532.2	496.5	15.93	15.97	15.88
2011	158.79	82.95	75.84	1210.19	623.72	586.47	13.1	13.3	12.9

Source : *Census of India 2011, Office of Registrar General of India*

Table-1.2: Child population in the age-group 0-6 years by sex, India

Census	Persons	Male	Female	Decadal decline in child population		
				Persons	Male	Female
2001	163837395	85008267	78829128	-	-	-
2011	158789287	82952135	75837152	5048108 (3.1)	2056132 (2.4)	2991976 (3.8)

Source: *Census of India 2011, India, Office of Registrar General of India*

In 2011, the total number of children in the age-group 0-6 years is reported as 158.79 million which is down by 3.1 per cent compared to the child population in 2001 of the order of 163.84 million. The share of children (0-6 years) to the total population is 13.1 per cent in 2011 whereas the corresponding figures for male children and female children are 13.3 per cent and 12.9 per cent.[15]

The decadal decline in population was more for female children (3.8 per cent) than male children (2.4 per cent) in the age group 0-6 years.

Table-1.3: Proportion of children in the age-group 0-6 years to total population of India *(in per cent)*

Census	Persons	Male	Female	Decline in share of children to total population		
				Persons	Male	Female
1991	17.94	17.77	18.12	-	-	-
2001	15.93	15.97	15.88	-2.01	-1.8	-2.24
2011	13.12	13.3	12.93	-2.81	-2.67	-2.95

Source: *Census of India 2011, India, Office of Registrar General of India*

During 2001- 2011, the share of children to total population has been declined and the decline was sharper for female children than male children in the age group 0-6 year. While the size of child population in the age group (0-6 years) is declining with decline in the share of children in the total population, the share of girls in 0-6 years is declining faster than that of boys of 0-6 years.

1.1.2 Status of Children in India

India continues to have the highest number of malnourished children under five year in the world. Children are still far behind in terms of education, healthcare and other facilities. Children, especially girls faced many problems like lack of educational opportunities, malnourishment, infant mortality and early marriages. According to National Health Survey 2005-06 the all India average for malnourished children is 47 per cent. Every second child under 5 years is malnourished. Even the prosperous states like Gujarat and Kerala there is rise in the number of malnourished children. Both states saw an increase of 2 per cent between 2001-2011.Other states for instance Madhya Pradesh registered a rise from 54 per cent in 2001 to 60 per cent in 2011[16].

Nearly three fourth of all infants between 6-35 months of age are anemic in the 19 states for which NFHS -3 data are available. Among all the children up to 3 years age over 1/3 are stunted and more than 1/6th are wasted. Two out of five children are underweight. This state of the youngest Indians points towards pervasive malnutrition. For most of these infants, malnutrition would have started in the womb itself. This is evident from the data about married and pregnant women. It is surprised that still 54 per cent of pregnant women and nearly the same proportion of married women were found anemic. In fact the Body Mass Index (ratio of weight to height-a measure of nutritional availability) of nearly 1/3rd of all women was below normal. What is alarming that the situation is worsening or at best not improving over the years. Comparison with NHFS-2 carried out five years ago manifest that the proportion of wasted children has increased while underweight children are only marginally less. Similarly, the proportion of anemic infants has marginally increased. The number of pregnant women who are weak has jumped from about 49 per cent to over 54 per cent in these five years in these 19 states. The prevalence of anemia among infants has declined in several states but it has not improved or even worsened in AP, Assam, Karnataka, Kerala, Meghalaya,

Orissa, Punjab and UP. In no state has the proportion fallen below 50 per cent. UP, Rajasthan, Punjab, Haryana, Karnataka, Gujarat and Assam all have shockingly high proportions of anemic infants-80 per cent or above. Incidentally nearly a third of married men in the eastern states of W. Bengal, Orissa, Assam and Meghalaya and in highly advanced Gujarat are anemic and have lower than normal BMI. Chattisgarh has the highest number of underweight children closely followed by Gujarat and Uttar Pradesh. However, while the numbers have declined in the former, they are increasing in the latter two over the past five years.[17] According to fourth National family Health (2015-16) survey states like Bihar, Madhya Pradesh and Meghalya have more than 40 per cent of their children still started.

1.1.3 ICDS in India: An Evolution

India continues to have the highest rate of malnutrition and the largest number of undernourished children in the world.[18] India's concern to address the needs of children is evident from the First Five-Year Plan itself when the Planning Commission of India adopted a planned approach by introducing child welfare programmes in the country. Since then, various child welfare programmes were launched related to education, health, nutrition, welfare and recreation in subsequent Five- Year Plans. Special programmes to meet the needs of children with special needs, destitute and other groups of children were also undertaken. Some of these programmes were related to the health and development of children, especially children belonging to the pre-school age group of below six years. However, such child care programmes with their inadequate coverage and very limited inputs could not make much dent in the problems of children. As comprehensive and integrated early childhood services were regarded as investment in the future economic and social progress of the country, it was felt that a model plan which would ensure the delivery of maximum benefit to the children in a lasting manner should be evolved.[19]

The National Policy for Children (1974) lay down that the State should provide adequate services to children before and after birth and during the period of growth to ensure their full physical, mental and social development. This was in response to a shift in focus from 'child welfare' to Child Development' during the Fifth Five Year Plan (1974-79) with emphasis on integration and coordination of a multitude of inter-related services within the scope of a broad-based objective. In implementation of this policy, Integrated Child Development Services (ICDS) Scheme was launched on 2 October, 1975 by the Government of India as a centrally sponsored scheme of the Ministry of Women and Child development (earlier a department under Ministry of Human Resource Development). It is one of the world's largest programmes for Early Childhood Care and Education and represents country's commitment to its children and nursing mothers, its response to the challenge of providing Pre-school non-formal education on one hand and breaking the vicious cycle of malnutrition, morbidity, reduced learning capacity and mortality on the other. The ICDS is a self-selecting scheme and is open to all children below six years of age for their holistic development and pregnant and lactating mothers, disregarding their economic status.[20]

Table-1.4: Detail of ICDS Projects, Anganwadi Centres and Mini-Anganwadi Centres in India (as on 2017)

Sr. No.	State/UT	Number of ICDS Projects		Number of AWCs/Mini AWCs	
		Sanctioned by GOI	Operational	Sanctioned by GOI	Operational
1	Andhra Pradesh	257	257 (100.00)	55607	55574 (99.94)
2	Telamana	149	149 (100.00)	35700	35353 (99.03)
3	Arunachal Pradesh	98	98 (100.00)	6225	6028 (99.84)
4	Assam	231	231 (100.00)	62153	62153 (100.00)
5	Bihar	544	544 (100.00)	115009	91677 (79.71)
6	Chhattisgarh	220	220 (100.00)	52474	49941 (95.17)

7	Goa	11	11 (100.00)	1262	1260 (99.84)
8	Guiarat	336	336 (100.00)	53029	52065 (98.18)
9	Haryana	148	148 (100.00)	25962	25962 (100.00)
10	Jammu Kashmir	141	141 (100.00)	31938	29599 (92.68)
11	Jharkhand	224	224 (100.00)	38432	38432 (100.00)
12	Kamataka	204	204 (100.00)	65911	64558 (97.95)
13	Kerala	258	258 (100.00)	33318	33115 (99.39)
14	Madhya Pradesh	453	453 (100.00)	97135	91822 (94.53)
15	Maharashtra	553	553 (100.00)	110486	108010 (97.76)
16	Manipur	43	42 (97.67)	11510	9883 (85.86)
17	Meghalaya	41	41 (100.00)	5896	5309 (90.04)
18	Naqaland	60	59 (98.33)	3980	3455 (86.81)
19	Orissa	338	338 (100.00)	74154	71204 (96.02)
20	Punjab	155	154 (99.35)	27314	26656 (97.59)
21	Rajasthan	304	304 (100.00)	62010	60133 (96.97)
22	Sikkim	13	13 (100.00)	1308	1275 (97.48)
23	Tamil Nadu	434	434 (100.00)	54439	54439 (100.00)
24	Tripura	56	56 (100.00)	10145	9911 (97.69)
25	Uttar Pradesh	897	897 (100.00)	190145	187997 (98.87)
26	Uttrakhand	105	105 (100.00)	20067	19430 (96.83)

27	West Benqal	576	576 (100.00)	119481	116390 (97.41)
28	Chandigarh	3	3 (100.00)	500	500 (100.00)
29	Delhi	95	95 (100.00)	11150	10897 (97.73)
30	Dadra & N Haveli	2	2 (100.00)	302	282 (93.38)
31	Daman & Diu	2	2 (100.00)	107	107 (100.00)
32	Lakshadweep	9	9 (100.00)	107	107 (100.00)
33	Puducherry	5	5 (100.00)	855	788 (92.16)
All India		**7075**	**7072 (99.96)**	**1400000**	**1346186 (96.16)**

Source: *ICDS Status Report 2016-17, Ministry of Women and Child Development, Government of India.*

Note: i) UT= Union Territory; GOI = Government of India; AWC= Anganwadi Centre.

In 1975 the scheme of ICDS (as mentioned earlier) was launched with 33 projects and 4891 anganwadi centres and was gradually expanded to 5652 projects and 6 lakh sanctioned AWCs in the country by the end of Ninth Plan.[21] With a view to universalizing the scheme, the Supreme Court of India in its order of April 29,2004, and reiterated in its order dated Dec. 13,2006, has inter alia, directed the Government of India to sanction and operationalizea minimum of 14 lakh AWCs in a phased and even manner. To comply with the directions of the Supreme Court and to fulfill the commitment of the Government of India (GoI) to universalize the ICDS Scheme, it has been expanded in three phases in the years 2005-06, 2006-07 and 2008-09, so as to cover all habitations, including

Scheduled Caste (SC)/Scheduled Tribe (ST) and Minority, across the country.[22]

As on 2005 the scheme launched through a network of 7067 fully operational projects and 13.42 lakh AWCs (see Table 1.4). The services were currently being provided to 1045.08 lakh beneficiaries out of which 849.40 lakh were children under six and 195.68 lakh were Possible and Lactating Mothers. 370.70 lakh children of 3-6 years were provided pre-school education of which 188.19 were boys and 182.51 lakh were girls.[23]

1.2 Children in Himachal Pradesh: Demographic Profile

Himachal, one of the most dynamic hill states of India with remarkably high indicators of human development. Its natural resources and physiography, separate administrative identity, and notable accomplishments in literacy hold the promise of great progress. The socio-economic base of the state at the time of its formation and even earlier has a bearing on the level of its development. Like other hill areas, it has been neglected in the past because of its peripheral location. Himachal Pradesh started with a weak economic and institutional base and a low level of human skills essential for modern development. The state has tried to overcome this inadequacy by turning to horticulture, power generation and tourism.[24]

The word HIMACHAL derives its origin from two Hindi words, 'Him' and 'Anchal' meaning 'Snow' and 'Lap' respectively. Thus etymologically, Himachal Pradesh (Hill State) stands for the region which lies in the slopes of foot-hills of snow, that is, Himalaya.[25] Himachal Pradesh, the *Dev Bhumi* as it is known to the ancients, lies in the heart of the Western Himalaya.[26] Himachal literally means 'Land of Snowy-Mountains'.[27] Himachal situated in the heart of the western Himalaya, identified as "Dev Bhumi" and is believed to be the abode of Gods and Goddesses. The entire State is punctuated with stone as well as wood temples. The rich culture and traditions have made Himachal unique in itself.

The shadowy valleys, rugged crags, glaciers and gigantic pines and roaring rivers and exquisite flora and fauna compose the symphony that is forever Himachal.[28] Now, it is known as 'the Country's Orchard', 'Nature's Paradise' and an 'Abode of Peace'.

Himachal Pradesh is the third largest hill state of India, which is situated in the western Himalayan region.[29] Its location is between 30°22¢ 40^2 to 33°12¢40^2 North latitude and 75°45¢55^2 to 79°04¢20^2 East longitudes.[30] To the East, it forms India's border with Tibet, to the North lies state of Jammu and Kashmir, Uttrakhand in South-East, Haryana in the South and Punjab in the West. The entire territory of Himachal Pradesh is mountainous with altitude varying from 350 to 7000 meters above the mean sea level.[31]

The economy of Himachal Pradesh started its development journey from scratch, today the state has not only emerged as a model of development of hill areas in the country, but has also emerged as a pioneer in various fields of development. Himachal has emerged as a leading economy in the country and also a leader in hill area development. The state has made tremendous progress in industries, power, horticulture, agriculture and allied activities.[32]

Agriculture, the principal occupation of most of the people of Himachal Pradesh and has an important place in the economy of the state. The state of Himachal Pradesh is only state in the country whose 89.96 per cent of population lives in rural areas as per 2011 Census. Therefore, dependency on agriculture/horticulture is eminent as it provides direct employment to about 70 per cent of total workers of the state. Agriculture happens to be the premier source of State Income (GSDP). About 10.4 per cent of the total Gross State Domestic Product comes from agriculture and its allied sectors. Out of the total geographical area of 55.67 lakh hectares, the area of operational holdings is about 9.55 lakh hectares and is operated by 9.61 lakh farmers. The average holding size is about 1.00 hectare. Distribution of land holdings, according to

Agricultural Census 2010-11, shows that 87.95 per cent of the total holdings are of small and marginal farmers, 11.71 per cent of holdings are owned by semi-medium and medium farmers and only 0.34 percent by large farmers.[33]

The rich diversity of agro-climatic conditions, topographical variations and altitudinal differences coupled with fertile, deep and well drained soils favors the cultivation of temperate to sub- tropical fruits in Himachal Pradesh.

Table-1.5: District-wise Area, Total population, Sex ratio and Density of Population in Himachal Pradesh

District	Area (in Sq. Kms.)	Total population (in Number)	Sex ratio (women per 'ooo males)	Density of population (in per sq. Kms.)
Bilaspur	1167	381956	918	327
Chamba	6522	519080	986	80
Hamirpur	1118	454768	1095	407
Kangra	5739	1510075	1012	263
Kinnaur	6401	84121	819	13
Kullu	5503	437903	942	80
LahaulSpiti	13841	31564	903	2
Mandi	3950	999777	1007	253
Shimla	5131	814010	915	159
Sirmaur	2825	529855	918	188
Solan	1936	580320	880	300
Una	1540	521173	976	338
Total	**55673**	**6864602**	**972**	123

Source: *Department of Economics and Statistics, Economic Survey 2016-17 7(Part-II), Table 8, p. 7.*

The region is also suitable for cultivation of ancillary horticultural produce like flowers, mushroom, honey and hops. This particular suitability of Himachal has resulted in shifting of land use pattern from agriculture to fruit crops in the past few decades. The area under fruits, which was 792 hectares in 1950-51 with total production of 1200 tons has increased to 2,24,352 hectares during 2014-15. The total fruit production in 2014-15 was 7.52 lakh tons, which during 2015-

16 (upto December 2015) has been reported as 8.19 lakh tons. Apple is so far the most important fruit crop of Himachal Pradesh, which constitutes about 49 per cent of total area under fruit crops and about 85 per cent of the total fruit production. The area under apple has increased from 400 hectares in 1950-51 to 3,025 hectares in 1960-61 and 1,09,553 hectares in 2014-15.[34]

The population of Himachal Pradesh has been continuously increasing over the years. However, the growth rate of total population shows a decrease trend over the last three decades. In 2011 the total population of Himachal Pradesh is 68,64,602 out of which 34,81,873 were males and 33,82,729 were females. The composition of the population shows that 90 per cent of the population is rural and only 10 per cent is urban.[35]The number of women per 100 men is 972. The highest sex ratio has been observed in district Hamirpur (1095). Density per square km., as per population census, is 123 persons.

1.2.1 Demographic Profile of Children in Himachal Pradesh

The Social Justice and Empowerment Department of the State is engaged in socio-economic and educational uplift of scheduled castes, scheduled tribes, other backward classes, infirm, handicapped, orphans, children, widows, destitute, poor children and women etc.[36]

In pursuance of the National Policy for Children and India's commitment to provisions enshrined in the Directive Principles of the Constitution, Integrated Child Development Services Programme, on experiment basis, was introduced On 2nd October 1975in 33 projects including one in Pooh of Kinnaur district throughout the country.[37] Integrated Child Development Services (ICDS) programme, is being implemented in all Developmental Blocks of the State through 78 ICDS projects. ICDS services are being provided to children and pregnant/ lactating mothers through 18,385 and 515 Mini Anganwadi Centres in the State. The department is providing supplementary nutrition, nutrition and health education' immunization, health check-ups referred services and non-formal pre-school education[38] to the masses in the state. The scheme is being implemented on 90:10 (Centre: State) basis.

The population in age group '0-6' in Himachal Pradesh as per Census 2011 (provisional) has been given in Table 1.6.

Table-1.6: Population in the Age-Group 0-6 in Himachal Pradesh (Census 2011)

District	Area (in Sq. Kms.)	Total population (in Number)	Sex ratio (women per 'ooo males)	Density of population (in per sq. Kms.)
Bilaspur	1167	381956	918	327
Chamba	6522	519080	986	80
Hamirpur	1118	454768	1095	407
Kangra	5739	1510075	1012	263
Kinnaur	6401	84121	819	13
Kullu	5503	437903	942	80
LahaulSpiti	13841	31564	903	2
Mandi	3950	999777	1007	253
Shimla	5131	814010	915	159
Sirmaur	2825	529855	918	188
Solan	1936	580320	880	300
Una	1540	521173	976	338
Total	**55673**	**6864602**	**972**	123

Source: *http://censusindia.gov.in/2011-prov-resuls/prov_data_oridycts_ himachal. html*

The child population (0-6 age group) of Himachal Pradesh is 7,63,864 out of which 4,00,681 are males and 36183 are females as per Census 2011. The child population constitutes 11.14 per cent of total population of Himachal Pradesh. Kangra has the highest child population, while Lahaul and Spiti has the lowest child population in Himachal Pradesh. Mandi followed by Shimla and Chamba ranks 2nd, 3rd and 4th respectively in child population. In terms of both male and female it has been observed that Kangra tops the list followed by Mandi, Shimla and Chamba.

The proportion of child to its total population in Himachal Pradesh has been shown in Table 1.6 Chamba has the highest child proportion to its total population. It is also clear from the Table 1.5 that Chamba has highest female proportion to its total population in Himachal Pradesh. Kangra, which is the most populated district of Himachal Pradesh, ranks seventh in terms of percentage of child population to its total population.

During 2001-2011, the share of children (0-6 age group) to total population has been declined. In 2011, the proportion of children in the age-group 0-6 years is reported as 11.14 per cent which is down by 1.9 per cent compared to the child population in 2001. The figures for male children and female children, as per Census 2011, are 11.53 per cent and 10.74 per cent respectively.

The proportion of child population in age group '0-6' in Himachal Pradesh as per Census 2011 (provisional) has been given in Table 1.7.

Table-1.7: Proportion of Child Population in the Age-group 0-6 to Total Population

Sr. No.	District	Census					
		2001			2011		
		Person	Male	Female	Person	Male	Female
1.	Chamba	15.1	15.13	15.06	13.38	13.64	13.11
2.	Kangra	12.29	13.56	11.06	10.67	11.47	9.88
3.	Lahul &Spiti	11.03	10.13	12.15	9.5	9.04	10
4.	Kullu	13.84	13.61	14.09	11.44	11.37	11.51
5.	Mandi	13.31	13.96	12.66	11	11.57	10.44
6.	Hamirpur	12.28	13.94	10.78	10.5	11.7	9.41
7.	Una	13.32	14.48	12.16	11.17	11.81	10.52
8.	Bilaspur	12.58	13.31	11.58	10.89	11.4	10.37
9.	Solan	13.27	12.93	13.67	11.51	11.41	11.61
10.	Sirmaur	14.92	14.66	15.21	12.82	12.72	12.93
11.	Shimla	11.78	11.58	12	9.93	9.9	9.97
12.	Kinnaur	11.88	11.15	12.73	9.47	8.82	10.27
Himachal Pradesh		**13.05**	**13.55**	**12.53**	**11.14**	**11.53**	**10.47**

Source: *http://censusindia.gov.in/2011-prov-sults/prov_data_products_himachal.html.*

District-wise child sex ratio of Himachal Pradesh has been shown in Table 1.8 which reveals that that Lahaul & Spiti has the highest positive decadal growth (5.41) followed by Kangra (4.43) and Una district (3.94). Whereas district Kinnaur registered highest negative decadal growth rate (-2.66). Out of total district, half of the districts registered negative growth rate and rest of district registered positive growth rate in the state.

Table-1.8: District-wise Child Sex Ratio in Himachal Pradesh: 2001-2011

Sr. No.	District	Child Sex ratio in age group 0-6 years (Number of females per 1,000 males)		Decadal Growth Rate (In %age)
		2001	2011	
1	Chamba	955	950	-0.52
2	Kangra	836	873	4.43
3	Lahul&Spiti	961	1,013	5.41
4	Kullu	960	962	0.21
5	Mandi	918	913	-0.54
6	Hamirpur	850	881	3.65
7	Una	837	870	3.94
8	Bilaspur	882	893	1.25
9	Solan	900	899	-0.11
10	Sirmaur	934	931	-0.32
11	Shimla	929	922	-0.75
12	Kinnaur	979	953	-2.66
Himachal Pradesh		**896**	**906**	**1.12**

Source: *Series-3 Provisional Population Totals Paper- 1 Of Census 2011*

Note: *For calculation of sex ratio, others have been considered as males*

$$GDR = \left(\frac{P_x - P_o}{P_o}\right) \times 100$$

In overall, Himachal Pradesh have shown a positive trend. The decadal growth for the state has been observed 1.12, which is a positive sign.

Graph 1.1
Child Sex Ratio in Himachal Pradesh: 2001-2011

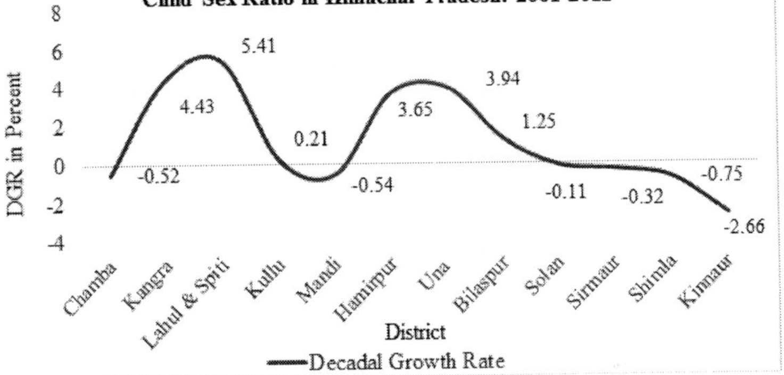

1.2.2 Integrated Child Development Services (ICDS) in Himachal Pradesh

ICDS is a Centrally-sponsored Scheme implemented through the State Governments/UT Administrations. Prior to 2005-06, 100 per cent financial assistance for inputs other than supplementary nutrition, which the States were to provided out of their own resources, was being given by the Government of India. Since many States were not providing adequately for supplementary nutrition in view of resource constraints, it was decided to support to States up to 50 per cent of the financial norms or to support 50 per cent of expenditure incurred by them on supplementary nutrition, whichever is less. in 2005-06. [39]

From the financial year 2009-10, Government of India has revised the funding pattern of ICDS between Centre and States. The sharing pattern of supplementary nutrition in respect of North-eastern States between Centre and States has been altered from 50:50 to 90:10 ratio. So far as other States and UTs, the existing sharing pattern of 50:50 continues. However, for all other components of ICDS, the ratio has been modified to 90:10 (100 per cent Central Assistance earlier).[40]

The programme proposes a holistic child health comprising nutrition, health and education components for pregnant women, lactating mothers, and children less than six years of age. The programme is implemented through a network of community- level Anganwadi Centers. The range of services targeted at young children and their mothers for growth monitoring, immunization, health check-ups and supplementary feeding, as well as nutrition and health education to improve the childcare and feeding practices that mothers adopt. Pre-school education is provided to children between three and six years of age.[41]

In inforcement of the National Policy for Children and India's commitment to provisions enshrined in the Directive Principles of the Constitution, Integrated Child Development Services Programme, on experiment basis, was introduced on 2nd October 1975 in 33 projects including one in Pooh of Kinnaur district throughout the country. During Sixth and Seventh Plan period, more projects were sanctioned to the State. In 1995-96 during universalization phase of the scheme, the Government of India sanctioned 29 new ICDS projects. Four new ICDS projects, namely, Shimla (urban), Haroli, Tauni Devi and Sulah were sanctioned during 2005-06. Thereafter, during 2009-10, two new projects at Dharamshala and Nankhari were sanctioned. Today the scheme is operating in 78 ICDS projects. Out these 70 projects come in the definition of Rural Projects, one in Urban Projects and remaining 7 in Tribal Projects.[42]

Integrated Child Development Services (ICDS) programme, is being implemented in all Developmental Blocks of the State through 78 ICDS projects. The department is providing supplementary nutrition, health and nutrition education' immunization, health check-ups referred services and non-formal pre-school education.[43]

For better governance in the delivery of the Scheme, convergence is, therefore, one of the main features of the ICDS Scheme. This convergence is in-built in the Scheme which

Table-1.9: Detail of the delivery of services to the beneficiaries

Services	Target Group	Service provided by
(i) Supplementary Nutrition	Children below 6 years, Pregnant & Lactating Mothers (P&LM)	Anganwadi Worker and Anganwadi Helper [MWCD]
(ii) Immunization*	Children below 6 years, Pregnant & Lactating Mothers (P&LM)	ANM/MO [Health system, MHFW]
(iii) Health Check-up*	Children below 6 years, Pregnant & Lactating Mothers (P&LM)	ANM/MO/AWW [Health system, MHFW]
(iv) Referral Services	Children below 6 years, Pregnant & Lactating Mothers (P&LM)	AWW/ANM/MO [Health system, MHFW]
(v) Pre-School Education	Children 3-6 years	AWW [MWCD]
(vi) Nutrition & Health Education	Women (15-45 years)	AWW/ANM/MO [Health system, MHFW & MWCD]

Source: *http://icds-wcd.nic.in/icds/icds.aspx*

* AWW assists ANM in identifying the target group

provides a platform for providing all services under the Scheme in the form of Anganwadi Centres.[44]

The concept of providing a package of services is based primarily on the consideration that the overall impact will be much larger if the different services develop in an integrated manner as the efficacy of a particular service depends upon the support it receives from related services.

1.3 Demographic Profile of Children in District Kangra

Kangra district derives its name from Kangra town that was known as *Nagarkot* in ancient times. Kangra proper originally was a part of the ancient *Trigarta (Jallundhur)*, which comprises of the area lying between the river *"Shatadroo"* (probably Sutlej) and Ravi. A area of land to the east of Sutlej that probably is the area of *Sirhind* in Punjab also formed a part of *Trigrata*. Trigrata had two provinces, that is, one in the plains with headquarters at *Jallundhur* and other in the hills with headquarters at *Nagarkot* (the present Kangra).[45]The present Kangra district came into existence on the 1st

September, 1972 consequent upon the re-organization of districts by the Government of Himachal Pradesh.[46]

Kangra district lies between 31°21 to 32°59 N latitude and 75°472 552 2 to 77°452 E longitude. It is situated on the southern escarpment of the Himalayas. The entire area of the district is traversed by the varying altitude of the Shivaliks, Dhauladhar and the Himalayas from north-west to south-east. The altitude varies from 500 metres above mean sea level to around 5000 metres. It is encapsulated in the north by the districts of Chamba and Lahaul and Spiti, in the south by Hamirpur and Una, in the east by Mandi and in the west by Gurdaspur district of Punjab.[47]

According to the Surveyor-General of India the area of the district is 5,746 square kilometers. In terms of area, the district constitutes 10.31 per cent of the state area and ranks fourth among the districts. According to the Census of India 2011, the total rural population of the district is 14,23,794 persons with the population density of 248 people per square kilometer. Out of total population of the district, 3,19,385 persons are scheduled castes and 84,564 persons are scheduled tribes. As per the Census of India 2011 the population of the male and female is 7, 05,365 and 7, 18,429 respectively. The sex ratio is 1019 female per 1000 male in the district.

Area wise, Baijnath (1,301 square kilometer) is the biggest block in the district Kangra. The percentage of rural population is highest in Nagrota Bagwan block (8.91 per cent) and lowest in Fatehpur block (4.44 per cent). Regarding density of population the Table 1.9 shows that the highest density of population (that is, 639 persons per square kilometer) is in Fatehpur block and lowest density of population (that is, 69 persons per square kilometer) is in Baijnath block. Block-wise area, rural population and density of population has been shown in Table 1.10.

Table-1.10: Block-wise Area, Rural Population, Density of Rural Population and Sex Ratio in Kangra District (as per 2011 Census)

Block	Area of Blocks (sq. kms.)	Total Rural Population	%age to total rural population	Density of population (persons per sq. kms.)	Sex ratio (women per '000 male)	Literacy rate
Baijnath	1301	90374	6.35	69	993	73.84
Bhawarna	259	91376	6.42	353	1006	79.91
Dehra	236	76469	5.37	324	1185	79.15
Dharamshala	203	68341	4.80	337	971	80.41
Fatehpur	99	63223	4.44	639	1009	79.22
Indora	252	104710	7.35	416	998	81.03
Kangra	183	83005	5.83	454	1019	77.63
Lambagaon	426	104115	7.31	244	1036	76.29
Nagrota Bagwan	713	126804	8.91	178	1064	80.36
Nagrota Surian	416	112689	7.91	271	1045	83.43
Nurpur	309	99101	6.96	321	1041	80.89
Panchrukhi	374	118668	8.33	317	968	80.39
Pragpur	404	105351	7.40	261	927	79.31
Rait	399	109948	7.72	276	985	80.18
Sullah	172	69620	4.89	405	1097	81.20
Total	**5746**	**1423794**	**100.00**	**248**	**1019**	**79.62**

Source: *Block Indicators, District Statistical Office, Dharamshala, Kangra District.*

Kangra, being the largest district accounting for more than one fifth of the state population and 10.31 per cent of the total geographical area, plays an significant role in the economy of this hilly state. The economy of district is primarily agrarian with two-thirds of the population directly dependent on agriculture.[48]The district is covered by fertile valleys and agriculture is the main occupation of the rural population. The agro-climatic conditions obtaining in the district are most suitable for the growing of food crops such as Wheat, rice, maize, oil seeds, sugarcane, potatoes and tea. With implementation of various programmes, the government has endeavored to increase the agricultural production by the introduction of improved variety of seeds, increased fertilizers, chemical pesticides, improved agricultural implements, etc.[49]

1.3.1 Children in District Kangra Demographic Profile:

Block-wise child population and sex ratio in Kangra district have been depicted in Table 1.11.

Table-1.11: Block Wise Child Population and sex ratio in Kangra district, 2011

Block	Area of Blocks (sq. kms.)	Total Rural Population	%age to total rural population	Density of population (persons per sq. kms.)	Sex ratio (women per '000 male)	Literacy rate
Baijnath	1301	90374	6.35	69	993	73.84
Bhawarna	259	91376	6.42	353	1006	79.91
Dehra	236	76469	5.37	324	1185	79.15
Dharamshala	203	68341	4.80	337	971	80.41
Fatehpur	99	63223	4.44	639	1009	79.22
Indora	252	104710	7.35	416	998	81.03
Kangra	183	83005	5.83	454	1019	77.63
Lambagaon	426	104115	7.31	244	1036	76.29
Nagrota Bagwan	713	126804	8.91	178	1064	80.36
Nagrota Surian	416	112689	7.91	271	1045	83.43
Nurpur	309	99101	6.96	321	1041	80.89
Panchrukhi	374	118668	8.33	317	968	80.39
Pragpur	404	105351	7.40	261	927	79.31
Rait	399	109948	7.72	276	985	80.18
Sullah	172	69620	4.89	405	1097	81.20
Total	**5746**	**1423794**	**100.00**	**248**	**1019**	**79.62**

Source: Census of India 2011, Himachal Pradesh, District Census Handbook, Series-03.

Table 1.11 shows block-wise sex-ratio of rural child population in the age-group 0-6 years in thedistrict. The sex-ratio is 877 for the district (rural). The sex-ratio of C.D. block varies from 814 to 931. It is highest in NagrotaBagwan C.D. block with 931 and is followed by 928 in Sulah C.D. block and lowest 814 is found in Nurpur C.D. block. Except for Pragpur, Kangra, Indora, NagrotaSurian, Fatehpur and Nurpur C.D. blocks, the sex-ratio for 0-6 age group is higher than the district rural average sex-ratio of 877.

Block-wise decadal growth in Kangra district has been shown in Table 1.12.

Table-1.12: Block Wise Decadal Growth in Kangra district, (Census of India 2001-11)

Block	Child Sex Ratio in age group 0-6 years (number of females per 1000 males)		Decadal Growth (in %age)
	Census 2001	Census 2011	
Baijnath	1029	993	-3.499
Bhawarna	1008	1006	-0.198
Dehra	1069	1064	-0.468
Dharamshala	987	971	-1.621
Fatehpur	1013	985	-2.764
Indora	917	927	1.091
Kangra	1038	998	-3.854
Lambagaon	1189	1185	-0.336
N/Bagwan	1043	1019	-2.301
N/Surian	1047	1041	-0.573
Nurpur	984	968	-1.626
Panchrukhi	1055	1009	-4.360
Pragpur	1036	1045	0.869
Rait	1041	1036	-0.480
Sulah	1101	1097	-0.363
Total	**1032**	**1019**	**-1.260**

Source: *District Statistics Office, Kangra*
Note: *For calculation of growth rate following formula has been used*

$GDR = \left(\frac{P_n - P_o}{P_n}\right) \times 100$; Where P_n = present year; P_o = Base year

Data in Table 1.12 depicts that the decadal growth remained negative in almost all the blocks of Kangra district. The decadal

Graph 1.2
Decadal Growth of Child Sex Ratio in Himachal Pradesh: 2001-2011

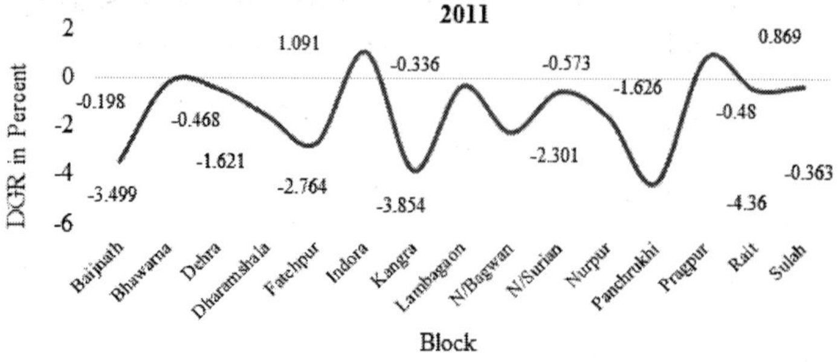

growth of child sex ratio was positive in Pragpur and Indora block. In these blocks the growth was 0.869 per cent and 1.091 per cent respectively.

1.4 Review of Literature

A literature review is a body of text that aims to review the critical points of current knowledge including substantive findings as well as theoretical and methodological contributions to a particular topic. Knowledge of existing and up-to date relevant literature related to the studies and their critical and comprehensive review helps a researcher to formulate research project on scientific lines. It guides the investigator to solve the researchable issues of the study. Literature review acts as a searchlight to guide the course of prospective research activity. Keeping in view this logical thinking, here an effort has been made to make analytical review of the relevant literature.

Gupta and Rohde (2004)[50] discussed about the negative consequences on child health due to malnutrition. He gave the solution by the need to understand the distinction between hunger and malnutrition. As according to the oxford dictionary hunger is an uneasy sensation caused by want of food. But malnutrition is much more severe situation. He quote that malnutrition is not necessarily non availability and accessibility of food but lack of breast feeding during the first two years mainly the first 6months also leads to malnutrition. He suggested spending infant and young child nutrition to improve their health for enhancing their development.

Chatterjee (2006)[51] demonstrate that adequate child care encourages school going among children and tackle social barriers such as caste. Employment to women as crèche teachers helps them forge that causes a child to be hurt killed. The term child abuse refers to as physical, emotional or mental harm inflicted on children of all ages. Another form of child abuse is sexual abuse that exp. The children should be provided with the food, clothing warmth so that they are shattered.

Chowdhury (2006)[52] in her study entitled, "ICDS: India's Response to Early Child Development", opined that ICDS has reached a stage where it has become essential to harmonize the expansion of the programme and its content enrichment, in order to accelerate the, implementation in achieving the core objectives of the programme especially to reduce the child malnutrition and help reduction in mortality rates. The trend in reduction in malnutrition as observed between NFHS-I & NFHS-II is not significantly positive towards achieving the MDGs by the end of 2015. In order to accelerate the pace of reduction in prevalence of child malnutrition, a concerted effort is required during the 11th Plan in some of key areas. Addressing issues like prevention and management of malnutrition (especially severe cases), poor maternal and adolescent nutrition, lack of nutrition and health education, and inadequate community participation in the programme, continues to be a major challenge during the Eleventh Plan. During the 11th Five Year Plan, the overall objective for 'ICDS could be Strengthening ICDS for Reduction of Child Malnutrition'. In order to have a faster and sustained achievement of child and women nutritional goals, a paradigm shift is required to reform the ICDS in respect of overall programme management. During the Eleventh Plan, while we rededicate ourselves to promoting early childhood care for survival and development of the children, an attempt would be made to re-structure the ICDS programme implementation framework to suit the current nutritional needs of the women & children and to strengthen the existing service delivery mechanism.

Mehrotra (2006)[53] focused that the rate of child nutrition are higher in India, Pakistan and Bangladesh as in sub-saharan countries of Africa. The focus of all interventions has to be on improving ten health status of women in general and the target of most inventions is on the first three years of life as in the case of infants. The universal school feeding programmes will ensure to save the cost of atleast one square meal for its children belonging to poor families and there is a need of rapid action to the access to safe drinking water and sanitation facility to the entire population.

Gautam (2006)[54] has emphasized that children constitute one third of the country's population and children are the human resources and assets of a country. So development of children has to be priority item in the country's development agenda. Various policies and legislations have also been introduced in India to ensure protection of children and improvement in their status like Rajiv Gandhi National Creche Scheme, Shishu Greh Scheme and Scheme for Working Children in need or Care and protection. The country is on the threshold bonds with other women and for the promotion of allover community development. Child care is essential to make children to attend shook the older siblings, particularly girls, can also take care for their young sisters and others if the crèche is located in school compound. This will encourage children to go school. The little exposure to learning through play, learning, through play way method, earning from others and exploring the world outside can be helpful in blooming the poor children having few opportunities.

Gragnolati, et.al. (2006)[55] in a study concluded that ICDS has great potential to improve the nutritional status of India's children is undeniable, but it needs to overcome some challenges if this potential is to be realized. Three major mismatches between what an effective nutrition interventions should do and what ICDS is currently doing are preventing the programme from achieving better results. Consequently, despite its national infrastructure, ICDS is not making the expected contribution to reducing the prevalence of malnutrition in India. It might be more beneficial to focus energies on improving service delivery within existing AWCs projects, rather than just on expanding coverage. There are some possible alternatives to the current overall implementation strategy adopted by ICDS that, while still firmly rooted within the broad programmatic approach and overarching aims of the intervention, may help to resolve some of these issues. To conclude, greater clarity and focus are needed if the ICDS programme is to make a substantial dent in the problem of persistent undernutrition in India. In particular, the three mismatches identified earlier need to be resolved so that a nutrition intervention is implemented that (a) provides the most effective services to address the most important determinants of malnutrition; (b) reaches younger children and the most vulnerable segments of the population; and (c) is well targeted to areas where the prevalence of under nutrition is highest.

Sinha (2006)[56] in her paper generalizes that ICDS programme in India reaching nit to most neglected sections of the population. She suppressed the need of its scansion to include every child, pregnant and nursing mothers and adolescent girls. It is also important to set clear goals so that achievements can be assessed and work can give direction. The recommendation such as keeping Anganwadi centers open for whole day, setting up crèches for younger children, providing take-home rations for less than three years of age etc. The vision of good health and wellbeing of mot children must be recognized as an overwhelming priority. Clear vision along political commitment in this regard could play a key role towards the development country.

Nayak and Saxena (2006)[57] in their article expose the apathy of the state governments of Bihar and Jharkhand towards this scheme, particularly in terms of coverage, financial procedures and practices adopted in the appointment of personnel. While they limiting their discussion of the implementation of sanctioned ICDS projects, they found that the problems appear at several levels. Further, to the operationalization of these projects, financial allocations need to be effectively utilized, vacancies need to be filled and staff needs to be trained and given vision. Very importantly, the programme needs to be given priority and effectively supervised. In its objectives and original structure, the ICDS set out to achieve laudable goals. Since 2001, the vision of the scheme has been strengthened by the interim orders of the Supreme Court. The poor administrative arrangements for implementation of ICDS in Bihar and Jharkhand are especially unfortunate, given the fact that many other poor states have managed to get the scheme off the ground. Procedural corrections are critically required for positive change.

Chandra and Reddy (2007)[58] argued that the main trap for engaged in the industries like state mine is the structure of employment and segmented nature of work. The adult workers especially female workers who are engaged in industry has reinforced the child workers. The technical advancement tends to reduce child labour as machines do the routine and repetitive work efficiently and the people, often children and it demand for more highly skilled workers like adults in the slate industry because of diversification in designing slates has reduced drastically but the demand for more raw material for designing slate phenomenally increased the involvement of children in the slate mines. If the change in income of the parent could be made then the practice of child labour will ultimately end the child labour.

Reddy (2007)[59] generalized the child labour as the byproduct of our social economic conditions. In the pretext of socio-economic conditions the evil can be aired rather than be eliminated. The ban on child labour can cause harm to the real of the families of the working children. Formal education should be given to the children indulge in some work as a form of evening or night school. Thus, it is a society need India and indispensable in a society like India and complete abolition.

Sirinivasan and Bedi (2009)[60] provides a brief review of the pattern of daughter elimination in Tamil Nadu and then goes on to focus on the role played by the government's Girl Child Protection Scheme in particular, in shaping sex ratios influencing daughter elimination has declined sharply between the late 1990s and 2003. In Tamil Nadu, daughter elimination in the form of female infanticide first gain public attention in the mid-1980s. Initially it was felt that the practice was limited to certain groups and certain geographical areas but subsequent several researched.

Gairola and Chauhan (2009)[61] in their article observed that healthy society raises children to be responsible citizens rather than mere consumers. It is probably impossible to compltetly, shield children from marketing message. The ice by the parents and help by the government in this regard can stop children by local targeting. Children need counseling, time and lot of patience by their parents to make them to understood the ill effects of certain food commodities available in the market, by stressing the need of a supportive family system so that children do not fall prey to advertisement and marketing gimmicks very easily.

Programme Evaluation Organization (2011)[62] of Planning Commission has conducted an evaluation study to assess the gaps and impact of implementation of ICDS programme in achieving its aims and objectives. The study has been conducted in 100 districts of 35 States and UTs and has covered 19,500 households. The study concluded that the performance of ICDS programme has been found to be mixed in selected sample states. There is wide divergence between official statistics on nutritional status, registered beneficiaries and number of days food/ supplementary nutrition served vis-a-vis ground-reality with regard to these indicators. Around half of the total eligible children are currently enrolled in anganwadicentres and the effective coverage as per norms is only 41% of those registered for the ICDS benefits. Anganwadi workers are over-burdened, under-paid and mostly unskilled, which affects the implementation of the scheme. Inadequate infrastructure to deliver the six designated services under the ICDS at majority of anganwadicentres have adversely affected the service delivery.

Arokiasamy and Goli (2012)[63] examining the direct relevance of the landholding-patriarchy hypothesis to the dynamics of sex discrimination and family-building strategies in rural India, This paper presents evidence that indicates the child sex ratio varies greatly when stratified by size of household landholdings. Among many structural factors, the landholding size emerges as an inûuential determinant of the sex ratio imbalance in rural India. The key effect of landholding is consistently established across categories of the principal socio-economic determinants of sex ratio imbalance. The CSR consistently increased with the size of household landholding. The SRB for last and last two births increased steeply with the size of landholding, as an outcome of both the strong preference for sons to maintain the large-sized landholdings and the greater economic utility assigned to boys in household agricultural activities. Women in large landholding families do not have much socio-economic freedom or decision-making powers. Among states where land distribution is more uniform (for example, Kerala), the sex ratio is favourable to females. In contrast, the results for Gujarat, Punjab and Haryana substantiate the pattern of skewed distribution in household landholdings and sex ratio. Madhya Pradesh, Chhattisgarh and West Bengal fall in a third category, where traditionally women were allowed to participate in decision-making.

Ao and Lhungdim (2014)[64] in their paper entitled, "Re-Estimating Malnourishment and Inequality among Children in North-east India" have tried to re-estimates the prevalence of child malnutrition among the under-five age group in eight north-east states using the composite index of anthropometric failure method as proposed by P Svedberg, using the National Family Health Survey-3 data. The study highlights that children's characteristics do inûuence their nutritional status, but the mother's characteristics, such as education or BMI, have a stronger relationship with child nutritional status. There is also a strong relationship indicated between wealth index and malnutrition, and a substantial poor-rich gap in all domains of malnutrition with a disproportionate burden of child malnutrition on the poor. Also interesting is the ûnding that suggests no signiûcant association between macroeconomic growth and child malnutrition. Economic development per se would not ensure good nutritional status of the children unless it is through inclusive growth. Unless there is proper monitoring and coordination at the household and community levels, there would be no improvement in child nutritional status. Among the eight states in the region, Meghalaya has been a surprise by being the state with the highest percentage of child malnutrition (in all measures - underweight, stunting, wasted and CIAF), but at the same time as having lowest inequality in child malnutrition across all socio-economic groups

Aguayo, Singh and Badgaiyan (2014)[65] in their study made an attempt to present a child under-nutrition index (CUI) that captures the multidimensional nature of child under-nutrition in India and reûects which states face the greatest nutrition risk, to present a child nutrition score (CNS) that captures the performance of Indian states in delivering proven essential nutrition interventions for infants and young children; and to assess the links between under-nutrition risk and nutrition performance as measured by the CUI and the CNS, respectively. Both the index and the score use data from India's NFHS-3. Their study clearly indicates that levels of child under-nutrition in India are strongly associated with the performance of states in delivering proven nutrition interventions for children. Almost without exception, the higher the state's CNS - measuring the overall coverage of essential nutrition interventions for children - the lower the state's CUI. What is relevant to policy is the fact that the CNS tends to be signiûcantly lower among the most vulnerable children and population groups. CNS is lower in the states with higher proportions of people surviving below the poverty line, among children from the poorest wealth quintiles, those who belong to SC/ST families, and/or those who live in rural areas. Further, they found that in India child under-nutrition levels are lower where the economic growth dividend has been directed to reduce poverty and the proportion of children surviving in households below a minimum standard of living; and improve the coverage and equity of proven essential nutrition interventions, particularly for the most vulnerable children. Therefore, the challenge ahead for India is to ensure that national nutrition policies and social transfers are aimed at reducing inequalities and the disproportionate impact of under-nutrition among the poorest and most vulnerable groups in society and that nutrition intervention are delivered through effective governance systems that privilege evidence-based and cost-effective interventions.

Khera (2015)[66] in her paper studied the two children's schemes in four districts in and reports how they perform and identifies areas for further action.The level of functionality achieved in the ICDS in Odisha is remarkable because as recently as 2009, when anganwadis opened, the main activity was providing supplementary nutrition (Government of India 2011a). A study in 2009 in seven districts found that the "Take Home Ration under Supplementary Nutrition Programme is found to be the only activity that is going on everywhere. The gains in the implementation of ICDS are largely on account of creative policymaking in the ûeld of child nutrition in Odisha. Simple measures such as providing uniforms for the ANM, AWW, AWH and ASHA as well as anganwadi children helps create an environment of seriousness associated with, say, schooling or at health centres. Another example is decentralized procurement for items required for Supplementary Nutrition Programme (SNP). Instead of routing funds through the CDPO's ofûce, the money goes straight into a joint account operated by the AWW and a GP member. This has freed AWWs from the tyranny of CDPOs, a common complaint elsewhere. Along with decentralized devolution of funds, the state has also introduced a model of decentralized procurement for THR. The most interesting initiative as far as nutrition is concerned, of course, has been the introduction of eggs as THR. It is more nutritious than chhatua and given that its shelf life is longer than most other foods with comparable nutritive value, it can be given as THR.

Duflo (2016)[67] Women's empowerment and economic development are closely related: in one direction, development alone can play a major role in driving down inequality between men and women; in the other direction, empowering women may benefit development. Does this imply that pushing just one of these two levers would set a virtuous circle in motion? This paper reviews the literature on both sides of the empowerment-development nexus, and argues that the inter-relationships are probably too weak to be self-sustaining, and that continuous policy commitment to equality for its own sake may be needed to bring about equality between men and women

Dhas (2016)[68] The paper argued that lack of women education can be an impediment to the country's economic development. Education for women is the best way to improve the health, nutrition and economic status of a household that constitute a micro unit of a nation economy. The paper also explores that the changes in the policies and infrastructural support on primary, secondary and higher education reflect the initiatives of the govt. of India towards education. Section 1 discusses the trends in female literacy levels in India. The sec. 2 presents the investments on education and the infrastructural is support in India. The last section provides the summery of the findings and conclusions.

Raghurajan 2016[69] The book highlights the impact of the government welfare programmes being implemented for the upliftment of women, especially in rural areas. The author makes an incisive analysis to understand the status and the living standard of the poor and downtrodden rural women and the way they are coming forward to avail benefits of these programmes and scheme. This will have researched work brings out an understanding not only about the expectation and suggestions of the beneficiary's women in the context of more effective implementation of the programmmes.

Desai (2017)[70] This paper addresses the conceptual and methodological issues related to women's empowerment, the trends in women's empowerments over last 20 years in key areas such as education, health, economic and political participation, and finally the best practices of state and non-state actors in empowering women.

Mishra (2017)[71]conducted a study in three tribal districts, namely, Alirajpur, Barwani and Khandwa, of Madhya Pradesh. This study assesses child malnutrition, its causal analysis and also reviews the Integrated Child Development Services (ICDS) scheme which is aimed at the reduction of child malnutrition in tribal areas. The study reveals that the conversion of malnourished children (SUW and MUW) of AWCs to normal category, and at the same time, normal children converting to malnourished category after a span of two years had stated a dismal picture. There was no significant difference between malnutrition level of children availing supplementary nutrition and children who were not availing the same from AWCs. The study concluded that despite certain IYCF practices (colostrum feeding and early initiation of breastfeeding) being traditionally strong among tribals, there was a high level of child malnutrition in the tribal area due to short period of breastfeeding, delayed initiation of supplementary nutrition, and most importantly, poor growth monitoring and poor implementation of malnutrition reduction interventions, including information, education and communication (IEC) activities under ICDS. Barring ANC services, other nutrition and health services for women were not found satisfactory. Low BMI of women and low birth weight of children had also shown a strong association with high child malnutrition stating the need for more emphasis on nutrition care of women in a way to reduce child malnutrition. Poor health condition had registered a positive association with child malnutrition, and moreover, malnutrition was found to be one of the important factors responsible for child deaths in tribal areas.

Sharma (2017)[72] conducted a study to know the impact of socio-economic status on nutritional status of pregnant women in Patna. She found that more than three fourth of pregnant women consumed meals thrice a day, but largest share of pregnant women taking meals twice a day was in the low income group and least in the high income group. The mean intake of rice, wheat and other cereals was almost at par among the pregnant women of all income groups but it was much less than the recommended dietary Allowances given by the Indian Council of Medical Research. Further, she concluded that mean daily intake of calcium, iron and Vitamin-C was significantly low in all income groups. The study also indicate that pregnant women of high income groups suffered less from deficiency diseases as they seem to have more nutritional awareness and have a more balanced diet during pregnancy.

Sharda and Bedi (2018)[73] provides a brief review of the pattern of daughter elimination in Tamil Nadu and then goes on to focus on the role played by the government's Girl Child Protection Scheme in particular, in shaping sex ratios influencing daughter elimination has declined sharply between the late 1990s and 2003. In Tamil Nadu, daughter elimination in the form of female infanticide first gain public attention in the mid-1980s. Initially it was felt that the practice was limited to certain groups and certain geographical areas but subsequent several researched.

Sampagaran dand Lakhkar (2018) [74] their article observed that proves that it is possible to breastfeed a child with any severity of cleft lip and palate. However, these children are prone to malnutrition as well as developmental delay. Delay was more common in syndromic children and in those with unilateral defect, but factors such as malnutrition, recurrent respiratory infections, and repeated hospitalization also added to the developmental delay. School performance was good in majority of the children.

Henrik and Camille, (2018)[75] The book highlights the impact of study despite considerable gender convergence over time, substantial gender inequality persists in all countries. Using full-population administrative data from Denmark and a quasi-experimental event study approach, we show that most of the remaining gender inequality can be attributed to the dynamic effects of children. We have presented three main sets of results. First, we have shown that the impact of children on women is large and persistent across awide range of labour market outcomes, while at the same time men are unaffected. The female child penalty in earnings is close to 20% in the long run. Underlying this earnings penalty, we find sharp impacts of children on labour force participation, hours worked, wage rates, occupation, Sector, and firm choices. Together, these findings provide quite complete pictures of the behavioural margins that adjust in response to parenthood and how strongly gendered these margins are. We have laid out the identification assumptions of our event study approach, providing two important robustness checks that support our strategy: a difference-in-differences extension of the event study and an IV-approach based on sibling sex mix.

Dandotiya, et.al.(2018)[76] have conducted a cross-sectional study on 40 anganwadis in Bhopal city. They took a sample of 240 beneficiaries. The study concluded that 69.16 per cent of beneficiaries were satisfied with the services and rest of the beneficiaries were not satisfied with the services provided under ICDS. They concluded that improvement in the quality of services is the need of the hour to keep the satisfaction and utilization level.

Sampagaret. et.al. (2018)[77] conducted a study to assess the factors associated with development delay and nutritional status among the children with cleft lip and/or cleft palate. The study concluded that it is possible to breastfeed a child with any severity of cleft lip and palate. However, these children are prone to malnutrition as well as developmental delay. Delay was more common in syndromic children and in those with unilateral defect, but factors such as malnutrition, recurrent respiratory infections, and repeated hospitalization also added to the development delay.

Reddy (2018)[78] generalized the child labour as the by product of our social economic conditions. In the pretext of socio-economic conditions the evil can be aired rather than be eliminated. The ban on child labour can cause harm to the real of the families of the working children. Formal education should be given to the children indulge in some work as a form of evening or night school. Thus, it is a society need India and indispensable in a society like India and complete abolition.

1.5 Selection of Problem

As India races towards achieving superpower, its children are still far behind in terms of healthcare, education and other facilities. Children, especially, girls are faced with lack of educational opportunities, malnourishment, infant mortality and early marriages. Every second child under 5 years is malnourished. Child malnutrition is, mostly, the result of high levels of exposure to infection and in appropriate infant and young child feeding and caring practices, and has its origins almost entirely during the first years of life. To prevent recurrence and to overcome the effects of chronic malnutrition, these children need extra attention both during the early rehabilitation phase and over the longer term.

Integrated Child Development Scheme is one of the best expressions of India's commitment for children. It is, today, the largest and unique and integrated programme of the world for early child development, converging interventions for health, nutritional well-being, psycho-social and cognitive development linked to other sectoral operations for safe drinking water, environmental sanitation and women's development. As the government is investing huge sum of money in this programme, it is important that it will provide better services to the society.

Many scholars had attempted to study the schemes of child welfare and development at the national level. But, in Himachal Pradesh very little work was initiated to study Integrated Child Development scheme. The present study was initiated to fill this gap. As the success of any programme depends on the effective implementation and its impact on the target group, hence, it is important to study the implementation and impact of ICDS so that strategy can be chalked about effective functioning of ICDS & can lay foundation of healthy childhood for the future of bright India. It is in this background that the present study is conducted. This topic is also studied under social Welfare Administration and therefore will be beneficial for the students of Public Administration.

1.6 Importance of the Study

As the ICDS is one of the major concerns of India's commitment to child development and welfare, the present study was conducted to evaluate the implementation and impact of ICDS in Himachal Pradesh in general and in Kangra district in particular. The present study will be important as it will contribute, theoretically and empirically, to a better understanding of the issues involved in designing child welfare programme. It would be critical in designing not only appropriate policies for child welfare but also for women development. Moreover, the present study will be a great help to planner, policy makers and administrators in making efforts to streamline the process of implementation of ICDS. And also it will provide the real picture of implementation and impact of ICDS in Himachal Pradesh.

1.7 Scope of the Study

The scope of the present study was confined to analyze the implementation and impact of Integrated Child Development Services in Himachal Pradesh in general and in Kangra district in particular. The study was based on the responses obtained from the Anaganwadi Workers and ICDS beneficiaries.

1.8 Objectives of the Study

The present study was conducted to achieve following objectives.

1. To study the organizational set up for the implementation of ICDS.
2. To study and examine the child welfare programmes ,policies & legislations
3. To analyse the functioning of ICDS in Himachal Pradesh
4. To examine perception of Aanganwari Workers about ICDS
5. To study and analyse the perception of beneficiaries regarding working of ICDS in Himachal Pradesh
6. To find out the constraints and shortcoming which are hampering the effective functioning of ICDS.
7. To suggest measures that would help in enhancing the effectiveness and streamlining the effective functioning of ICDS in Himachal Pradesh

1.9 Hypotheses of the Study

To achieve aforementioned objectives, following hypotheses were tested during the study.

1. Integrated Child Development Services has not been implemented as per its spirit.
2. There is a lack of awareness among the people about the ICDS
3. There is a lack of proper infrastructure & facilities in the anganwadi centres.
4. Proper training is not imparted to anganwadi workers related to the ICDS objectives.
5. Community participation is not effective at ICDS level.
6. There is lack of proper monitoring and supervision of Anganwadi centres.

1.10 Research Methodology

The application of appropriate methods and adoption of scientific form of mind is an essential requirement for any systematic study. The methodology for the present study was as under:

1.10.1 Methodology for Data Collection

With a view to achieve the objectives and testing the hypotheses, the present study was based on the primary as well as secondary data. The methodology of data collection was as under:

1.10.1.1 Collection of Primary Data

In the present study, primary data was collected through a sample survey by administering the interview schedules. For this, well-designed schedules were prepared and administered to the respondents selected through sampling method.

1.10.1.2 Collection of Secondary Data

In the present study secondary data has been obtained from the office records of the Department of women and Child welfare, Department of Economics and statistics, Planning Department of Government of Himachal Pradesh, Block office.

It includes annual progress reports, economic surveys, annual administrative reports, etc. The secondary data has also been collected from the various books, research papers, journals and internet sites.

1.10.2 Sampling Design

A sample design is a definite plan for obtaining a sample from a given population. It refers to the technique or the procedure the researcher would adopt in selecting items for the sample. For the collection of relevant first hand data in the present study multistage random-cum-purposive sampling technique has been used.At the first stage one district was selected, at the second stage five blocks were selected, at the third stage Anganwadi centres were selected and at the fourth stage respondents were selected.

1.10.3 Selection of District

At the first stage, Kangra District was selected to represent Himachal Pradesh. To choose a representative district all the districts have been arranged on the basis of three indicators. These indicators were: total anganwadi centres, population of 0-3 years child, beneficiaries of ICDS (lactating and pregnant mothers), 3-6 years boys and girls beneficiaries.

All the twelve districts have been given ranks from 1 to 12. The ranks ranged from 1 to 12. 1st rank was given to the highest number and thus in descending order 12 to the lowest number. Then ranks were converted into scores. Maximum scores of 12 was assigned to 1st ranks, 11 to 2nd ranks, 10 to 3rd ranks and so on. After this, individual scores were added to get the total scores with respect to each district separatrly. Thereafter, final ranking of the district was made. The district that attained first ranks was selected for the study (see Table 1.13). This district was Kangra district.

Table 1.13: Procedure for the Selection of Sample District

Selection of District	Total AWC			Child Population						Beneficiaries									Total Score	Re-ranking
	AWC	Rank	Score	0-3 years	Rank	Score	3-6 Years	Rank	Score	Women Lac/Prag	Rank	Score	Boys 3-6 years	Rank	Score	Girls 3-6 years	Rank	Score		
Bilaspur	1111	9	4	16219	10	3	10229	8	5	5987	10	3	4874	8	5	4821	8	5	25	9
Chamba	1495	4	9	25658	5	8	22757	3	10	9805	4	9	10271	3	10	10225	3	10	56	4
Hamirpur	1351	7	6	17090	8	5	6989	10	3	6569	9	4	3536	10	3	3437	10	3	24	10
Kangra	4225	1	12	54742	1	12	36925	2	11	21732	1	12	12766	1	12	12373	1	12	71	1
Kinnaur	234	11	2	3105	11	2	2420	11	2	944	11	2	234	12	1	630	11	2	11	11
Kullu	1095	10	3	16848	9	4	14067	6	7	6582	8	5	5321	7	6	5482	7	6	31	8
Lahaul spiti	123	12	1	897	12	1	850	12	1	273	12	1	347	11	2	329	12	1	7	12
Mandi	3004	2	11	40915	2	11	37194	1	12	15243	2	11	10661	2	11	10377	2	11	67	2
Shimla	2152	3	10	29482	3	10	19019	4	9	10024	3	10	8515	4	9	8506	4	9	57	3
Sirmaur	1485	5	8	24317	4	9	15862	5	8	9688	5	8	7941	5	8	7921	5	8	49	5
Solan	1281	8	5	22172	6	7	11358	7	6	8238	6	7	5841	6	7	5588	6	7	39	6
Una	1364	6	7	20390	7	6	9450	9	4	7643	7	6	4740	9	4	4710	9	4	31	7

Source: Directorate of Women and Child Development, Department of Social Justice and Empowerment, Government of Himachal Pradesh, Shimla

1.10.4 Selection of Blocks

At the second stage five blocks were selected. The selection of blocks have been made after ranking all the blocks of the selected district on the basis of three indicators. These indicators were: total anganwadi centres, population of 0-3 years child, beneficiaries of ICDS (lactating and pregnant mothers), 3-6 years boys and girls beneficiaries These indicators and the procedure of ranking was the same as in case of selection of district.

There are fifteen blocks in Kangra district. All the 15 blocks were given ranks from 1 to 15. The ranks were ranged from 1 to 15. 1st rank was given to the highest number and thus in descending order 15th to the lowest number.

Then ranks were converted into scores. A maximum score of 15 was assigned to 1st rank, 14 to 2nd rank and so on. After this, individual scores were added to get the total points with respect to each block separately. Thereafter, final ranking of the block was made. The blocks that attained first five ranks were selected (see Table 1.14). These blocks were Dehra, Fatehpur, Indora, Nurpur and Pragpur.

1.10.5 Selection of Anganwadies and Respondents

At the third stage, anganwadi centres were selected from the five selected blocks of Kangra district. Ten Anganwadies were selected from each block. This anganwadi centre were selected on the basis of highest number of beneficiaries.

Thus after selecting five blocks 50 Anganwadi Centres (10 from each block) were selected. A total 350 respondents were selected for the present study. The respondent included 100 anaganwadi workers (2 from each anganwadi centre) and 250 ICDS beneficiaries, (five from each anganwadi centres) Informal discussions with officials (CDPO/ACDPO and supervisor) were also conducted (see Table 1.15).

Table 1.14 : Procedure for the selection of Sample Blocks

Block	Total AWC			Child Population						Beneficiaries									Total Score	Re-ranking
	AWC	Rank	Score	0-3 years	Rank	Score	3-6 Years	Rank	Score	Women Lac/Prag	Rank	Score	Boys 3-6 years	Rank	Score	Girls 3-6 years	Rank	Score		
Baijnath	278	8	7	3050	9	7	2967	5	11	1126	12	4	610	10	6	622	10	6	41	8
Bhawarna	230	13	3	2930	12	4	1784	12	4	1140	10	6	515	12	4	513	12	4	25	13
Dehra	387	1	15	5178	1	15	2042	7	9	2168	1	15	1018	4	12	1024	4	12	78	3
Dharmshala	182	14	2	2278	15	1	1238	14	2	987	14	2	733	9	7	705	9	7	21	14
Fatehpur	278	9	8	4427	5	11	4304	2	14	1607	7	9	1583	2	14	1412	2	14	70	4
Indora	314	5	11	4769	3	13	3179	3	13	1743	4	12	1687	1	15	1497	1	15	79	2
Kangra	295	6	10	3342	8	8	2046	6	10	1503	8	8	435	14	2	452	14	2	40	9
Lamba Gaon	276	10	6	2997	10	6	1214	15	1	1082	13	3	522	11	5	593	11	5	26	12
Nagorta Suryan	325	4	12	4223	6	10	2008	8	8	1621	5	11	919	6	10	847	8	8	59	6
Nagrota Bagwan	254	11	5	2971	11	5	1890	10	6	1127	11	5	463	13	3	489	13	3	27	11
Nurpur	349	3	13	4898	2	14	5295	1	15	2010	2	14	1193	3	13	1202	3	13	82	1
Pnachrukhi	169	15	1	2407	14	2	1973	9	7	929	15	1	357	15	1	376	15	1	13	15
Pragpur	364	2	14	4043	7	9	3160	4	12	1616	6	10	924	5	11	949	5	11	67	5
Rait	282	7	9	4455	4	12	1708	13	3	1765	3	13	902	8	8	876	6	10	55	7
Sulah	240	12	4	2774	13	3	1847	11	5	1308	9	7	905	7	9	870	7	9	37	10

Source: Directorate of Women and Child Development, Department of Social Justice and Empowerment, Government of Himachal Pradesh, Shimla

Table-1.15: Selection of Angawadi Centres and Respondents

Selected Blocks	Total number of Anganwadi Centres	Sample Anganwadies (Ten from each block)	Respondents		
			Anganwadi Workers	Beneficiaries (5 from Each Anganwadi	Total Respondents
Dehra	387	10	20	50	70
Fatehpur	278	10	20	50	70
Indora	314	10	20	50	70
Nurpur	349	10	20	50	70
Pragpur	364	10	20	50	70
Total	**1692**	**50**	**100**	**250**	**350**

Thus total sample will be consist 350 respondents (see Table 1.16)

Table-1.16: Sample for Study

Anganwadi Workers	100
ICDS Beneficiaries	250
Total	350

1.11 Data Analysis and Interpretation

Percentage is the most commonly used tool for the analysis and interpretation of collected data. Therefore, the present study employed percentage as a mean for data analysis and interpretation. A percentage has also been used in making comparison between two or more series of data. More over percentages has also been used to compare the relative terms of the distribution of two or more series of data. The formula for calculating percentage will be as below:

$$Percentage = \frac{No.of\ respondent\ s}{Total\ no.respondent\ s} \times 100$$

1.12 Scheme of Chapterization

Chapter I : Introduction

Chapter II : Organizational Set up of Integrated Child Development Services in Himachal Pradesh

Chapter III : Constitutional Provisions, Plans, Policies, Programmes and Machinery for Child welfare

Chapter IV : Functioning of Integrated child development Scheme (ICDS)

Chapter V : Socio-Economic Profile of the Respondents

Chapter VI : Perception of Anganwadi workers

Chapter VII : Perception of Beneficiaries

Chapter VIII : Conclusions and Suggestions

References

1 Sears R.R., Identification as a Form of Behavioural Development, Ed. book by D.B. Harris, 'The Concept of Development', University of Minnesota Press (1957).

2 Lai, Sunder., "Child Bangles for Screening of Severely Malnourished Children", Indian Journal of Preventive Medicine and Social Medicine, 10(1), (1979) pp.165-167.

3 Gupta, J.R., Manchanda, V.K., Juyal, R.K., and Joshi, C.B."Integrated Child Development Services Scheme: A Study of its Health Component in a Delhi Anganwari' Indian Journal of Public Administration, 25. (1978). pp 734-749.

4 Meera Mishra (February, 2016), "Reducing malnutrition: Women's health holds the key", *Yojana*, Vol. 60, New Delhi: Ministry of Information and Broadcasting. p. 46.

5 Ranjan Ray (February, 2014), "Child Health in India: Some Inconvenient Facts", in *Yojana*, Vol. 58, New Delhi: Ministry of Information and Broadcasting. p. 57.

6 Gill, Sukhdeep. 'Childcare Programme in India: Changing Trends in Human Development and Family Study in India, (Ed)by T.S. Sarswati and Baljeet Kaur. Sage Publication New Delhi, (1993) p. 18.

7 Programme Evaluation Organization (2015), *A Quick Evaluation Study of Anganwadis under ICDS*, NitiAyog, Government of India, p. 1.

8 Government of India (2012), *Children in India 2012- A Statistical Appraisal*, Social Statistics Division, Statistics Office, Ministry of Statistics and Programme Implementation, New Delhi, p. 17.

9 Rajlakshmi Murlkiharan and Vanita Kaul., 'Early Childhood Care and Education: Current Status and Problems', in "Human Development and Family Study in India', (Ed)by T.S. Sarswati and Baljeet Kaur, Sage Publicatwn, New Delhi, (1993) p. 249.

10 Vasudeva, Y.L. and Lai, Sunder, "Health and Nutrition Education at Frontline by Anganwari Workers and ANMs in Integrated Child Development Services Block Kathura", Haryana Health Journal, 10(39), 1979pp.6-9.

11 Baiokhra, Jag Mohan, The Wonderland Himachal Pradesh, H.G. Publications, New Delhi, 1992. pp. 273, 299-300

12 Vandana Khullar (March, 1998). "Integrated Child Development Services: A Critique of Evaluation Techniques". *Economic and Political Weekly*. XXXIII(10). p. 537

13 Baiokhra, Jag Mohan 'The Wonderland of Himachal Pradesh', H.G. Publications, New Delhi, (1992), p. 5

14 Government of India (2012), op.cit., p. 7.

15 Tandon, B.N., "Evaluation of Health Care Planning with Special Reference to Integrated Child Development Services",National Conference on Evaluation of Primary

Health Care Progranune, New Delhi, ICMR, April, 1980, pp. 321-330.

16 Khalakdina, M., "Evaluation of Impact of ICDS Services on the beneficiaries in the selected blocks of Himachal Pradesh", unpublished MSC thesis. Department of Child Development, Himachal Pradesh.

17 Economics and Statistics Department (2016), *Economic Survey 2015-16*, Government of Himachal Pradesh, Shimla

18 Sanjeev Kumar and Sainath Banerjee (January-March, 2015), "Integrated Child Development Services (ICDS) Programme in the Context of Urban Poor and Slum Dwellers in India: Exploring Challenges and Opportunities" in *The Indian Journal of Public Administration*, Vol. LXI, No. 1, New Delhi: Indian Institute of Public Administration. p. 94.

19 Manisha Desai, "Hope in Hard time: Women empowerment and Human Development" ,2017.

20 Public Accounts Committee (2015), *Integrated Child Development Services (ICDS) Scheme*, 14th Report (PAC No. 2045), New Delhi: Lok Sabha Secretariat, p. 1.

21 Ibid, p. 5.

22 Sanjeev Kumar and Sainath Banerjee (January-March, 2015), op.cit., p. 97.

23 Public Accounts Committee (2015), loc.cit., p. 5.

24 Planning Commission (2005), *Himachal Pradesh Development Report*, Government of India, New Delhi: Academic Foundation, , p.26.

25 M.S. Ahluwalia (1993), *History of Himachal Pradesh (2nd ed.)*, New Delhi: Intellectual Publishing House, , p. 2.

26 MianGoverdhan Singh (1999), *Wooden Temples of Himachal Pradesh*, Indus Publishing Company, New Delhi, p. 13.

27 Jag Mohan Balokhra (2010), *The Wonderland Himachal Pradesh: An Encyclopedia on the State of Western Himalayas*, New Delhi: H.G. Publications, p. 5.

28 Lai, Sunder, (1986), "Problem of Malnutrition in Pre-school Children in Rural Areas of Himachal Pradesh, Himachal Health Journal, 1(X39), 1979, pp. 13-15.

29 A.K. Tiwari (2007), *Spatial Dimension of Socio-Economic Development: A Case Study of Himachal Pradesh,* New Delhi: Kanishka Publishers and Distributors, p. 21.

30 Planning Department (2010), *Draft Annual Plan 2010-11,* Government of Himachal Pradesh, Shimla, p. 2.

31 Jag Mohan Balokhara (2010), *loc.cit.*, p. 5.

32 Economics and Statistics Department (2015), *Economic Survey 2014-15*, Government of Himachal Pradesh, Shimla, p. 2.

33 Santosh Mehrotra (March 2006), "Child Malnurition and Gender Discrimination in South Asia", *Economic and Political Weekly*, XLI(10), pp. 11-17.

34 Economics and Statistics Department (2016), *Economic Survey 2015-16*, Government of Himachal

Pradesh, Shimla,p.21

35 Economics and Statistics Department (2015), *Socio-Economic Indicators of Himachal Pradesh 2016-17*, Shimla: Government of Himachal Pradesh, p. 1.

36 Department of Statistics and Economics (2015), *Economic Survey 2014-15*, Government of Himachal Pradesh, Shimla, p. 129.

37 Planning Department (2012), *Draft 12th Five Year Plan 2012-17 and Annual Plan 2013-14*, Government of Himachal Pradesh, Shimla, p. 122.

38 Economics and Statistics Department (2015), op.cit. p. 137.

39 Roa, P.S.S., Prasad, K.R. and Indira Bai, K. , "A Study of Leprosy among Urban and Rural School Children " Leprosy in India, 54(1), 1982; pp.100-109.

40 Lai, Sunder, (1986), "Problem of Malnutrition in Pre-school Children in Rural Areas of Himachal Pradesh, Himachal Health Journal, 1(X39), 1979, pp. 13-15.

41 Planning Department (2010), *Draft Annual Plan 2010-11,* Government of Himachal Pradesh, Shimla,

42 Planning Department (2012), *Draft 12th Five Year Plan 2012-17 and Annual Plan 2013-14,* Government of Himachal Pradesh, Shimla, p. 122.

43 Economics and Statistics Department (2016), loc.cit., p. 130-131.

44 Nair, Narayan. and Bansal, R.D., "Evaluation of Integrated Child Development Service Scheme " M.D. thesis. Department of Preventive and Social Medicine, Jawaharlal Institute of Post Graduate Medical Education and Research, Pondicheary, NIPCCID, New Delhi

45 Planning Department (2009), *District Human Development Report: Kangra,* Government of Himachal Pradesh, Shimla., p. 5.

46 *Ibid.*

47 Gupta, S.B., Shrivastava, B.C., Bhushan, B.C. and Sharma, P., "Impact of Child Development Services ", Indian Journal of Medical Research, (1984) pp. 363

48 Planning Department (2009), *op.cit.,* p. 32.

49 *Ibid.*

50 Arun Gupta and Jon E. Rohde, "Infant and Young Child under Nutrition", *Economic and Political weekly,* 29(49), pp.

51 Mirai Chatterjee (August -September 2006), "Decentralized Children Services", *Economic and Political Weekly,* 41(34), pp. 3660-3669.

52 Renuka Chowdhury (2006). "ICDS: India's Response to Early Child Development", *Yojana.* 50(11). pp. 5-9.

53 Santosh Mehrotra (March 2006), "Child Malnurition and Gender Discrimination in South Asia", *Economic and Political Weekly*, XLI(10), pp. 11-17.

54 Manjulika Gautam (November, 2006), "Chile Development in India", *Yojna*, 50(11), pp. 25-30.

55 Michele Gragnolati, Caryn Bredenkamp, Monica Das Gupta, Yi-Kyoung Lee, Meera Shekar (March 25, 2006). "ICDS and Persistent Undernutrition Strategies to Enhance the Impact". *Economic and Political Weekly*. XLI(12). pp. 1193-1201.

56 Deepa Sinha (August-September, 2006), "Rethinking ICDS: A Right based Perspective", *Economic and Political Weekly*, 41(34), p. 3689.

57 Nandini Nayak and Naresh C Saxena (August 26, 2006). "Implementation of ICDS in Bihar and Jharkhand". *Economic and Political Weekly*.XLI(34). pp. 3680-3684.

58 Suman K. Chandra and V. Gang Reddy (2007), Segmented labour Market for Children- Is it a demand side Creation? A case Study of Industry in Makapur.

59 D. Channa Reddy (2007) " ChildLabour: A Challenge to the Nation", *Rural Development and Empowerment of Weaker Sections – Practice, Promotion and Programmes*, New Delhi: The Associated Publishers.

60 Sharda Srinivasan and S. Arjun Bedi (November-December 2009), "Girl Child Protection Scheme in Tamil Nadu", *Economics and Political Weekly*, XLIV(48). pp. 10-12.

61 Yogesh Gairola and Amita Chauhan (January – March, 2009), *Think India Quarterly*, 12(1).

62 Programme Evaluation Organization (2011), *Evaluation Report on Integrated Child Development Services Volume I & II*, Planning Commission, New Delhi: Government of India

63 PerianayagamArokiasamy, Srinivas Goli (October 20, 2012). "Explaining the Skewed Child Sex Ratio in Rural India Revisiting the Landholding-Patriarchy Hypothesis". *Economic and Political* Weekly. XLVII(42). pp. 85-94.

64 MoatulaAo, HemkhothangLhungdim (February 8, 2014). "Re-Estimating Malnourishment and Inequality among Children in North-east India". *Economic and Political* Weekly. XLIX(6). pp. 53-63.

65 Victor Aguayo, Gayatri Singh, Nina Badgaiyan (April 5, 2014). "Scoring Child Nutrition in India: Measuring the Performance of States", *Economic & Political Weekly*.XLIX(14), pp. 97-103.

66 Reetika Khera (October 3, 2015). "Children's Development Baby Steps in Odisha". *Economic and Political Weekly.* l (40). pp. 44-49.

67 Esther Duflo "Women Empowerment and Economic Development" Journal of Economic Literature 2016

68 Raghuvansh Dhas "programmes for women" new delhi 2016

69 Y.K. Raghurajan, "Women welfare Programmes", Omega Publication, 2016.

70 Manisha Desai, "Hope in Hard time: Women empowerment and Human Development" ,2017.

71 Rajesh Mishra (February, 2017), Determinants of Child Malnutrition in Tribal Areas of Madhya Pradesh, *Economic & Political Weekly*. LII(5). pp. 50-57.

72 Kukum Kumari Sharma (November, 2017) "A Study of the Impact of Socio-economic Status on the Nutritional of Pregnant Women in Patna". *Journal of Community Guidance & Research*, 34(3).

73 Sharda Srinivasan and S. Arjun Bedi (November-December 20018), "Girl Child Protection Scheme in Tamil Nadu", *Economics and Political Weekly*, XLIV(48). pp. 10-12.

74 Abhilasha Sampagar,bhavana Lakhhar. "Indian J Child Health." A Study to Assess Factor Associated with Development Delay and Nutritional Status among the Children with Cleft Lip and / or Cleft Palate vol 5, issue 6, June 17, 2018

75 Kleven, Henrik Landais.Camille, ." national bureau of economics research "Children and Gender Inequality: Evidence From Denmark, January 1, 2018.

76 Dileep Dandotiya, Angeline Priya, Manju Toppo, Veena Melwai and Soumitra Sethia (2018), "A study on Utilization and Satisfaction of ICDS Services in Aanganwadis of Urban Bhopal". *Indian Journal of Youth & Adolescent Health.* 5(1). pp. 30-33.

77 AbhilashaSampagar, Bhavana Lakhakar, Tanvi Bafna and Niranjan S Mahantashetti (June, 2018), "A Study to assess the factors associated with development delay and nutritional status among the children with cleft lip and/or cleft palate". *Indian Journal of Child Health,* 5(6). pp. 407-412.

78 D. Channa Reddy (2018) "ChildLabour: A Challenge to the Nation", *Rural Development and Empowerment of Weaker Sections – Practice, Promotion and Programmes,* New Delhi: The Associated Publishers.

2

ORGANIZATIONAL SETUP OF INTEGRATED CHILD DEVELOPMENT SERVICES IN HIMACHAL PRADESH

Organization plays an important role in the administration. Without proper organization, whole system of administration would get collapsed. These are interlinked and interconnected as well as interdependent to each other[1]. An organization set out a proper and identifiable boundary, a normative order, authority ranks, communications system, and work for achieving the goals or a set of goals.[2]

We can say that an organization is a purposeful system with several sub-systems where individuals are organized to achieve certain predetermined goals by proper division of labour and coordination of activities.[3] Organization can be said as the combination of group of activity in the enterprises. In this sense organization structure can be thought of as the machine through which management works to accomplish its tasks.[4]

The various characteristics of an organization are communication, co-operative efforts, common objectives and rules and regulations. The persons who form the organization must be in a position to communicate with each other and through proper coordination among them the goal can be achieved easily.

However, practically formal organizations deviates from the lines expected from the established structures because of informal relationships. Thus, both the structure and informal relationships at a point of time determines the effectiveness of an organization[5].

Organizational success depends on its structure. It is the structure in which human beings can perform most effectively. It is important to define the areas of authority and responsibility of administrative units, so that they can function properly subject to constitutional and political controls. Worse organizational structure of ministries often a major cause of inefficient implementation of government policies and programmes[6].

Integrated Child Development Services (ICDS) in India is the world's largest integrated early childhood programme, with over 40,000 centres nationwide. Since its inception in 1975, the programme has matured and expanded, despite difficulties in adapting to the vastly different local circumstances found on the Indian subcontinent. UNICEF helped launch the ICDS programme and provided financial and technical assistance along with the World Bank. The programme today covers over 4.8 million expectant and nursing mothers and over 23 million children under the age of six. Of these children, more than half participate in early learning activities.[7]

Hence, in this chapter, an attempt has been made to discuss the organizational structure for the implementation of Integrated Child Development Services .Ministry of Women & Child Development is the main Ministry at the central level working with implementation of ICDS in India as discussed below.

2.1 Ministry of Women and Child Development

The Ministry of Women and Child Development has nodal responsibility to highlight the rights and issues of women and children and promote their survival, protection, development and participation in a proper manner. The Ministry has core objective of addressing gaps in State action for women and children and for promoting inter-Ministerial and inter-sectoral convergence to create gender equitable and child-centred policies, programmes, schemes and legislation.[8] The Department of Women and Child Development was set up in the year 1985 as a part of the Ministry of Human Resource Development to provide more resources for development of women and children.[9]

The Ministry of Women and Child Development, Government of India, was established as a separate Ministry with effect from 30th January, 2006. In 2014, the Ministry was headed for the first time by a Cabinet rank Minister. It has the nodal responsibility to advance the rights and concerns of women and children who keep total of 67.7% of the country's population, as per 2011 Census.[10]The prime motto of the Ministry is to have holistic development of Women and Children. As a nodal Ministry for the advancement of women and children, the Ministry formulates plans, policies and programmes; enacts/ amends legislation, guides and coordinates the efforts of both governmental and non-governmental organizations working in the field of Women and Child Development. Besides, playing its nodal role, the Ministry implements certain innovative programmes for women and children. These programmes cover welfare and support services, training for employment and income generation, awareness generation and gender sensitization. These programmes play a supplementary and complementary role to the other general developmental programmes in the sectors of health, education and rural development etc.[11]

2.1.1 Organizational Structure of Ministry of Women and Child Development

Minister of Women and Child Development is the head of the Ministry of Women and Child Development at the centre level. He/ She is assisted by a Secretary (WCD), who is the administrative head of the ministry. Secretary (WCD) is assisted by two Additional Secretaries, four Joint Secretaries, a Financial Adviser, an Economic Adviser and a Statistical Adviser. The Organizational chart of the Ministry has been shown in Chart 2.1.

2.1.2 Subjects allocated to the Ministry of Women and Child Development

Subject allocated to the Ministry of Women and Child Development (MahilaAur Bal VikasMantralaya) vide Government notification dated 16.2.2006[12], are as follows:

1. Welfare of the family.

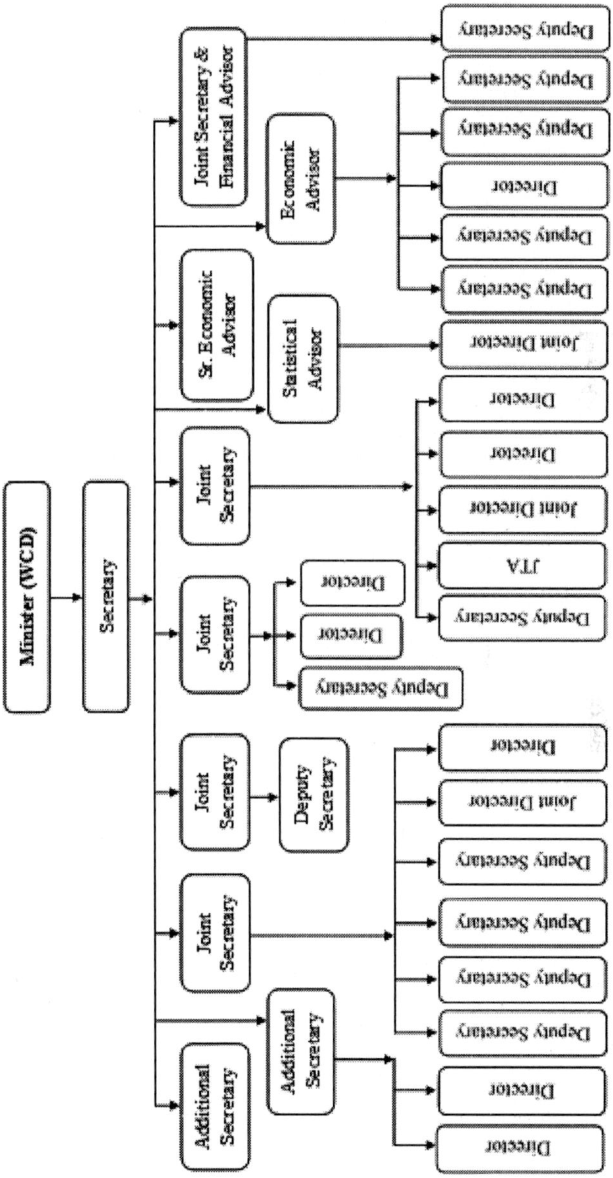

Chart 2.1Organizational Structure for the Implementation of ICDS at the Centre Level

Source: Ministry of Women and Child Development. *Annual Report 2016-17.*

2. Women and Child welfare and co-ordination of activities of other Ministries and Organisations in connection with this subject.

3. Reference from the United Nations Organizations relating to traffic in women and children.

4. Care of pre-school children including pre-primary education.

5. National Nutrition Policy, National Plan of Action for Nutrition and National Nutrition Mission.

6. Charitable and religious endowments pertaining to subjects allocated to this Department.

7. Promotion and development of voluntary effort on subjects allocated to this Department.

8. Implementation of following Acts

a) The Immoral Traffic (Prevention) Act, 1956 (as amended up to 1986);

b) The Indecent Representation of Women (Prevention) Act, 1986 (60 of 1986);

c) The Dowry Prohibition Act, 1961 (as amended up to 1986);

d) The Commission of Sati (Prevention) Act, 1987 (3 of 1988), excluding the administration of criminal justice in regard to offences under these Acts.

9. Proper coordination of activities and programmes of Cooperative for Assistance and Relief Everywhere (CARE).

10. Implementation of the Infant Milk Substitutes, Feeding Bottles and Infant Food Regulation of Production, Supply and Distribution) Act, 1992 (41 of 1992).

11. Planning, Research, Evaluation, Monitoring, Project Formulations, Statistics and Training relating to the welfare

and development of women and Children, including of gender sensitive data base.

12. United Nations Children's Fund (UNICEF).

13. Central Social Welfare Board (CSWB).

14. National Institute of Public Cooperation and Child Development (NIPCCD).

15. Food and Nutrition Board.

16. (i) Development and popularization of subsidiary and protective foods.

    (ii) Nutrition extension.

17. Women's Empowerment and Gender Equity.

18. National Commission for Women.

19. Rashtriya Mahila Kosh.

20. Juvenile delinquency and vagrancy.

21. Probation of Juvenile offenders.

22. Issues relating to adoption, Central Adoption Resource Agency and Child Help Line (Childline).

23. The Children Act, 1960 (60 of 1960).

24. The Juvenile Justice (Care and Protection of Children) Act, 2000 (56 of 2000).

25. The Child Marriage- Restraint Act, 1929 (19 of 1929).

26. Institutional and non-institutional services for the care and development of children in need including orphans and orphanages.

The Ministry is working according to the Five Year and Annual Plans for inclusive growth and development of women and children and implementing them with the support of State Governments/UTs, Government and Non-Government Organizations for achieving its mandate.[13]

2.1.3 Objectives of the Ministry

The objectives of the Ministry have been discussed as under:

1. Laying foundation for development of children below 6 years with focus on Supplementary Nutrition and pre-school, non-formal education and to enhance the awareness and capability of mothers for nutritional and health needs of the child's.
2. Empowering adolescent Girls and Boys to meet the day to day challenges.
3. Providing a safe and secure environment for overall development of children who are in need of care and protection and children in conflict with law.
4. Review of existing laws and forming new laws to check discrimination against women.
5. Mainstreaming gender concerns in the policies and programmes of Government of India and State Governments through gender budgeting.
6. Promoting the rights based approach in the formulation of policy for children.
7. Socio-economic empowerment of marginalized women.[14]

2.2. Machinery for implementation of ICDS in Himachal Pradesh

Department of social Justice& Empowerment is the main Department concerned with implementation of ICDS in Himachal Pradesh as given below:

2.2.1 Organizational Structure of Department of Social Justice & Empowerment in Himachal Pradesh

Department of Social Justice and Empowerment has the sole responsibility of implementing the Integrated Child Development Scheme in Himachal Pradesh. This department implements the scheme through directorate of Women and Child development, which was set up in the year 2011. The programme was first started in Pooh Development Block. At present this programme is being run in all 77 development blocks of the state and a child development project is being run in Shimla city. Under this program, 18386 Anganwadi centres and 539 mini Anganwadi centres are sanctioned in the state, out of which 18385 Anganwadi centres and 522 mini Anganwadi centres are working properly.[15]

The Department of Social Justice and Empowerment has the overall responsibility of implementing Integrated Child Development Services in the State. It works for the socio-economic development of the women, child and weaker section of the society. In the year 2011, a new Directorate, namely, Directorate of Women and Child Development, has been established level under the Department of Social Justice and Empowerment. All the matters concerning socio-economic development and protection are given to this directorate. It implements all the programmes relateding to child development and protection of women empowerment.

The organizational structure for the implementation of ICDS in Himachal Pradesh has been shown in Chart 2.2.

Chart-2.2 Organizational Structure of the Department of Social Justice and Empowerment in Himachal Pradesh

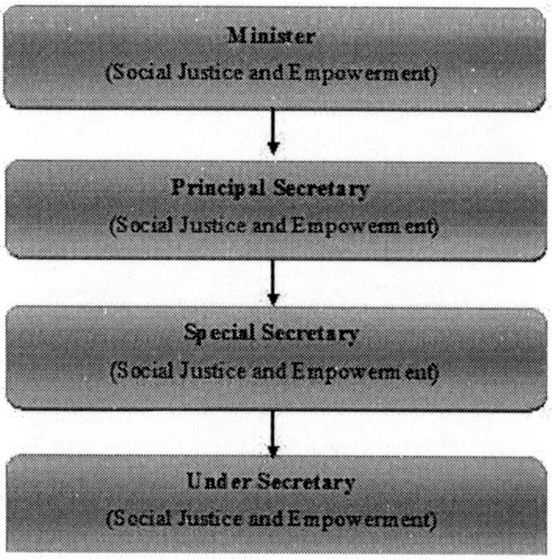

Source: *http://admis.hp.nic.in/himachal/welfare/secttlevel.htm*

The department of Social Justice and Empowerment is headed by a Minister (Political Head). He is assisted by Principal Secretary (Administrative Head), Special Secretary and under Secretary. The Principal Secretary is responsible for the formulation and implementation of policies, plans and programmes relating to social justice and empowerment. He acquaints Minister-in-Charge with all the activities of the department. Special Secretary and Under Secretary helps the Principal Secretary in the administration and control of the department.

2.2.2 Functions of the Department of Social Justice and Empowerment

Department of Social Justice and Empowerment implements the following policies of Directorate of Women and Child Development in coordination with various departments / stakeholders / coordinators: -

1. National Policy for Children
2. National Policy for Nutrition
3. National Policy for empowerment of women

In view of above, the Department of Social Justice and Empowerment has been given the following areas for the implementation and monitoring of following schemes& programme -[16]

Implementation of State sponsored schemes such as Beti Hai Anmol Scheme, Chief Minister Kanyadan Yojana, Women Self Employment Assistance, Women Development Corporation, Widow Rehabilitation Scheme, Mother Teresa Helpless Maternal sambal Scheme, Nari Seva Sadan, Special Women's Upliftment Scheme, Rape Victim Financial Assistance and Support Services Women Development Incentive Scheme, by the department.

1. The Central Sponsored Schemes are like Indira Gandhi Matritva Sahayog Yojana, the Rajiv Gandhi Kishori Sashakti Karan Yojana Beti Bachao Beti Padhao scheme are being implemented by the department for the upliftment of women and adolescent girls.

2. For the development of children, central sponsored schemes such as Integrated Child Protection Scheme and Integrated Child Development Schemes are implemented through the department. It also ensures implementation of Acts relating to Children and Women[17]

a) Himachal Pradesh Marriage Registration Act of 1996

b) Domestic Violence Act 2005 for the protection of women.

c) Child Marriage Immigrant Act of 2006

d) Juvenile Justice Act 2006

e) Sexual Harassment Act 2012 for the protection of children.

f) Act related to prevent sexual harassment of women at work level (2013)

(a) Functions of Different officials at Departmental Level

i) Functions and responsibilities of Principal Secretary (Social Justice and Empowerment)

According to the mandate of the department Principal Secretary has the responsibility for fixation and implementation of policies, programs, schemes, rules and regulations. He/She is also responsible for presenting the following types of cases related to the department, before the Minister in charge of the department.[18]

a) All those matter which have placed in front of the Council of Ministers.

b) All Legislative Assembly cases

c) Such matters which are to be placed before the Governor or under Rule 58 which are to be placed before Chief Minister.

d) All statutory proposals and the proposals of new schemes

ii) Functions of Special/Additional/Joint/Deputy/Under Secretary

a) To help the Principal Secretary in total control and administration of powers of the Department of Social Justice and Empowerment.

b) Help the Principal Secretary in making Decisions and plans.

c) Present all cases and schemes in the proper manner with the possible solutions and suggestions in front of the High Authorities.

d) To take steps on decisions taken by the government and to coordinate with the related agencies for the implementation of the policies and programs.

e) To fulfil the responsibilities handed over by senior officials so that they can give their time on important matters.

f) Issuing the orders with certification as per the decisions taken by competent authorities.

2.3 Organization structure for implementation of ICDS at the Directorate Level in Himachal Pradesh

Directorate of women and child development functions under the Department of Social Justice and Empowerment. The directorate is headed by a director. He/She is assisted by Additional Director and Joint Director (ICDS). Under Joint Director (ICDS) there are two Programme Officers and one Special Nutrition Officer. The directorate of women and child development has the overall responsibility of implementation and monitoring ICDS in the State.[19] The organizational Structure of Directorate of Women and Child Development in Himachal Pradesh has been shown in Chart 2.3.

Chart-2.3: Organizational Structure of Directorate of Women and Child Development

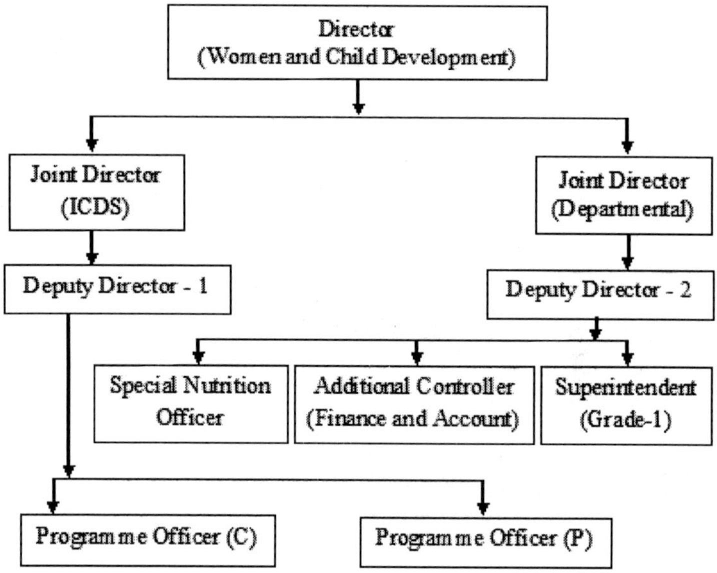

2.3.1 Objective of Directorate of Women and Child Development

The objectives of Directorate of Women and Child Development of Himachal Pradesh are as follows.

1. To improve the nutritional and health status of children in the age groups of 0-6 years and to increase the capacity of mothers to look after the normal health and nutritional needs of children through proper nutrition and health education;

2. To built an infrastructure and support system to prevent abuse, violence and also to provide safe environment to children in conflict with law;

3. Empowering adolescent girls (11-18 years) through nutrition, health care & life skill education; and

4. Proper execution of law are required to stop discrimination against women, policies & programmes for promoting social, economic and political empowerment of women.[20]

2.4 Functions of Directorate of Women and Child Development

Directorate of Women and Child Development of Himachal Pradesh performs following functions.

1. Implementation of legislation, policies, programmes and schemes for social and economic empowerment of women, protection and development of children;

2. To provide an institutional mechanism and structures in the State for implementing the Integrated Child Protection Scheme (ICPS);

3. Proper access of women to Micro Finance for Economic Empowerment and capacity building through skill development and market support;

4. Implementation of Protection of Women from Domestic Violence Act, 2005, Implementation of Rajiv Gandhi Scheme for Empowerment of Adolescent Girls – SABLA in four districts of the State i.e. Chamba, Kangra, Kullu and Solan and Beti Bachao Beti padhao scheme was also implemented.

5. Advocacy and awareness generation about rights of women and children particularly the girls child;

6. Institutionalization of Gender Budgeting process, capacity building of officers of State Government Departments;

7. Implementation of Indira Gandhi Matritva Sahyag Yojana (IGMSY) in Hamirpur District on pilot basis for health care of mothers and infants; and

8. Implementation of State Specific Schemes – Beti Hai Anmol, Mata Shabari Mahila Sashakti karan Yojan etc.[21]

2.5 Organizational structure at the District level and below

The organizational structure for the implementation of Integrated Child Development Services at the district level and below has been shown in Chart 2.4.

Chart-2.4: Organizational Structure for ICDS at District, Block and Village Level

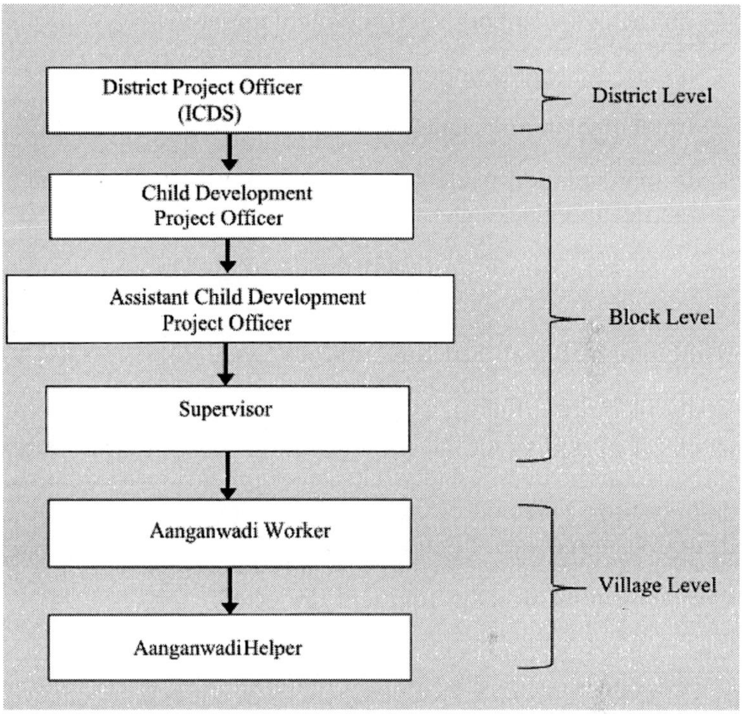

Source: *Directorate of Women and Child Development Shimla, Government of Himachal Pradesh*

2.5.1 District Level

At the district level District Programme Officer (ICDS) has the responsibility for the proper working of Integrated Child development Services. District Programme Officers performs the following functions:

1. Maintains record of establishment of the office of District Program Officer.
2. Receipt and distribution of food items under special nutrition program.
3. Receipt and distribution of medicine Kit / Pre-school Kit.

4. As drawing and disbursing officer maintain and provide full information about the amount / budget received.
5. The achievement of each component under ICDS.
6. Notice of Benefits under State Schemes.
7. Implementation of state schemes at the district level.
8. Implementation of departmental testing programmes at district and block level.
9. Reviewing the monthly progress of ICDS and State Schemes.[22]

2.5.1(i) Organizational Structure at Block Level

At the block level, there is a Child Development Project Officer (CDPO) is responsible for the implementation ICDS at the block level. He is assisted by Assistant Child Development Project Officer and supervisor. Function of Child development Project Officer and supervisor has been discussed as under:

(a) Functions of Child Development Project Officer

The CDPO have to play an important role in the scheme of ICDS. He/She is responsible for the organization of services and administration and implementation of the scheme at the field level.[23] The Child Development Project Officer will:

1. Be the Principal executive functionary of the ICDS team at the project level.
2. Allocate monthly and yearly budgets to each Anganwadi Centre and release funds.
3. Supervise and guide the work of the entire project team, including Supervisors and AWWs
4. Help the AWWs at initial stages to collect the primary data of the project.
5. Look after all the equipment and material supplied are accounted for and used and maintained properly.

6. Acts as the Convenor of the Project Coordination Committee or Functional Committee.
7. Ensure proper maintenance of registers and records both at Project and at AWC level and inspect the records periodically
8. Make necessary arrangements for procurement, transportation, storage and distribution of various supplies.
9. Act as an integral part of the Block team.
10. Incur contingency expenditure on articles, materials etc. required by AWWs and other Project functionaries and would act as DDO for ICDS scheme, excluding health inputs.
11. Make effort to obtain local community's involvement and participation in programmes and services.
12. Conduct educational programmes such as nutrition and hygiene.
13. Responsible for preparing and dispatching periodical progress reports to concerned higher officials.
14. Help AWWs informing and operating village level coordination committees.
15. Take all necessary measures for staff recruitment and development in the capacity of in charge ICDS team and the block level. He will depute Supervisors and AWWs for training/ orientation as and when required.
16. Undertake field visit periodically and will submit his monthly tour programme to higher officials.

Additional Responsibility

She/ He will make effort to costruct own building of AWC. Coordinate with Urban Development Department to install smokeless chullah, sanitary latrines and water filters at AWCs in urban areas. She/he will coordinate with Rural Water Supply/ PHE department to install hand pumps in those AWCs where no drinking water facility is available. She/he will help/ coordinate with AWWs undertaking literacy classes under NAEP. She/ he will remain in close contact with DRC where referrals will be made by AWWs. Coordinate Demonstration on Nutrition and Health Education. Ensure that each AWC is provided with a Community Growth Chart. Guide AWWs to involve Adolescent Girls in the activities of AWWs and service to be provided to them. Training programme for Adolescent Girls. She/he will arrange for field placements of ICDS functionaries. She/he will develop a Resource Centre in his office. Materials on Pre-school Education, Health and Nutrition and Community Participation will be included in the library of the centre[24].

(b) Functions of Supervisor

Supervisor at the block level performs the following functions in the implementation of ICDS:

The functions and responsibility of supervisor are as follows:[25]

1. Inspection of Anganwadi centres.
2. To provide the services of Anganwadi workers, select the target group, list the beneficiaries and assist in the maintenance of the records.
3. Work as mediator between Child Development Project Officer and Anganwadi Workers.
4. Provide help and facilities to the anganwadi workers to identify malnourished and unhealthy children.
5. Monthly inspection of Anganwadi centres.
6. Collaborate with the Child Development Project Officer in the implementation of various works and programmes of project administration.

2.5.2 Organizational Structure at Village Level

Anganwadis started by the Indian government in 1975 as part of the Integrated Child Development Services programme to reduce child hunger and malnutrition. Anganwadi is a government sponsored child-care and mother-care center in India. It caters to children in the 0-6 age group. The Anganwadi system is managed by the Anganwadi worker who is a health worker selected from the community and provided four months training in health, nutrition and child-care. She is incharge of an Anganwadi which covers a population of 1000. 20 to 25 Anganwadi workers are supervised by a Supervisor. Four supervisors are headed by a Child Development Projects Officer (CDPO). They provide proper services to poor families in need of immunization, healthy food, clean water, clean toilets and a learning environment for infants, toddlers and pre-schoolers. They also provide similar services for expectant and nursing mothers. Anganwadis are India's primary tool against the scourges of child malnourishment, infant mortality and curbing preventable diseases such as polio. As a result of its efforts infant mortality rate has declined in recent years.[26]

(a) Population Norms for setting ICDS Project and Aanganwadi Centre

The revised Population norms for setting up a Project, Anganwadi Centre and Mini-AWC are as under:

(i) ICDS Projects:

(a) Community Development Block in a State should be the unit for sanction of an ICDS Project in rural/tribal areas, irrespective of number of villages/population in it.

(b) The existing norm of 1 lakh population for sanction of urban project is there

For blocks with more than two lack population, States could opt for more than one Project (@ one per one lack population) or could opt for one project only. In the latter case, staff could be suitably strengthened based on population or number of AWCs in the block. Similarly, for blocks with population of less than 1 lack or so, staffing pattern of CDPO office could be less than that of a normal block[27].

(ii) Anganwadi Centres for Rural/Urban Projects

Population 400-800 = 1 AWC

Population 800-1600 = 2 AWCs

Population 1600-2400 = 3 AWCs

Thereafter in multiples of 800 = 1 AWC

For Mini-AWC

Population 150-400 = 1 Mini-AWC

For Tribal /Riverine /Desert, Hilly and other difficult areas/ Projects

Population 300-800 = 1 AWC

Mini- AWC

Population 150-300 = 1 Mini AWC

(b) Functions and Responsibilities of Anganwadi worker

For effective implementation of the programmes the Anganwadi Worker (AWW), who has to be a local woman belonging to the same village/ward, required to perform the following functions:

1. To conduct community survey and enlisting beneficiaries. The community to be covered should be surveyed to find out the number of children below six years of age, pregnant and nursing mothers. Data about the number of families, family members and income should be obtained. Broader statistics particularly of new births and deaths (especially child and maternal deaths) is maintained. Handicapped, exploited and destitute children should also be listed. In the collection and compilation of all this information, the supervisor would be guiding and helping the AWWs.

2. Supplementary feeding of 0-6 years of children and pregnant and nursing mothers.

3. Organise awareness camps for women, children and community awareness of population control with suitable education system.

4. Non-formal pre-school education of the children between 3 to 6 years of age.

5. Primary health care and first aid to children under six and pregnant and nursing mothers.

6. Assisting health staff in immunization and health check-up.

7. Providing referral services for severely under-nourished/ mal-nourished, sick and at-risk children and cases of communicable diseases and children with impairments.

8. Maintaining records/ registers particularly weight cards, child health cards, supplementary nutrition records, anganwadi attendance records etc.

9. Detection of impairments among children in the early stage and help in the prevention of disabilities.

10. Contacting the parents of children coming to the Anganwadi through home visits and ensuring their participation in the programme.

11. Coodination with other institutions in the village/urban e.g. Panchayats, Mahila Mandals, Schools, Local organizations etc. and seeking their support and participation in the ICDS programme.[28]

Additional Responsibilities of Anganwadi worker

Conduct annual village level Educational Survey of all households along with Primary School Teachers. Provide information on growth of each child from the Growth Chart maintained by her. Also educate Community about Mahila Samridhi Yojana and Rashtriya Mahila Kosh and motivate them to adopt the schemes where the schemes are applicable. Assist in activities of Village Bal Vikas Samiti constituted at the village level.

Act like Village Rehabilitation Worker, she will create awareness for early detection of disability, its prevention and making appropriate referrals. She will involve adolescent girls in the various activities of AWCs and provide services under the schemes for Adolescent Girls.

2.5.3 Functions of Anganwadi helpers[29]

1. Cooking and service the food to children and mothers;
2. Cleaning the Anganwadi premises daily; fetching water for Anganwadi;
3. Cleanliness of small children;
4. Collection of small children from village at the Anganwadi.

In addition, anganwadi helpers should develop following skills:

1. Training children to be hygienic in their personal and toilet habits;
2. Assist AWW in health check-ups, weighing of children and immunization of pregnant women and children;
3. Preparation of simple recipies, conservation of nutrients through correct methods of sanitation, storage and cooking;
4. Organizing and conducting simple play and creative activities for the overall development of children;
5. Organising group activities like singing songs with music and actions, storytelling dramatization etc. using folk media;
6. Disposal of food wastes, peels etc;
7. Developing a small kitchen garden
8. Ensuring participation of mothers in the Anganwadi Programme;

9. Creating an awareness among mother about nutrition, health and play needs of their children;

10. Arrange equipment in the Anganwadi

Conclusion

The analysis of organizational structure clearly reveals that for the achievement of goals and objectives of Integrated Child Development Services a well-organized structure has been established both at the Center & State level. .At the central level Ministry of women and Child development is responsible for the implementation of Integrated Child Development Services in the Country. The Department of Women and Child Development was set up in the year 1985 as a part of the Ministry of Human Resource Development to give the much needed impetus to the holistic development of women and children. In the year 2006, the Department has been upgraded to a Ministry. In Himachal Pradesh Department of Social Justice and Empowerment has the overall responsibility of implementing Integrated Child Development Services. It works for the socio-economic development of the women, child and weaker sections of the society. Himachal Pradesh has shown its concern for the welfare of children through setting a new. Directorate of Women and Child Development. All the matters concerning socio-economic development and protection are given through this Directorate. It implements all the programmes concerning child development, protection and women empowerment. In other words, it has the overall responsibility of implementation and monitoring of ICDS in the state. Then there is ICDS team comprising of Child Development and Project Officer (CDPO), Assistant Child Development and Project Officer (ACDPO), Supervisors, Anganwadi Workers and Anganwadi Helper who are engaged in providing adequate services to women and children to ensure their physical, mental and social development. These services are being provided through a network of Anganwadi centres spread throughout the State.

References

1 N. Jayapalan, *Public Administration*, New Delhi: Atlantic Publishers and Distributors, 2000,p. 46.

2 Richard H. Hall, *Organization: Structure and Process*, New Jersey: Prentice Hall, Inc., Englewood Cliffs, 1972, p. 9.

3 Uma Sekaran, *Organizational Behaviour: Text and Cases (2nd ed.)*, New Delhi: Tata McGraw Hill Publishing Company Ltd., 2004, pp. 1-2.

4 Oliver Sheldon quoted in K.D. Trivedi, *Organization and Administrative Theories*, Jaipur: Research Publication, , 1999, p. - 10

5 A.S. Malik, "Rural Development Administration in India", in Surat Singh and Mohinder Singh, ed., *Rural Development in the 21st Century: A Multi-Dimensional Study*, New Delhi: Deep and Deep Publications Pvt. Ltd., 2006, pp. 224 and 225.

6 Girish Malhotra, *op.cit.*, 2006, pp. 65 and 66.

7 *India - Integrated Child Development Services (ICDS)*, retrieved from https://www.unicef.org: https://www.unicef.org/earlychildhood/files/india_icds.pdf

8 Ministry of Women and Child Development. *Five Year Strategic Plan (2011-2016)*, New Delhi: Government of India, p. 8.

9 http://www.performance.gov.in/?q=ministry/wcd

10 Ministry of Women and Child Development. *Annual Report 2016-17*, New Delhi: Government of India, p. 3.

11 *India - Integrated Child Development Services (ICDS)*, retrieved from https://www.unicef.org: https://www.unicef.org/earlychildhood/files/india_icds.pdf.

12 Ministry of Women and Child Development. *Annual Report 2016-17*, New Delhi: Government of India, pp. 207-2010.

13 Ministry of Women and Child Development. *Annual Report 2016-17*, New Delhi: Government of India, pp. 205-207.

3

CONSTITUTIONAL PROVISIONS, PLANS, POLICIES, PROGRAMMES AND MACHINERY FOR CHILD WELFARE

The children- of today will make the India of tomorrow. The way we bring them up will determine the future of the country.

Jawaharlal Nehru

Children are the real assets of any country. Children's development is extremely necessary for the development of Nation.[1] In the 21st century the role of the child welfare system is to ensure the security, permanency, and well-being of children and youth whose families are not able to meet these needs.[2]Children are not only the future of a nation, but they are the future of the world and mankind also. They are real asset of the nation. Children should be nurtured and cared for in its tender and vulnerable age to enable him to become a dynamic citizen of tomorrow. Children are found working in the most inhuman, hazardous and hostile circumstances where they may be abused harassed and exploited due to their vulnerability.[3]

According to the United Nations convention on the right of child, child means a person male or female who is below 18 years of age. In India, it is found that, around 440 million are children which constitute around 40 percent of country's population. India has high rate of neo-natal deaths which is around 35 percent in the world. Around 50 percent of child mortality occurs in the country. Keeping in view the problems and challenges faced by the Indian children, laws have been introduced and various policies and programmes are being implemented for the welfare of children in India.[4]

3.1 Definitions of Child

Definition of the child (Article 1) (THE CONVENTION ON THE RIGHTS OF THE CHILD): The Convention defines a 'child' as a person below the age of 18, unless the laws of a particular country set the legal age for adulthood younger.

According to the (Legal-dictionary)

Child is:

1) A person's natural offspring.
2) person 14 years and under. A "child" should be distinguished from a "minor" who is anyone under 18 in almost all states.

According to Cambridge Dictionary child means "A boy or girl from the time of birth until he or she is an adult."

The Child Labour (Prohibition and Regulation) Act, 1986 defines a child as a person who has not completed fourteen years of age.

The Census of India considers children to be any person below the age of 14, as do most government programmes.

As per the ILO (International labour organisation) in case of Hazardous work the minimum age is to be 18 years and only under strict conditions it is to be reduced to 16. It further states that the basic minimum age of work should not be below the age of finishing compulsory school which is generally 15 years of age. In this case there is exception for the developing countries where the minimum age is 14 years. Children between the ages of 13-15 years may do light work that does not jeopardize their health and safety or hinder their educational or vocational orientation and training. In the case of developing countries it is between 12 -14 years of age.[5]

The National Policy for Children, 2013 adopted on April 26, 2013: Government of India for the first time gives a definition to the Child and recognises that a child is any person below the age of 18 years. All aspects of the development and welfare of the child are included in this policy and Definition of the children as provided in this policy is in conformity with the definition given by the United Nations Convention for the Rights of the Child.

3.2 Child Right

The UN conventions on the Rights of Child which India ratified in December 11, 1992, list the following as the Rights of the Child:

3.2.1 The Right to Survival

According to the convention, the "Right to Survival includes all those right like life, the attainable standard of health, nutrition and an adequate standard of living. It also includes the right to name and nationality". These rights seek to ensure that children have nutritious food, portable drinking water, a secure home and access to health facilities.

3.2.2 The Right to Protection

According to the convention, this right includes freedom from all forms of exploitation, abuse and inhuman or degrading treatment. This includes the right to special protection in situations of emergency and armed conflict and external aggression. The aim is simple, to protect vulnerable children from those who treat them as slave and to safeguard their minds and bodies.

3.2.3 The Right to Development

This right includes the right to be educated, to receive support for development and care during early childhood and to social security. It also includes the right to leisure, to recreation and to cultural activities. This right seeks to ensure that children can study and play with whomever they want practice their own religion and culture and accept their own uniqueness of other cultures and religion.[6]

3.2.4 The Right to Participation

According to the convention, the Right to Participation includes the child access to appropriate information and the freedom of thought and expression, conscience and religion. In addition to this, one ought to respect the views of the child. The main objective behind this is that children will be able to set his own values and principles and will get proper opportunity to express themself and their own opinion.[7]

The Government of India has additionally adopted the National Charter for children, that has been ready after getting the views/comments and suggestions of the State governments/ UT Administrations, involving Ministries and Departments and specialists within the field. The document emphasizes Government of India's commitment to children's rights to survival, health and nutrition, pattern of living, play and leisure, time of life care, education, protection of the girl child, empowering adolescents, equality, life and liberty, name and nationality, freedom of expression, freedom of association and peaceful assembly, the right to a family and also the right to be protecting against economic exploitation and every form of abuse and harassment.[8] In Constitution of India Special provisions are made for children as given below:

3.3 Constitutional provisions for children in India

The framers of the Constitution of India realized that children are the most vulnerable section of society and thus are at the maximum risk of being exploited. In order to safeguard children against exploitation the Constitution makes the following provisions:

3.3.1 Fundamental Rights

Article 21 A: Right to Education "The State shall provide free and compulsory education to all children of the age of six to fourteen years in a manner as the State may, by law, determine."

Right of Children to Free and Compulsory Education Act, 2009, has been passed by the Parliament on 4th August 2009, which describes in detail of the provision of free and compulsory education for children of the age of six to fourteen years. The Act comes into force w.e.f. 1.04.2010.

Article 23 (1): Prohibition of traffic in human beings and forced labour "Traffic in human beings and 'beggar' and other similar forms of forced labour are prohibited and any contravention of this provision shall be an offence punishable in accordance with law."

Article 24: Prohibition of employment of children in factories, etc."No child below the age of fourteen years shall be employed to work in any factory or mine or engaged in any other hazardous employment."

3.3.2 Directive Principles

Article 39: Certain Directive principles of state policy to be followed by the State: The State shall, in particular, direct its policy towards securing- "..... (e) that the health and strength of workers, men and women, and the tender age of children are not abused and that citizens are not forced by economic necessity to enter vocations unsuited to their age and strength; (f) that children are given opportunities and facilities to develop in a healthy manner and in conditions of freedom and dignity and that childhood and youth are protected against exploitation in any form."

Article 45: Provision provides for early childhood care and education to children below the age of six years "The State shall endeavour to provide early childhood care and education for all children until the age of six years."

3.3.3 Duty of Parent/Guardian towards the Child

Article 51A(k) on Fundamental Duties states that it shall be the duty of every citizen of India, who is a parent or guardian to provide proper opportunities for education to his child in the age group of six to fourteen years.

Article 243G provides for institutionalizing child care to boost the amount of nutrition and living, improve public health and monitor the event and well-being of children within the Country.[9].

3.4 Child Welfare and Development through Five Year Plans

In Five year Plans various initiatives have been taken for welfare of children as discussed below. Child development and child welfare has been primary concern of India's designing. Here an endeavour has been created to judge the state of child development throughout completely different five-year plan in India.[10]

3.4.1 First Five Year Plan (1951-56)

The first five year plan (1951-56) major area of concern with regard to children was health, nutrition and education. Within the initial years, the responsibility of child care services had primarily untried with voluntary organizations below the charge of a national apex body, viz., In 1953 the Central Social welfare Board was set up, to meet the needs, of children, woman and person with disabilities. The World Health Organization, with the Indian government, self-addressed children's health and reduced infant mortality, indirectly helpful to growth of population. In September 1955, the Ministry of Education implanted a National Advisory Council for the education of the physically disabled[11].

3.4.2 Second Five Year Plan (1956-61)

Second five year plan aimed at strengthening the child welfare systems. The Central Bureau of Correctional Services (CBCS) was set up in 1961 for assortment and compilation of national statistics and preparation of guide books and model schemes.. These centres organized for the regular training of maternal and child health personnel and conjointly provide periodic refresher courses. The second five year plan provides for a bigger focus on basic education, growth of instruction, diversification of instruction, improvement of standards of school and university education, extension of facilities for technical and vocational training and also the implementation of social education and cultural development programmes[12].

3.4.3 Third Five Year Plan (1961-66)

During the third five year plan the child was recognised as a human being with special needs and special efforts were made to coordinate between sectors to ensure these needs. The Central Institute of analysis and training publicly Cooperation was established in 1966 for research and training on issues concerning popular participation. In the Third plan, several primary schools were started in rural areas. Holiday homes children were secure and far social concern was shown towards children. Drawback of child beggary was to be isolated and brought care of. Services were developed within the following lines[13]:

i. teaching handicapped persons in their homes;

ii. providing recreational facilities for the handicapped, and the infirm;

iii. Providing assistance by way of special aids.

3.4.4 Fourth Five Year Plan (1969-74)

The Fourth five year Plan (1969-74), focused on getting basic services to children. All efforts were made to consolidate the initiatives taken within the previous plans. Additionally to the 3 National Institutes for the Blind, the Deaf and therefore the Mentally Retarded, a National Institute of Orthopedically Handicapped was started. For the position of Disabled persons in employment, special employment exchanges were started.[14].

3.4.5 Fifth Five Year Plan (1974-78)

The Fifth Plan (1974-78) proved to be the landmark in the field of child development through the adoption of a National Policy for Children (1974), and launching of the Integrated Child

Development Services (ICDS) with a shift from welfare to development in the approach towards development of children. The programme of ICDS, launched in 33 experimental blocks in 1975, aimed to provide a package of 6 basic services, i.e. health check-up, immunization, referral services, supplementary feeding, non-formal pre-school education and health and nutrition education for children below 6 years and expectant and nursing mothers living in the most backward areas through a single window delivery agency called 'Anganwadi Centre'. The Central and State Governments provided scholarships to the physically disabled. The State Governments extended institutional and non-institutional services for the socially and physically disabled. Very high priority had been given to elementary education programme. Adequate provision has been made for additional enrolment in terms of teaching personnel and construction of class-rooms, especially in backward areas. There were scholarships provided with upto 12000 awards given every year since 1975-76. University education was laid emphasis upon under the plan[15].

3.4.6 Sixth Five Year Plan (1980-85)

The Sixth plan, For the first time planners took into consideration the needs of working children .Programme were undertaken to improve the health ,nutrition and educational status of working children. The National Policy of Health adopted in 1983 set sure specific targets like transfer down the high rates of infant and child Mortality. By the year 2002 A.D., the National Policy on Education of 1986 emphasised universal entry and retention of children within the schools particularly the girl children. Non-formal education programmes were additionally promoted intensively. Pre-school education centres were supported within the educationally backward states by extending grants to voluntary organizations. The Children's Acts (the present JJ Act of 2000) were enacted .The Central welfare Board continuing to perform as a focal and apex agency within the voluntary sector. In 1982 The Voluntary Action Bureau was started to satisfy the challenge of crimes and atrocities against women and children. The purpose was to ensure to all equal chance for education for up the standard of life and their participation within the tasks of promoting the final well-being of the society. It absolutely was planned that the programme of universalization of education would lean serious thought, particularly within the educationally backward States and for reaching the socially underprivileged United Nations agency represent the majority of the non-attending children and of the drop-outs.Within the comparison below to see the rise within the range of enrolments w.r.t. the planning years.[16]

3.4.7 Seventh Five Year Plan (1985-90)

The Seventh Plan strengthen the functioning of ICDS and continued the major strategy of promoting early childhood survival and development through programmes in different sectors, universal immunization, maternal and child care services, nutrition, preschool education, protected drinking water, environmental sanitation and hygiene, and family planning. The Ministry of Health and Family Welfare, the universal immunization programme were started to protect children from six major diseases which affect early childhood mortality and morbidity, viz. diphtheria, whooping cough, tetanus, polio, measles and childhood tuberculosis was strengthened for the development of children as a whole. ICDS continued to be the single nation-wide programme for early childhood survival and development during Seventh Plan. The Juvenile Justice Act (JJA) was enacted in 1986, to deal effectively with the problem of neglected or juvenile delinquents and provide for a standardized framework for dealing with such children. The Government of India enacted the Child Labour Prohibition and Regulation Act, 1986 and in 1987, the National policy on Child Labour was formulated. Projects were sanctioned to voluntary organizations for the welfare of working children to provide non-formal education, supplementary nutrition, health care and skill training[17].

During the Seventh plan and Annual Plans 1990-92, a big growth of programmes and services for the welfare of the

Disabled passed. For education of the Disabled most the states enforced programmes to supply stipends and alternative incentives to the Disabled at the primary school stage. Additionally to four National Institutes for Disabled, two alternative organizations, i.e., the Institute for the Physically incapacitated (Delhi) and also the National Institute of Rehabilitation training and research (Cuttack) also offered a large varity of services for the rehabilitation of the Disabled and arranged men training. The medical and health care facilities for children were additional increased within the urban areas with not therefore smart results[18].

3.4.8 Eighth Five Year Plan (1992-97)

Development of human resources was the most important focus of the Eighth five year plan, policies and programmes concerning 'child survival, protection and development' reduction in infant and child mortality is an essential pre-requisite for acceptance of small family norm. This initiative ensured that the inter linkages between Family Welfare Programme and Development was kept in focus in state plans. Following the agreement of the 'Convention on the Rights of the Child', in 1992 the Government of India Government of India developed two National Plans of Action (NPA) - one for children and therefore the different completely for the Girl-Child, whereas the terrorist organization for children sets out quantitative goals to be achieved by 2000 AD within the priority areas of health, nutrition, education, water, sanitation and atmosphere, the terrorist organization for the lady child (1991-2000) geared toward removal of gender bias and enhances the standing of girl child within the society, therefore on offer them the equal opportunities for survival, protection and development. Each the Plans of Action adopted an inter-sectoral approach in achieving sectoral goals set down within the Action Plans in shut uniformity with the most important goals of 'Health For All', 'Education For All' etc. The Seventh plan gave more emphasis for the realisation of the target of UEE by 1990. It had been calculable that for achieving the goal, over five cores extra children would need to be registered. Visible of the most thrust of the Eighth plan policies and programmes concerning survival, protection and development of all sections of the population particularly those of the Disabled and deprived were enforced. The most important thrust was towards enabling the disabled to become active, self-dependent and productive members of the state by extending opportunities for education, and economic rehabilitation etc. The enactment of a comprehensive legislation, namely, The Persons with Disabilities (Equal Opportunities, Protection of Rights and Full Participation) Act, 1995, was a land mark action within the history of the welfare of the Disabled. The Rehabilitation Council of India (RCI) was created as a statutory body below the RCI Act of 1992, with the target of upgrading and standardizing the program and guaranteeing uniform standards of training of execs for the welfare of the Disabled[19]

3.4.9 The Ninth Five Year Plan (1997-2002)

Under Ninth five year plan Special focus was given on young child by placing child on top agenda by instituting National Charter for Children ensuring that no Child remains illiterate, hungry or lacks medical care; ensuring Survival, and implementation of the two National Plans of Action - one for the Children and the other for the Girl Child; early age first six years as critical for the development of children, therefore, special thrust on the three major areas of child development i.e. health, nutrition and education; universalizing ICDS as the main-stay of the Ninth Plan for promoting the over-all development of the young children, especially the Girl Child and the mothers all over the country; fixing the declining sex ratio and curb its related problems of female foeticide and female infanticide; bringing down the IMR to less than 60 and the CMR to below 10 by 2002 through providing easy access to health care services including RCH services and 100 per cent coverage of immunization in respect of all vaccine preventable diseases; In order to achieve these commitments/ strategies, efforts were being made during the Ninth five year Plan through various policy/programmatic interventions, in all child-related sectors through effective coordination and convergence of services and personnel. Efforts were made to strengthen the on-going approach of convering the basic services of health, nutrition and preschool education towards promoting the holistic development of the young child through Integrated Child Development Scheme (ICDS). Though universalization of ICDS was contemplated by the end of 1995-96 through expanding its services in all the 5652 Blocks all over the country, yet only 4200 could become operational at the beginning of Ninth Plan, before the ban on further operationalization of ICDS projects was imposed by the Ministry of Finance i.e. 16.5.97. However, the ban was finally removed and now the Government has decided to universalize ICDS all over the country by the end of the Ninth Plan. The other efforts has been taken as follow[20]:

i. **Balika Samriddhi Yojana** was launched to extend a special package to girl children belonging to these families living below the poverty line to ensure that all girl children should take admission in schools. Special incentives, i.e. '500 to the mother and annual scholarships ranging from '300 to '1000 for girl children in classes I to X.

ii. **Kishori Shakti Yojana** was introduced as an enriched version of the scheme for Adolescent Girls

iii. **UDISHA** was launched to strengthen the on-going ICDS Training Programme into a dynamic, responsive and comprehensive training-cum-human resource development programme. For the implementation of UDISHA, World Bank increased financial assistance to the extent of '600.55 crore.

iv. **The scheme of Crèches and Day Care Centres for children** of working/ailing mothers being a non-expanding scheme, maintained the same level of 12470 crèches benefiting 3.12 lakh children.

v. **Nutrition Programme**: improving the dietary intake and through a change in the feeding practices and intra-family food distribution and preventing they from the deficiency diseases

vi. **The Reproductive and Child Health (RCH) Programme,** being operated by the Ministry of Health and Family Welfare since October 1997 aimed at integration and expansion of family welfare services, up-gradation of their quality and making them easily accessible to the people.

vii. **Mid-Day Meals Programme** for school going children implemented by the State Governments.

viii. **A Child Line Foundation** was planned to extend child line 77 services in major cities to protect children facing abuse, exploitation and neglect and preventing them from social harassment.

ix. **A Programme for Juvenile Justice** aimed at strengthening the implementation of Juvenile Justice Act 1986 and to bring about a qualitative improvement in the services provided for both neglected as well as delinquent children.[21]

3.4.10 Tenth Five Year Plan(2002-2007)

The Tenth 5 Year plan main focus & approach was to make sure the survival, development, protection and participation of children with priority to the young child and girl child. Programmes for children at a glance launched during 10th five year plan[22]:

Rajiv Gandhi National Crèche Scheme for children of working mothers was important initiative taken in this direction. Eight large integer crèches are needed to satisfy the child care wants of twenty two crore women within the informal sector. Integrated Programme for Street Children- Preventing destitution of children; providing shelter, nutrition, health care, education, recreation, and protection against abuse and exploitation was also kept main focus during this Five year Plan.

Welfare of Working Children in Need of Care and Protection: Through this initiative efforts were made to provide non-formal education, vocational training to working children to facilitate their entry/re-entry into mainstream education and prevent their exploitation, implemented through NGOs and other social welfare group working in this field.

Assistance to Homes (Shishu Greh) for Children: This initiative Provides grant-in-aid through Central Adoption Resource Agency to government institutions and NGOs for promoting adoptions within the country.

Nutrition Programme for Adolescent Girls: Launched by the Planning Commission, in 51 districts, on a pilot project basis, in 2002–03. It envisaged that all adolescent girls (10–19 years) will be weighed four times a year and families of girls weighing less than 35 kg will be given 6 kg of food grains/month for three months in order to promote nutritional status of adolescent girls.

3.4.11 Eleventh Five year plan (2007-2012)

The government took an altogether new stand with regard to children in the Eleventh Five Year plan. The stands adopted may be categorically tabulated as follows[23]:

1. **Child Rights-Apex of the plan:** The government adopt Child Rights to constitute centre of the plan & it pledges to provide child with the rights of survival, participation & development.
2. **Admittance:** Though India signed & morally obliged to abide by many International charters like Discrimination against Women & Child and UNCRC, the government accepted that women & children in India continue to suffer under the jaws of violence, neglect & injustice.
3. The children in India can be raised in an environment of development & make them a part of India's economic growth of swelling GDP in accordance with the roadmap laid forward by the National Plan of Action for Children 2005.

4. **Differential Approach:** The government accepts that courtesy to the vast diversity of India in terms of several parameters like social, regional and economic the children don't compose a homogeneous class in themselves & hence mapping & addressing of specific problems which should be treated timely.

In a nutshell, India aimed to achieve the following targets relevant to children during the plan period[24]:

i. Raise the sex ratio for age group 0–6 from 927 in 2001 to 935 by 2011–12 and to 950 by 2016–17, proper implementation & review of Pre-Conception and Pre-Natal Diagnostic Techniques Act (PC&PNDT). Monitoring appropriate authorities for granting, suspending or cancelling registration of Genetic Counselling Centres & review complaints.

ii. Make it sure that at least 33 per cent of the direct and indirect beneficiaries of all government schemes are women and girl children.

iii. Reduction in IMR from 57 to 28 per 1000 live births.

iv. Reduction in malnutrition among children of age group 0–3 to half its present level.

v. Reduction in anaemia among women and girls by 50 per cent

vi. Reduction in dropout rate for primary and secondary schooling by 10 per cent for both girls as well as boys.

3.4.12 Twelfth Five Year Plan (2012-17)

The major child relevant targets were laid in the Twelfth plan as given following:

i. Education

(a) Must aim at universalization of secondary education by 2017.

(b) Must focus on quality of education (11th Plan emphasis was on quantity).

(c) Education for life - Vocational/skill development to ensure employability in various sector.

(d) Response to changing market needs.

(e) Requirement of high tech training system.

(f) Significant reduction in social, gender and regional gaps in education.

(g) Development and operationalization of PPP models in School and Higher education.

(h) Education should be according to need of fast growing personal economy.

ii. Health

a) Focus on women and children; ICDS needs to be revamped.

b) Clean drinking water, sanitation and better nutrition, childcare.

iii. Resource allocation

a) Health, Education and Skill Development together in the Centre's Plan will have to be increased by at least 1.2 per cent point of GDP.

b) Health and Education received less than projected in Eleventh Plan. Allocations for these sectors will have to be increased in 12th Plan

3.5 Union Laws Guaranteeing Rights and entitlement to Children

Constitution of India provides the provision for the protection of the rights of the children. The age at which a person ceases to be a child varies under different laws in India. Under the Child Labour Prohibition and Regulation Act, 1986, a child is a person who has not completed 14 years of age. For the purposes of criminal responsibility, the age limit is 7 (not punishable) and above 7 years to 12 years punishable on the proof that the child understands the consequences of the act, under the Indian Penal Code. For purpose of protection against kidnapping, abduction and related offences, it's 16 years for boys and 18 for girls. And the Protection of Women from Domestic Violence Act 2005 defines a child as any person below the age of 18, and includes an adopted step- or foster child.[25]For special treatment under the Juvenile Justice (Care and Protection of Children) Act 2011, the age is 18 for both boys and girls. In India various laws are there for Children welfare some of them given below[26]

3.5.1 Important Union laws Guaranteeing Rights and Entitlement to Children

1. The Guardian and Wards Act, 1890
2. The Reformatory Schools Act,1897
3. The Children (Pledging of Labour) Act, 1933.
4. The factories Act 1948
5. The Hindu Minority and Guardianship Act, 1956
6. The Hindu Adoption and Maintenance Ac, 1956
7. The Immoral Traffic prevention Act, 1956
8. The Women's and Children's Institutions (Licensing) Act, 1956
9. The Young Person's harmful Publication's Act, 1956
10. The Probation of Offender's Act, 1958
11. Orphanages and Other Charitable Homes (Supervision and Control) Act, 1960
12. The Apprentices Act, 1961
13. The Child Labour (Prohibition and Regulation) Act, 1986

14. The Persons With Disabilities (Equal Opportunities, Protection of Rights and Full Participation)Act, 1995
15. The Juvenile Justice (Care and Protection of Children) Act, 2000, repealed the Juvenile Justice Act 1986. The 2000 act also has been amended in 2006 and 2010.
16. The Infant Milk Substitutes, Feeding bottles and Infant Foods (Regulation of Production, Supply Distribution) Act, 1992 and its amendment of 2003
17. The Pre- conception & Pre-natal Diagnostic Technique (Regulation, Prevention and Misuse) Act, 1994 and its amendment of 2002.
18. The Commissions For Protection of Child Rights Act, 2002
19. The prohibition of Child Marriage Act, 2006
20. Right To Education Act 2009
21. The Protection of Children from Sexual Offences Act, 2012
22. Juvenile Justice (Care and Protection of Children) Act, 2015

Some of these Laws are discussed in detail below:

3.5.2 Children (Pledging of Labour)

Act, 1933 declares any agreement by a parent or guardian to pledge the labour of a child below 15 years of age for payment or benefit other than reasonable wages, illegal and void. This Law also provided punishment for such parent or guardian as well as those who employ a child whose labour is pledged.

3.5.3 The Immoral Trafficking (Prevention)

Act (ITPA), 1956 is a vital contribution on trafficking in India. This act prohibits commercial sexual exploitation and all cases relating to prostitution under the Act. This Act defines a minor as a person between 16 to 18 years of age. The Act also says that if any person over the age of 18 years knowingly lives wholly or in part on the earning of the prostitution of any other person shall be punishable with imprisonment up to 2 years or with fine up to Rs1000 or both, or where such earnings relate to the prostitution of a child or a minor, shall be punishable with imprisonment for 7-10 years. The Act prohibits the activities relating to prostitution in a public place or within 200 metres from a public place[27].

3.5.4 The Bonded Labour System (Abolition) (1976)

Act, 1976 the objective of this act to make provisions for abolition of "Bonded Labour System" for preventing the exploitation economic and physical of weaker section of the population. The act extinguishes all debt agreements and obligations. It prohibits creation of any new bondage agreement and discharges bonded labourers from all debts for which they were bonded. Compelling a person to render bonded labour is punishable under the law. This includes punishment for parents who pledge their child or other family members to work as a bonded labourer.

3.5.5 The Child Labour (Prohibition & Regulation)

Act (CLPR Act) 1986 Prohibits employment of a child in 18 occupations and 65 processes and regulates the conditions of working of children in other occupations/ processes. As per this Act a child means any person who has not completed 14 years of age. The Act also provides punishment for the offence of employing or permitting employment of any child in contravention of the provisions of this Act.

3.5.6 Salient Features of the Child Labour (Prohibition and Regulation) Act, 1986:

The Act:

- Prohibits/bans the employment of any person who has not completed his fourteenth year of age in occupations and processes enlisted in Part A and B of the Schedule of the Act.

- Proper checks and regulation are made where children are not prohibited from working
- Lays down enhanced penalties for employment of children in violation of the provisions of the Act and other Acts
- Lays down a procedure to decide modifications to the Schedule of banned occupations or processes

Section 14 of the Act provides for punishment upto 1 year (minimum being three months) or with fine up to Rs. 20,000/- (minimum being ten thousand) or with both, to one who employs or permits any child to work in contravention of provisions in Section 3.

Children employed in occupations and processes, not banned by the Act are regulated by the following provisions:

- A child shall not be required to work for more than six hours a day which shall be inclusive of his/her half an hour break.
- No child shall be permitted or required to work between 7 p.m and 8 a.m.
- No child shall be required or permitted to work over-time.
- Every child shall get a weekly off to take rest.

There is an obligation on the part of the employer to furnish information to the inspector regarding the employment of children. It is mandatory for the employer to maintain a register on this matter.

Government had prohibited employment of children as domestic servants or (roadside eateries), restaurants, hotels, motels, teashops, resorts, recreational centres. The ban has been imposed under the Child Labour (Prohibition & Regulation) Act, 1986 and affected from 10th October, 2006. So far employment of children has been prohibited in 16 occupations and 65 processes including this.

3.5.6 The Pre-Conception and Pre-Natal Diagnostic Techniques Act-1994

The basic purpose of the Act is three-fold, with a focus on averting further decline in sex ratio:

- Regulation of Pre-Natal Diagnostic Techniques only for legitimate uses as prescribed under the Act
- Complete ban on misuse of Pre-Conception Diagnostic Techniques (PCDT) and pre-natal diagnostic techniques '(PNDT) for sex selection / determination
- Absolute prohibition of selection of sex of the foetus, both before and after conception, except for detecting sex-linked diseases.

The term "pre-natal diagnostic techniques" (PNDT) includes all pre-natal diagnostic procedures 'and prenatal diagnostic tests '.

- "Pre-natal diagnostic procedures" means all gynaecological, obstetrical or medical procedures, both invasive and non-invasive, for sex selection, both before and after conception:
- invasive pre-natal diagnostic procedures are utilized to remove samples from a woman or a man, both before and after conception, of amniotic fluid, chorionic villi, embryo, blood or any other tissue or fluid, for conducting any type of analysis or test like: amniocentesis, chorionic villi biopsy, foetal skin or organ biopsy, cordocentesis,
- non-invasive pre-natal diagnostic procedures include ultrasonography, foetoscopy .
- "Pre-natal diagnostic is a technique to determine whether a developing fetus is affected with a genetic disorder or other abnormality. Act provide for the prohibition of sex selection before or after conception and for regulation of pre-natal diagnostic techniques for detecting genetic or

metabolic disorders or chromosomal abnormalities or congenital anomalies or sex-linked diseases.

The term Sex selection includes: technique, administration, prescription and provision of anything for the purpose of ensuring or increasing the probability that an embryo will be of a particular sex.

3.6. Prohibition of Child Marriage Act, 2006

Child marriage is an age-old practice that has both social and religious sanction and cut across all sections of society. Child marriage is additionally related to different issues like dowry and child widowhood. It's additionally related to deficiency disease, poor health of mothers and high fertility and hence over-population. Hindu marriage act 1955 governs marriage in India, since the act does not prohibits child marriage ,child marriage were rampant and there was no legislation in order to prevent this social menace ,thus in order to prevent such marriages between non consenting minors the act The Prohibition of Child Marriage Act was enacted in 2006. Although marriage usually comes within the scope of non-public laws, this Act is an overall legislation that clearly states that marriage of a child.[28]

3.6.1 Right to Education Act 2009

Main features of Right to education Act are summarised below.

- Providing Free and compulsory education to all children of age group of 6-14 of years.
- No Child shall be required to pass Board examination till the completion of elementary education.
- A child shall be admitted in a class appropriate to his or her age if a child above 6 years of age has not been admitted in any school or could not complete his or her elementary education. However, if a case may be where a child is directly admitted in the class appropriate to his or her age,

then, in order to be at par with others, he or she shall have a right to receive special training within such time limits as may be prescribed. Provided further that a child so admitted to elementary education shall be entitled to free education till the completion of elementary education even after 14 years.

- Proof of age for admission: No child shall be denied admission in a school for lack of age proof. For this purpose the age of a child shall be determined on the basis of the birth certificate issued in accordance with the Provisions of Birth. Deaths and Marriages Registration Act 1856, or on the basis of such other document as may be prescribed.[29]
- A child who completes elementary education shall be awarded a certificate.
- Call need to be taken for a fixed student–teacher ratio.
- Twenty-five per cent reservations for economically disadvantaged communities in admission to Class I in all private schools is to be done.
- Improvement in the quality of education is important.
- Adequate professional degree will need to the School teachers within five years or else will lose job.
- School infrastructure need to be improved in every 3 years, else recognition will be cancelled.
- Financial burden will be shared between the state and the central government.[30]

3.6.2 The Protection of Children from Sexual Offences Act, 2012

Salient features of this Act are given below

- The Protection of the children from sexual offences Act,2012 defines a child as any person below the age of 18 years. The age of Act defines a child as any person below eighteen years of age, and regards the best interests and well-being of the child as being of paramount importance at every stage, to ensure the healthy physical, emotional, intellectual and social development of the child.

- It provide protection to different forms of sexual abuse, including penetrative and non-penetrative assault, as well as sexual harassment and pornography, and deems a sexual assault to be "aggravated" under certain circumstances, such as when the abused child is mentally ill or when the abuse is committed by a person in a position of trust or authority vis-à-vis the child, like a family member, police officer, teacher, or doctor.
- The Act provides the punishment provision to the people who are involved in trafficking of children for sexual purposes. The Act prescribes stringent punishment graded as per the gravity of the offence, with a maximum term of rigorous imprisonment for life, and fine.
- Punishments for Offences covered in the Act
- Penetrative Sexual Assault (Section 3) on a child – Punishment should not be less than seven years which may extend to imprisonment for life, and fine (Section 4)
- Aggravated Penetrative Sexual Assault (Section 5) – Not less than ten years which may extend to imprisonment for life, and fine (Section 6)
- Sexual Assault (Section 7) i.e. sexual contact without penetration – Not less than three years which may extend to five years, and fine (Section 8)
- Aggravated Sexual Assault (Section 9) by a person in authority – Not less than five years which may extend to seven years, and fine (Section 10)
- Sexual Harassment of the Child (Section 11) – Three years and fine (Section 12)

- Use of Child for Pornographic Purposes (Section 13) – Five years and fine and in the event of subsequent conviction, seven years and fine Section 14 (1)
- Special Courts established for the trial of offences under the Act, keeping the best interest of the child as of paramount importance at every stage of the judicial process.
- The Act provides child friendly procedures for reporting, recording of evidence, investigation and trial of offences. These include:
- Special Provision made for recording the statement of the child at the residence of the child or at the place of his choice, preferably by a woman police officer not below the rank of sub-inspector.
- Minor should not be detained in the police station in the night for any reason.
- Police officer should not be in uniform while recording the statement of the child.
- The statement of the child should be recorded as spoken by the child.
- Assistance of special educator or any person familiar with the manner of communication of the child in case child is disabled
- Assistance of an interpreter or translator or an expert as per the need of the child.
- The medical examination victim of a girl Child shall be conducted by a woman doctor. 13. Frequent breaks for the child during trial. Child should not be called repeatedly to testify.
- Medical examination of the child to be conducted in the presence of the parent of the child or any other person in whom the child has trust or confidence.

- No aggressive questioning or character assassination of the child in-camera trial of cases.
- The Act recognizes that the Intent to commit an offence, even when unsuccessful for whatever reason, needs to be penalized.
- The attempt to commit an offence under the Act has been made liable for punishment for up to half the punishment prescribed for the commission of the offence.
- The abetment of the offence is punishable under the Act, which is the same as for the commission of the offence.
- On the occurrence of offence Act makes it mandatory to report to the commission and also the recording of complaint and failure to do so would make a person liable for punishment of imprisonment for six months or / and with fine. 18.1t is a Punishable action if Police / Special Juvenile Police Unit fails to report a commission of the offence under this act [Section- 2141)]
- The burden of proof is shifted to the accused for heinous offences of Penetrative Sexual Assault, Aggravated Penetrative Sexual Assault, Sexual Assault and Aggravated Sexual Assault This provision has been made keeping in view the greater vulnerability and innocence of children.
- Punishment has been provided for making false complaint or proving false information with malicious intent and misuse of Act. Such punishment has been kept relatively light (six months) to encourage reporting. If false complaint is made against a child, punishment is higher (one year) (Section 22).
- The media has been barred from disclosing the identity of the child without the permission of the Special Court. The punishment for breaching this provision by media may be from six months to one year (Section 23).

- The Act provides speedy trial for the evidence of the child to be recorded within a period of 30 days. Also, the Special Court is to complete the trial within a period of one year, as far as possible (Section 35).
- Immediate Relief and rehabilitation is provided to the child, as soon as the complaint is made to the Special Juvenile Police Unit (SJPU) or local police, these will make immediate arrangements to give the child, care and protection such as admitting the child into shelter home or to the nearest hospital within twenty-four hours of the report. The SJPU or the local police are also required to report the matter to the Child Welfare Committee within 24 hours of recording the complaint, for long term rehabilitation of the child.
- The Act casts a duty on the Central and State Governments to spread awareness through media including the television, radio and the print media at regular intervals to make the general public, children as well as their parents and guardians aware of the provisions of this Act.
- The POCSO Act is only applicable to child survivors and adult offenders. In case two children have sexual relations with each other, or in case a child perpetrates a sexual offence on an adult, the Juvenile Justice (Care and Protection of Children) Act, 2000, will apply.[31]

3.6.3 Juvenile Justice (Care and Protection of Children) Act, 2015

- The main purpose and object behind-enactment the act in need of care and protection by the catering to their basic needs with proper care, protection, treatment, development, social reintegration, by adopting a child-friendly approach in the adjudication and disposal of matters in the best interest of children. The Juvenile Justice (Care and Protection of Children) Act, 2015 has come into force from January 15, 2016 and repeals the Juvenile Justice (Care and Protection of Children) Act, 2000.[32]

Key provisions

- Change in nomenclature from 'juvenile' to 'child' or 'child in conflict with law', across the Act to remove the negative connotation associated with the word "juvenile"
- Clarity in powers, function and responsibilities of Juvenile Justice Board (JJB) and Child Welfare Committee (CWC); clear timelines for inquiry by Juvenile Justice Board (JJB); The Act mandates setting up Juvenile Justice Boards and Child Welfare Committees in every district. Both must have at least one woman member each.
- **Special provisions for heinous offences committed by children above the age of sixteen years - under Section 15**, special provisions have been made to tackle child offenders committing heinous offences in the age group of 16-18 years. The Juvenile Justice Board is given the option to transfer cases of heinous offences by such children to a Children's Court (Court of Session) after conducting preliminary assessment. The provisions provide for placing children in a 'place of safety' both during and after the trial till they attain the age of 21 years after which an evaluation of the child shall be conducted by the Children's Court. After the evaluation, the child is either released on probation and if the child is not reformed then the child will be sent to a jail for remaining term. The law will act as a deterrent for child offenders committing heinous offences such as rape and murder and will protect the rights of victim.
- **Separate new chapter on Adoption to streamline adoption of orphan, abandoned and surrendered children -** The existing Central Adoption Resource Authority (CARA) is given the status of a statutory body to streamline adoption procedures for orphan, abandoned and surrendered children, to enable it to perform its function more effectively. Separate chapter (VIII) on Adoption provides for detailed provisions relating to adoption and

punishments for not complying with the laid down procedure. Processes have been streamlined with timelines for both in-country and inter-country adoption including declaring a child legally free for adoption. As per the provisions, a single or divorced person can also adopt, but a single male cannot adopt a girl child.

- **Inclusion of new offences committed against children** - Various offences committed against children, not covered strictly under specific law, are included in the Act. These include: sale and procurement of children for any purpose including illegal adoption, corporal punishment in child care institutions, use of child by militant groups, offences against disabled children and, kidnapping and abduction of children.

- **Penalties for cruelty against a child**, offering a narcotic substance to a child, and abduction or selling a child have been prescribed. Any official, who does not report an abandoned or orphaned child within 24 hours, is liable to imprisonment up to six months or fine of '10,000 or both. The penalty for non-registration of child care institutions is imprisonment up to one year or fine of one lakh rupees, or both. The penalty for giving a child intoxicating liquor, narcotic or psychotropic substances is imprisonment up to seven years or fine of one lakh rupees, or both.

- Children are provided with various services including education, health, nutrition, de-addiction, treatment of diseases, vocational training, skill development, life skill education, counselling, etc to help them assume a constructive role in the society. The variety of non-institutional options include: sponsorship and foster care including group foster care for placing children in a family environment which is other than child's biological family, which is to be selected, qualified, approved and supervised for providing care to children.

- **Mandatory registration of Child Care Institutions** - Every Institutions related to child care, whether run by State Government or by voluntary or non-governmental organisations, which are meant, either wholly or partially for housing children, regardless of whether they receive grants from the Government or not, are to be mandatorily registered under the Act within 6 months from the date of commencement of the Act otherwise stringent penalty is provided in the law in case of non-compliance.

Role of State Governments

- The Act provides for induction training of Members of Juvenile Justice Board and Child Welfare Committee within two months of their appointment (Section s 4 and 27). The Chief Judicial Magistrate or Chief Metropolitan Magistrate is to review pendency of cases in the Juvenile Justice Board once in three months and direct the Board to increase the frequency of sittings or recommend constitution of additional Board (Section 16). There is a provision for the constitution of a High Level Committee to review the pendency of cases in the Juvenile Justice Board.

- Under Section 36 of the JJ Act, 2015 Act provide Child Welfare Committees to submit quarterly reports to the District Magistrate regarding pendency and nature of disposal of cases. The District Magistrate is required to conduct quarterly review of the Child Welfare Committees and direct remedial measures to address the pendency. The District Magistrate shall send a report of his review to the State Government which may cause the constitution of additional committees, if required. If the pendency of cases continues even after three months, the State Government shall terminate the existing Committee and constitute a new Committee.

- The Act made mandatory to the State Governments to register all institutions within six months of the commencement of the JJ Act, 2015 whether such institutions are run by the Government or by an NGO and are meant either wholly or partially for housing children. These institutions should be registered irrespective of whether they are receiving grants from Government or not. The State Government is expected to issue a provisional registration certificate to the institution within one month from the date of application. There is also provision of penalty of one year imprisonment or fine of not less than '1 lakh for non registration of a Child Care Institution (Section 42).

- The State Governments are also, as per section 49 of the Act supposed to set up atleast one Place of Safety for placing persons above 18 years of age or children between the age of 16 - 18 years who have committed a heinous offence. Inspection Committees are to be appointed both for the state and the district level and these Inspection Committees are to mandatorily inspect all institutions atleast once in three months (Section 54). Under Section 55, the Central and State Government may conduct independent evaluation of the functioning of the Juvenile Justice Board, Child Welfare Committee, Special Juvenile Police Unit, registered institutions, fit facilities and fit persons through such persons or institutions as may be prescribed by the government.

- The State Government shall, under Section 65 of the Act, recognize one or more institutions in each district as a Specialized Adoption Agency. The State Agency has to furnish the name, address and contact details of the Specialized Adoption Agencies along with copies of certificate and letter of recognition or renewal to the Central Adoption Resource Authority (CARA). The state government should inspect Specialized Adoption Agency at least once in a year and take remedial measures. The Act provides a fine up to of '50,000/- in case of default by the Specialized Adoption Agency besides withdrawal of recognition in respect of repeated default.

- The Central and State Governments requires spreading awareness of the provisions of the Act to the general public, children, parents and guardians. Officers of the Government are to be imparted periodic training besides other concerned persons (Section 108).
- All institutions registered under the JJ Act, 2015 which may not have been recognized as Specialized Adoption Agency shall develop formal linkages with nearby Specialized Adoption Agency and get all orphans or surrendered or abandoned children declared legally free for adoption. Any contravention of this provision is also liable to fine of '50,000/- and de-recognition in case of persistent flouting of provisions (Section 66).

Institutional Care

- The Child Care Institutions in respect of children in conflict with law are the Observation Home, Special Home, Place of Safety and fit facility. For children in need of care and protection, Open Shelters, Children Home and Special Adoption Agencies have specific roles to play. All Child Care Institutions have to be mandatorily registered within six months from the date of commencement of the Act and failure to do so is a punishable offence. Registration applications of Child Care Institutions are to be disposed of within six months otherwise it would be considered as dereliction of duty and will invite departmental proceedings (Section 41)

3.6.4 Under Section 109 of the Juvenile Justice (Care and Protection) Act, 2015

1. Section 3 constitute the National Commission for Protection of Child Rights, or as the case may be, the State Commission for Protection of Child Rights constituted under section 17 (herein referred to as the National Commission or the

State Commission, as the case may be), of the Commissions for Protection of Child rights Act, 2005, shall, in addition to the functions assigned to them under the said Act, also monitor the implementation of the provisions of this Act, in such manner, as may be prescribed.

2. The National Commission or, as the case may be, the State Commission, shall, while inquiring into any matter relating to any offence under this Act, have the same powers as are vested in the National Commission or the State Commission under the Commissions for Protection of Child Rights Act, 2005.

3. The National Commission or, as the case may be, the State Commission, shall also include its activities under this section, in the annual report referred to in section16 of the Commissions for Protection of Child Rights Act, 2005.[33]

3.6.5 Under Rule 91 of Model Juvenile Justice (Care and Protection) Rules, 2016

i) Periodical review of the institution set-up under the Act.

ii) Develop Information, Education and Communication (IEC) material on child rights and gender sensitivity;

iii) Develop protocol for reformation and rehabilitation of children;

iv) Create awareness about identification and reporting of crimes against children such as drug abuse, trafficking, child sexual abuse and exploitation including child marriage, and other aspects of violence against children;

v) Panchayat and municipalities should have to play a core role on crimes against children including identification and reporting of crimes for enhanced protection;

vi) Formulation of detailed information regarding victim child right or witnesses and their families, and containing useful information in local languages, which may be provided to the victim and her/his family;

vii) Develop training module for stakeholders along with the State Child Protection Societies and NIPCCD, etc.

3.6.6 Linkages between the Juvenile Justice (Care and Protection of Children) Act, 2015 and the POCSO Act, 2012

(a) Child victims under the POCSO Act can also be children in need of care and protection.

(i) Section 30 (xiii) of the Juvenile Justice Act, 2015 requires the CWCs to take action for rehabilitation of sexually abused children who are reported as children in need of care and protection to the Committee by SJPU or local police under the POCSO Act, 2012

(ii) Under Section 19 (6) of the POCSO Act, the local police or the SJPU should report the commission of a sexual offence against a child to the CWC within 24 hours of receiving information and should also indicate if the child is in need of care and protection; and steps taken by them in this regard. Rule 4 (3) of the POCSO Rules, 2012 specifies 3 situations in which a child must be produced before a CWC viz. a) there is a reasonable apprehension that the offence has been committed or attempted or is likely to be committed by a person living in the same or shared household;

(b) Child is without parental support; c) the child is found to be without any home and parental support.

(iii) Upon production, as per Rule 4 (4), POCSO Rules, the CWC should determine within 3 days whether the child needs to be taken out of the custody of the family or shared household and placed in a Children's Home or Shelter Home. CWC can take the assistance of a social worker to make this determination.

(iv) Rule 4 (5), POCSO Rules specifies 7 factors that should be considered by the CWC along with preferences and the best interests of the child while deciding whether or not the child should be removed from the custody of the family or shared household. CWC should ensure that the child is not inconvenienced or exposed to injury during this inquiry.

3.6.7 Child Labour (Prohibition and Regulation) Amendment Act, 2016

In July 2016, the Parliament has passed the Child Labour (Prohibition and Regulation) Amendment Bill, 2016.To regulate the child labour practice in India by widening its scope against child labour and provides for stricter punishments for violations. The 1986 act prohibits employment of children below 14 years in 83 hazardous occupations and processes.

Salient provisions

- The act has completely banned employment of children below 14 in all occupations and enterprises, except those run by his or her own family, provided that education does not hampered. Whereas the 1986 act prohibited the employment of children less than 14 years in certain occupations like bidi-making, mines, domestic work, power looms, automobile workshops, carpet weaving etc.
- Addition of a new category of persons called "adolescent". It defines children between 14 to 18 years as adolescents and bars their employment in any hazardous occupations.
- The act makes child labour a cognizable offence. Employing children below 14 years will attract a jail term between 6 months to two years (earlier 3 months to 1 year) or a penalty between twenty-thousand to fifty thousand rupees or both for the first time. Repeat offenders will attract imprisonment between 1 year to 3 years (6 months to 2 years). In case, the offender is a parent, it provides a relaxed penal provision and proposes a fine of Rs.10,000 for repeat offence committed by parent.
- The act has a provision of creating Rehabilitation Fund for the rehabilitation of children.

- Help the the government to make periodic inspection of places at which employment of children and adolescents are prohibited.
- Government may confer powers on a District Magistrate (DM) to ensure that the provisions of the law are properly carried out and implemented. The Child Labour (Prohibition and Regulation) Amendment Act, 2016 suffers from several flaws
- The number of hazardous occupations has been decreased from 83 to 3. The three occupations are mining, inflammable substances, and hazardous processes under the Factories Act. It empowers Union Government to add or omit any hazardous occupation from the list included in the act.
- After discussing in detail various laws for child protection an attempt has been made in present chapter to discuss Institutions set up in India for Child welfare

3.6.8 Institutional mechanism for Children in India

National Commission for Protection of Child Right (NCPCR)

To protect, promote and defend child rights in the country, The National Commission for Protection of Child Rights (NCPCR) was constituted by the Government of India, Ministry of Women & Child Development as a statutory body in March, 2007 under the Commissions for Protection of Child Rights (CPCR) Act, 2005.

Functions

Section 13 lists out the following functions of the Commission

Under Section 13(1) of the CPCR Act, 2005

i) Examine and review the safeguards provided by or under any law for the time being in force for the protection of child rights and recommend measures for their effective implementation;

ii) Present to the Central Government, annually and at such other intervals, as the Commission may deem fit, reports up on the working of those safeguards;

iii) Look into the matters relating to children in need of special care and protection including children in distress, marginalized and disadvantaged children, children in conflict with law, juveniles, children without family and children of prisoners and recommend appropriate remedial measures;

iv) Inquire into violation of child rights and recommend initiation of proceedings in such cases;

v) Examine all factors that inhibit the enjoyment of rights of children affected by terrorism, communal violence, riots, natural disaster, domestic violence, HIV/AIDS, trafficking, maltreatment, torture and exploitation, pornography and prostitution and recommend appropriate remedial measures;

vi) Study treaties and other international instruments and undertake periodical review of existing policies, programmes and other activities on child rights and make recommendations for their effective implementation in the best interest of children;

vii) Undertake and promote research in the field of child rights;

viii) Do awareness regarding child rights literacy among various sections of the society and promote awareness of the safeguards available or protection of these rights through publications, the media, seminars and other available means;

ix) Inspect or cause to be inspected any juvenile custodial home, or any other place of residence or institution meant for children, under the control of the Central Government or any State Government or any other authority, including any institution run by a social organization;

where children are detained or lodged for the purpose of treatment, reformation or protection and take up with these authorities for remedial action, if found necessary;

x) Inquire into complaints and take SVO motto notice of matters relating to-

a) Deprivation and violation of child rights;

b) Non-implementation of laws providing for protection and development of children;

c) non-compliance of policy decisions, guidelines or instructions aimed at mitigating hardships to and ensuring welfare of the children and to provide relief to such children, or take up the issues arising out of such matters with appropriate authorities.

xi) Such other functions as it may consider necessary for the promotion of child rights and any other matter incidental to the above functions.

3.6.9 The National Institute of Public Cooperation and Child Development (NIPCCD)

NIPCCD is a premier organisation which acts as an autonomous body under the Ministry of Women and Child Development, Establishment in New Delhi in the year 1966 under Societies Registration Act of 1860, To promote voluntary action, research, training and documentation on women and child development. The institution was established at New Delhi with its four Regional Centres at Guwahati, Banaglore, Lucknow and Indore. The thrust areas of the Institute relates to child care interventions relates to maternal and child health and nutrition, early childhood care and education, childhood disabilities, positive mental health in children and child care support services.

3.6.10 Central Adoption Resource Authority (CARA)

The Central Adoption Resource Authority (CARA) is an autonomous body under Ministry of Women and Child

Development, Government of India. CARA is a govt body which primarily deals with adoption of orphan, abandoned and surrendered children through recognised agencies. As per the provisions of Hague Convention on Inter-country Adoptions, 1993, CARA is designated as the Central Authority to deal with in-country and inter-country adoption of children[34]Central Adoption Resource Authority (CARA), earlier an autonomous agency, has now become a Statutory Body as per the provisions under Section 68 of the Juvenile Justice (Care &Protection of Children) Act, 2015 (Act No. 2 of 2016), which was notified on 31 December 2015 and has come into force w.e.f. 15th January, 2016.[35]

Objective of Central Adoption Resource Authority

To make sure best interest of children; citizen centric approach enabling prospective adoptive parents (PAPs) to take informed decision; online registration, referral (based on seniority), reservation & matching system and eliminating offline matching for transparency. The new Child Adoption Resource Information & Guidance System (CARINGS) has leveraged technology for bringing greater transparency in the adoption process and also minimize delays in the adoption process through e-governance.

Functions of Central Adoption Resource Authority

It functions as a nodal body at the National level for promoting and regulating adoption of Indian children. As per the JJ Act, 2015, CARA has been mandated to undertake the following:

i) Ensure proper coordination between interstate and State Agencies.

ii) Regulate inter-country adoptions.

iii) Frame regulations on adoption and related matters from time to time, as may be necessary.

iv) Carry out the functions of the Central Authority under the Hague Convention on Protection of Children & Cooperation in respect of inter-country adoption.

v) Any other function as may be prescribed.

CARA has framed the Adoption Regulations, 2017, as mandated under section 68 (c) of JJ Act, 2015 which shall be effective from 16th January, 2017 and would replace the Adoption Guidelines, 2015. The Adoption Regulations have been framed keeping in mind the issues and challenges faced by CARA and other stake holders including the Adoption Agencies & Prospective Adoptive Parents (PAPs). This will further strengthen adoption programme in the country by streamlining the adoption process. Transparency, early deinstitutionalisation of children, informed choice for the parents, ethical practices and strictly defined timelines in the adoption process are the salient aspects of the Adoption Regulations. Important changes incorporated in the Adoption Regulations, 2017 are as enumerated underneath:

i) Ensure proper coordination between interstate and state agencies.

ii) Procedure related to adoption of stepchildren.

iii) Validity of Home Study Report has been increased from two to three years.

iv) The time period available to the domestic PAPs for matching and acceptance, after reserving the child referred, has been increased to twenty days from the existing fifteen days.

v) District Child Protection Unit (DCPU) shall maintain a panel of professionally qualified or trained social workers.

vi) There are 32 Schedules annexed to the Regulations including model adoption applications to be filed in the Court and this would considerably address delays prevalent in obtaining the Court order.

vii) CARA shall be facilitating all adoptions under the JJ Act, 2015 through Child Adoption Resource Information &Guidance System (CARINGS) and all kinds of adoptions, including adoptions by relatives shall be reported to CARA, which would enable safeguards for all adopted children by maintaining their record and ensuring post adoption follow up.

3.6.11 National Initiative for Child Protection

The National Initiative for Child Protection (NICP) is a campaign initiated by the Ministry of Social Justice and Empowerment through the National Institute of Social Defence (NISD) and CHILDLINE India Foundation (CIF).

NICP aims at building partnership with the Allied System for Child Protection and promotion of Child's Rights. These Allied Systems are:

- The police
- The health care system
- The judicial system especially
- The education system
- The labour department
- The media
- The department of telecommunication
- The corporate sector
- The elected representatives
- All of us

NICP hopes to achieve this by training who work within the Allied system. As awareness increase in the group, we believe that every child will get her or his rights.[36]

3.6.12 Child Line India Foundation

CHILDLINE India Foundation anchors the CHILDLINE service. It is a project of the Ministry of Social Justice and Empowerment (Government of India) and works in partnership with NGOs, UNICEF and the corporate sector. CIF is responsible for the establishment of CHILLDLINE centers across the country, for ensuring the quality of and monitoring the service throughout the country. CIF also functions as a center for awareness, advocacy and training on issues related to child protection.

(a) Child Line Services at National Level

The Child line service developed and managed by Child line India Foundation (CIF) is a free 24x7 phone outreach service. Under ICPS, the Ministry has undertaken expansion of the service to other parts of the country, with the final objective of covering all the districts. Child line is working in 413 locations. CIF is partnering with 667 organizations for running these Child line projects in 35 States/UTs.

Table No. 3.1: Status of Child Line Services

Year	No. of Cities/ Districts covered	No. of Partner Organisations	Grant Sanctioned (Rs. in Crores)
2009-10	83	188	9.33
2010-11	125	298	17.89
2011-12	205	449	23.16
2012-13	269	547	30.06
2013-14	278	544	30.15
2014-15	283	543	53.62
2015-16	396	646	56.73
2016-17**(as on 31.12.16)**	413	667	41.33

Source:*Annual Administrative Report Department of Women and Child Development, Government of India (2016-17)*

The above table shows the status of child line services in India. The number of cities/districts coverage under child line has shown a tremendous increase since 2009-10. As it was 83 in 2009-10 and as on 31.12.2016 the total number of covered cities and districts under child line is 413. The total number of partner organisations was 188 in the year 2009-10 and increased to 667 as on 31.12.2016. The sanctioned amount for run this service was Rs. 9.33 crore in 2009-10. In the year 2016-17 Rs.41.33 crore have been sanctioned for running the service.

(b) Track Child

The Union Woman and Child Development Ministry unveiled a portal Track Child to function as a central database of all those Children who have gone missing in different parts of the Country. The Ministry has been implementing the Track Child portal since 2011-12 which was developed by the National Informatics Centre (NIC) for tracking missing and recovered children all over the country. The Ministry will coordinate with police head, social welfare departments of various states and other agencies to establish this mechanism. Information of missing & recovered children is uploaded by the Police and information of children residing in Child Care Institutions is uploaded by Child Welfare Committees, Juvenile Justice Boards and functionaries of CCIs. Ministry of WCD and the State Governments monitor the functioning of the portal regularly. Recently, Track Child 2.0 a new version of the software was launched and the labels are available in Hindi and Bengali. The Track Child was designed & developed as per the guidelines provided under the Juvenile Justice (Care and Protection of Children) Act 2000 and Integrated Child Protection Scheme. On 23rd September 2016, the Juvenile Justice (Care and Protection of Children) Model Rules were notified by the Govt. of India and therefore, the modules available on Track Child are being updated by the NIC as per new rules.

The Khoya Paya Web portal is a citizen based website to exchange information on missing and found children. In the year 2015-16 the Ministry had developed another website i.e. Khoya-

Paya which was integrated as citizen's corner in the Track Child portal. The objective of creating a citizen centric platform was to enable citizens to report missing children as well as sightings of their whereabouts without losing much time. Found children can also be reported. Any citizen can register on KhoyaPaya by using an Indian Mobile number. Khoya-Paya is also made available in Hindi during 2016-17. A brief report of the cases reported on Khoya-Paya is as follows:

Table No. 3.2: Total Cases Reported on Khoya-Paya from 2.6.2015 to 31.12.2016

Classification	Numbers
Total number of registered users	7418
Total mobile App downloaded by citizens/parents	3774
Total missing/sighted cases published on the portal	6794
Number of total missing cases reported	1297
i. Number of cases published	942
ii. Number of cases rejected	355
Number of total sighted cases reported	6010
i. Number of cases published	5852
ii. Number of cases rejected	158
Total missing/sighted cases closed on the portal	2896

Source: *Annual Administrative Report Department of Women and Child Development, Government of India (2016-17)*

As on 31.12.2016, out of 16981 Police stations, 10715 are making entries of missing/recovered children in Track Child.

(c) Children Home/ Shelter Home

Creation of twenty establishments are established for children in want of care and protection within the state. All the establishments are running under the state sponsored scheme, namely, Mukhya Mantri Bal Udha Yojana – an Integrated theme for the children in need of Care and Protection. These establishments are brought beneath the range of Juvenile Justice Act by declaring these establishments as Bal/ Balika Ashrams-cum-Children Home/ Shelter Home.

(d) Shishu Grih

One Shishu Grih having Capacity of 15 children has been setup through Himachal Council for Child Welfare at US Club Shimla for the abandoned children. The Central Adoption Resource Authority is providing Grant-in-Aid to run the ShishuGrih.

(e) Adoption Agency

For all matters related with adoption of orphans and abandoned children, the Himachal Pradesh Council for child welfare has been declared as licenced Adoption Placement Agency for carring out adoptions within the state. So far, sixty six abandoned children are covered through this agency. [37]

3.7 National Policies and Programmes for Children in India

A number of Child centric policies and programmes are working in India, the issues of Child Survival, Child Development and Child Protection. The important among them are:[38]

1. National Policy for children 1974

Every Child has right to lead a decent life. The physical, mental, and social well being of a child depends upon the family to which she/he belongs. The National Policy for Children, 1974 was adopted on 22th August 1974 in order to address the emerging challenges relating to child rights. An advisory and Drafting Committee had been formed for the purpose. The regional consultations regarding drafting of working paper on Policy of Children had been held across the country with concerned Ministries and Departments from States and Union Territories, civil society organisations, government and non-government organisations, academicians and experts etc. Thrust Areas of the Policy

- Reducing Infant Mortality Rate.
- Reducing Maternal Mortality Rate
- Reducing Malnutrition among children
- Achieving 100 percent civil registration of births
- Universalisation of early childhood care and development and quality education for all children;
- Achieving 100 percent access and retention in schools including pre-schools;
- Complete abolition of female foeticide, female infanticide and child marriage and ensuring the survival, development and protection of the girl child;
- Improving water and sanitation coverage both in rural and urban areas.
- Securing for children all legal and social protection from all kinds of abuse, exploitation and neglect.
- Complete abolition of child labour with the aim of progressively eliminating all forms of economic exploitation of children.
- Monitoring, review and Reform of policies, programmes and laws to ensure protection of children's interest and rights.
- Ensuring child participation and choice in matters and decision affecting their lives. January 24th has been declared as the National Girl Child Day by the Ministry of Women and Child Development, since 2009[39]

2. National Policy on Education, 1986

National Policy on Education, 1986 was involved the removal of disparities and to equalize educational opportunity especially for woman, schedule tribes (ST) and the Schedule Cast (SC) communities. To achieve such a social integration the policy involved increasing scholarships, course of instruction, recruiting a lot of teachers from the SCs, incentives for poor families to send their children to high school often, development of latest establishments and providing housing and services. The NPE involved a "child-cantered approach" in primary education, and launched "Operation Blackboard" to boost primary colleges nationwide.

3. National Policy on child Labour, 1987

National Policy on child Labour, 1987 contains the action plan for handling the matter of child labour. It made provision for a legislative action plan focusing and convergence of general development programmes for benefiting children where doable and Project-based plan of action has been launched for the welfare of working children in areas of high concentration of child labour.

4. National Nutrition policy, 1993

This Policy was introduced to combat the problem of under - nutrition. This Policy aims to address this problem by utilizing direct (short term) and indirect (long term) interventions in the area of food production and distribution, health and family welfare, education, rural and urban development, woman and child development etc

5. National Population Policy, 2000

The national population policy 2000 aims at improvement in the status of Indian children. It emphasized free and compulsory school education up to age 14, , 100 per cent registration of birth, death, marriage and pregnancy, universal immunization of children against all vaccine preventable diseases ,substantial reduction in the infant mortality rate and maternal mortality ratio etc.[40]

6. National Health Policy, 2002

The main objective of this policy is to provide proper facilities to ensure fine health amongst the overall population of the country. The approach is to extend access to the redistributed public health system by establishing new infrastructure in deficient areas, and by upgrading the infrastructure within the existing establishments. Preponderant importance is given to making sure an additional just access to health services across the social and geographical expanse of the country.

7. National Charter for children (NCC), 2003

National Charter for children (NCC), 2003 it recognises the right of every child to survival, life and liberty and need for the state to protect these rights. This Charter secures for each child its inherent right to be a child and enjoy a healthy and happy childhood, to handle the main causes that negate the healthy growth and development of children, and to awaken the conscience of the community within the wider social group context to protect children from all varieties of abuse, whereas strengthening the family, society and therefore the Nation. Well-being of special teams like children of BPL families, street children, girl child, child-care programmes, and academic programmes for interference from exploitation realize special mention within the NCC. The Charter provides that the State and community shall undertake all doable measures to make sure and shield the survival, life and liberty of all children. For empowering adolescent, the Charter states that the State and community shall take all steps to produce the mandatory education and skills to adolescent children thus on equip them to become economically productive citizens.[41]

8. National Plan of Action for Children (NPA), 2005

National Plan of Action for Children (NPA), 2005 was adopted by Government of India in the pursuit of well-being of children. Child survival, Child development, child protection and child participation is the main objective of (NPA, 2005). Addressing and upholding the rights of children in difficult circumstances, Securing for all children legal and social protection from all kinds of abuse, exploitation and neglect.

9. National Plan of Action for Children 2016,

National Plan of Action for Children 2016, launched at a special function held to celebrate the National Girl Child Day in New Delhi. The Policy reaffirms National Policy for Children 2013; commitment to the realization of the rights of all children in the country. It recognizes every person below the age of eighteen years as a child and that childhood is an integral part of life with a value of its own, and a long term, sustainable, multispectral, integrated and inclusive approach is necessary for the harmonious development and protection of children.

The National Plan of Action for Children (NPAC), 2016 is based on the principles embedded in the National Policy for Children 2013. The Action Plan has four key priority areas; survival, health and nutrition; education and development; protection and participation. The National Plan of action for children therefore stands as the country's practical expression of commitment to national progress. As the children's vulnerabilities are multi-layered are inter-connected; it takes a multi-sectorial approach and focuses on convergence and coordination between all stakeholders, i.e.; relevant Ministries, State/UTs Governments, PRIs, civil society organizations, media, business houses and children themselves. It takes into account the Sustainable Development Goals and proposes a roadmap to achieve SDGs for children. The NPAC 2016 was released by Hon'ble Minister of Women and Child Development on 24th January 2017 on the occasion of National Girl Child Day.

10. Child Protection Policy 2019

The Ministry of Women & Child Development drafts Child Protection Policy on its website for comments & suggestions to curb instances of abuse of minors in Shelter homes & Child care institutions. Draft of the policy recommends that all organisations must have a code of conduct based on "Zero tolerance of Child abuse & exploitation"[42]

11. Integrated Child Protection Scheme (ICPS)

The Integrated Child Protection Scheme, a centrally sponsored Scheme, with the primarily aim of establishing a safety net of dedicated and quality personnel, structures and services for child Protection across the country. The government of India has started several programmes and policy for the welfare of children within the country. The Integrated Child Development Services (ICDS) programme continues to be the world's most unusual child development programme operated since three decades of its existence. The programme provides package services, comprising supplementary nutrition, protection, health check-up, referral services to children below six years older and expectant and nursing mothers. Non-formal pre-school education is imparted to children of the cohort 3-6 years and health and nutrition education to ladies within the cohort of 15-45 years. High priority is accorded to the wants of the foremost vulnerable younger children below 3 years older within the programme through capability building of caregivers to supply stimulation and quality infancy care.[43]

The programme is enforced through a network of community-level Anganwadi Centres. The variation of services targeted at young children and their mothers for growth observation, immunisation, health check-ups and supplementary feeding, similarly as nutrition and health education to enhance the service and feeding practices that mothers adopt. Pre-school education is provided to children between 3 and 6 years of age.[44]

ICDS was launched in 1975 in accordance to the National Policy for Children in India. Over the years it has grown into one of the largest integrated family and community welfare schemes in the world. Given its effectiveness over the last few decades, Government of India has committed towards ensuring universal availability of the programme.

The Ministry is implementing a Centrally Sponsored Scheme i.e. ICPS since 2009-10 through the State Government/UT Administrations on predefined cost sharing financial pattern. The objectives of the Scheme are to contribute to the improvement in the well-being of children in difficult circumstances, as well as reduction of vulnerabilities to situation and actions that leads to abuse, neglect, exploitation, abandonment and separation of children from parent.

a) Service Delivery Structures

For effectively working and implementation of the Scheme across the country, the scheme envisage a three tier service delivery structure at National, State and District level by setting up Central Project Support Unit, State Child Protection Societies(SCPS), State Adoption Resource Agencies (SARA) and District Child Protection Units (DCPU) respectively. Till now SCPS has been constituted in 35 States/ UTs, SARA in 34 States/ UTs and DCPUs in 664 district of the country.

b) Care, protection and rehabilitation services

The Scheme provides financial support to State Governments/ UT Administrations for running services for children either by themselves or through suitable NGOs. These services include(a) Homes of various types for children;(b)Outreach services through Childline; (c) Open Shelters for children in need of care and protection in Urban and Semi Urban Areas; (d) Family Based Non-Institutional Care through Sponsorship, Foster Care and Adoptions.

c) Statutory Support Services

Under the Scheme Financial assistance is also provided for setting up of statutory bodies under the JJ Act namely, (a) Child Welfare Committees (CWCs) and Juvenile Justice Boards (JJBs). As reported by State Governments/UT Administrations, 675 CWCs and 669 JJBs have so far been set up across the

d) Supplementary Nutrition Programme (SNP) under ICDS at national level

Through Anganwari Centres supplementary nutrition is provided in Centres to Children, pregnant/lactating mothers and BPL adolescent girls. The nutrition is provided for 300 days in a year. Rates has been fixed (per beneficiary per day) children, pregnant/ lactating woman, adolescent girls and severely malnourished children. Expenditure under this programme is borne by the Central and State Governments on 90:10 ratio bases. During the current financial year, there is a budget provision as State share of 6.80 crore and 61.21 crore have been received as Grant-in aid from Government of India and up to December, 2017,5.10 crore State share and 39.08 crore central share have been utilized under this scheme. 4, 44,738 children and 99,452 pregnant/ lactating mothers have been benefited.[45]

e) Poshan Abhiyan

The Union Cabinet has approved setting up of National Nutrition Mission (NNM) with a three-year budget of Rs.9046.17 crore commencing from 2017-18. The NNM, as an apex body, will monitor, supervise, fix targets and guide the nutrition related interventions across the Ministries. The proposal consists of: mapping of various Schemes contributing towards addressing malnutrition; introducing a very robust convergence mechanism; ICT based Real Time Monitoring system; incentivizing States/ UTs for meeting the targets; to provide incentives for Anganwadi Workers (AWWs) for using IT based tools; removing registers used by AWWs; introducing measurement of height of children at the Anganwadi Centres (AWCs); Social Audits; setting-up Nutrition Resource Centres, involving masses through Jan Andolan for their participation on nutrition through various activities, among others. The programme through the targets will strive to reduce the level of stunting, under-nutrition, anemia and low birth weight babies. It will create synergy, ensure better monitoring, issue alerts for timely action, and encourage States/ UTs to perform, guide and supervise the line Ministries and States/UTs to achieve the targeted goals. More than 10 crore people will be benefitted by this programme. All the States and districts will be covered in a phased manner i.e. 315 districts in

2017-18, 235 districts in 2018-19 and remaining districts in 2019-20.[46]

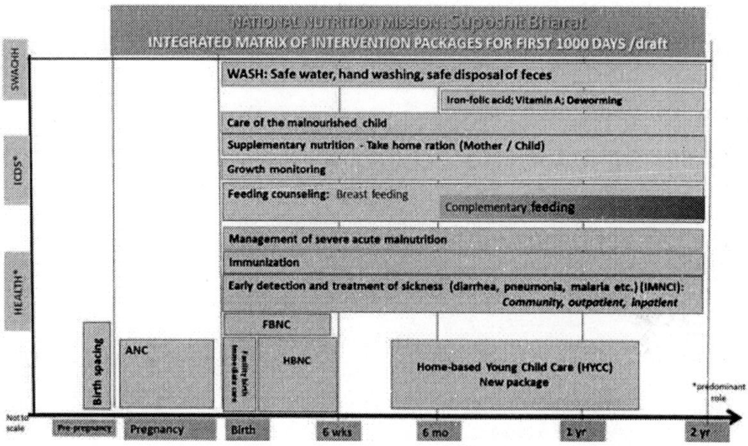

Source: Administrative Guidelines of National Nutrition Mission, Government of India

1 Mission Goals

The goals of NNM are to achieve improvement in nutritional status of Children from 0-6 years, Adolescent Girls, Pregnant Women and Lactating Mothers in a time bound manner during the next three years beginning 2017-18 with fixed targets as under:

Table- 3.3: Detail of Objectives and Target under National Nutrition Mission at National Level

Objective	Target
Prevent and reduce stunting in children (0-6 years)	By 6% @ 2% p. a.
Prevent and reduce under-nutrition (underweight prevalence) in children (0-6 years)	By 6% @ 2% p. a.
Reduce the prevalence of anaemia among young children (6-59 months)	By 9% @ 3% p. a.
Reduce the prevalence of anaemia among women and adolescent girls in the age of 15-49 years.	By 9% @ 3% p. a.
Reduce Low Birth Weight (LBW)	By 6% @ 2% p. a.

Source: Administrative Guidelines of National Nutrition Mission, Government of India

The Mission aims to reduce mal-nourishment from the Country in a phased manner, through the life cycle concept, by adopting a synergised and result oriented approach. The Mission will ensure mechanisms for timely service delivery and a robust monitoring as well as intervention infrastructure. Target of Mission is to bring down stunting of the children in the age group of 0-6 years from 38.4% to 25% by the year 2022.

Table-3.4 Detail of States/Districts to be Covered under National Nutrition Mission

Year	States/Districts to be Covered
2017-18	315 common district identified in the descending order of prevalence of stunting from amongst 201 districts identified by NITI Ayog on the basis of National Family Health Survey-4 data, 162 ISSNIP districts and 106 districts of schemes for adolescent girls.
2018-19	235 districts based on the status of under nutrition in various State/UTs to be identified generally based on prevalence of stunting.
2019-20	Remaining districts of all 36 State/UTs.

Source: Administrative Guidelines of National Nutrition Mission, Government of India

2 Functions of National Nutrition Mission

i) To act as an Apex body for nutrition related activities (for children under-six years of age, pregnant women, lactating mothers and adolescent girls).

ii) Monitor and review implementation of all nutrition related components across the line Ministries under Government of India/States/UTs.

iii) Fix targets of components relating to nutrition in each scheme implemented by various Ministries.

iv) Time to time review of nutritional status of States/UTs and provide policy directions.

v) Real Time Monitoring for alerts and prompt local interventions regarding Under-nutrition, Stunting, Wasting.

vi) BCC/ECCE – Audio-visual aids to be provided for effective interventions through BCC and ECCE for children.

vii) Identify relevant gap filling support to nutrition related programmes.

viii) Suggest/prescribe various nutrition related components/ actions to improve the nutrition status to concern agency.

ix) Prescribe/call periodical reports/returns on any nutrition related component from the line Ministries and States/ UTs (IT dash board).

x) Bring cohesion among various programmes run by various line Ministries and address convergence issues.

xi) Identify the nutrition related components in each scheme in consultation with the line Ministries

xii) ICDS-CAS/RCH Portal - synergy for data flow & interventions.

xiii) Assess causes of malnutrition in identified areas and plan for remedial actions.

xiv) Review the outcomes and suggest mid-course corrections that may be required in the policy design.

xv) Track progress in key outcomes with an analysis of lagging States/UTs and supportive action.

xvi) National Council for India's Nutrition Challenges will meet at least once in six months.

xvii) To perform any other function required for discharging the above functions assigned to the NNM.

Table-3.5: Nutrition Scheme to be monitored under National Nutrition Mission

Scheme	Components	Monitoring Criteria	Ministry/ Departmen
Anganwadi Services under Umbrella ICDS	* Supplementary Nutrition * Pre-school Education * Nutrition & Health Education	* Number of Beneficiaries enrolled and availed the scheme	MWCD
	* Immunization * Health check up * Referral Services	* Number of children immunized and left out * Number of children and PWD & LM availing the benefit	MH&FW/M CD
	* Weighing of Children * Measuring height of Children * Growth Monitoring chart * Nutrition Status	* Number of children weighed and found under-weight# * Number of children showing growth faltering (stunting)# * Number of wasted children#	MWCD
Pradhan Mantri Matri Vandana Yojana	Conditional cash transfer to pregnant women & lactating mothers	Number of enrolled and availed the benefits against eligible beneficiaries average delay in payment of installments	MWCD
National Creche Scheme	Providing day care services to the children of working women	Number of children availing the benefits	MWCD
Scheme for Adolescent Girls	Nutrition components for adolescent girls	Number of adolescent girls enrolled and availed the nutrition & IFA supplements	MWCD
National Health Mission	Institutional Delivery	* Number of deliveries in Hospitals * % of women received ante-natal health care * % of Low Birth Weight babies	Ministry of Health & Fam Welfare
	Anaemic Control Programme	* % of anaemic women of reproductive age# * % of pregnant women who consumed IFA tablets * % of anaemic children# * % of children consumed IFA	
	Rashtriya Baal Swasth Karyakram	* Number of AWCs covered	
Food Fortification	Functionaries of food Articles	Use of Fortified Food Articles in ICDS	MWCD in Collaboration with MH&FW DF&PD and FSSAI
Swachh Bharat Mission	Providing safe, clean and hygienic environment	Number of AWCs having toilets	Ministry of Drinking Wat & Sanitation
National Rural Drinking Water Programme	Providing safe, drinking water	Number of AWCs provided with drinking water facilities	Ministry of Drinking Wat & Sanitation
Targeted Public Distribution System	Access to household food to targeted beneficiaries	Number of beneficiaries covered	Department of Food & Public Distribution
Mid-Day Meal	Mid-Day Meal to school going children	Number of children benefited	Ministry of Human Resou Development
National Rural Livelihood Mission	Access to livelihood security giving resources to the poor to provide nutrition to the family	Number of poor families provided with livelihood resources	Ministry of Ru Development
Mahatma Gandhi National Rural Employment Guarantee Scheme	Construction of AWC building Access to livelihood security and poverty alleviation programme	Number of AWCs building constructed in convergence with MGNREGAS No. of unemployed persons provided job	Ministry of Ru Development MWCD

Panchayati Raj Institutions	Providing water facilities and toilets in the rural areas	No. of AWCs building, water facilities and toilets provided in the Rural Areas	Ministry of Panchayati Ra
Urban Local Bodies	Construction of AWCs building, water facilities and toilets in the urban areas	No. of AWCs building, water facilities and toilets constructed in the Urban Areas	Ministry of Ur Development
SarvaShikshAbhiyan	Providing Education to All	Number of persons provided education opportunities	Ministry of Human Resou Development
MNRE Home Based Care for Young Children (HBYC) Vitamin A Vitamin B Preferential Rotavirus and Pneumococcal Vaccine	Installation of Solar panels in AWCs	Number of AWC buildings where solar panels are installed	Ministry of Ne & Renewable Energy

Source: Administrative Guidelines of National Nutrition Mission, Government of India

 # Specific Targets Fixed under NNM

3 Monitoring of Schemes under NNM

NNM will ensure convergence of all nutrition related schemes on the target population. To create synergy, it will also monitor activities of health and other nutrition afective schemes from the habitation level upwards, being implemented by different Ministries and Departments. NITI Aayog will conduct monitoring and evaluation of NNM periodically through their 'Technical Support Unit' to assess the progress and impact of the programme.

4 Monitoring at National Level

There are some monitoring bodies in the country to monitor the National Nutrition Mission. The detail is following:

5 Council on India's Nutritional Challenges

A National Council has been established vide Government of India Letter No.NNM/2/2017-WBP dated 3rd January, 2018 with the following mandate:

a) Provide policy directions to address India's nutritional challenges through coordinated inter-sectoral action.

b) Review programmes for nutrition on a quarterly basis.

c) Coordinate and review convergence between Ministries.

The Council shall submit its report to the Prime Minister after every 6 months.

6 Executive Committee of NNM at National Level

An Executive Committee under the Chairpersonship of Secretary, MWCD has been established vide Government of India Letter No. NNM/50/2017-WBP dated 3rd January, 2018. The Executive Committee will be responsible for the Functions of NNM as given at Annexure II. The Executive Committee will report to the National Council of India's on Nutrition Challenges and will be the Apex body for nutrition related activities (for Children below six years age, Adolescent Girls and Pregnant Women and Lactating Mothers)providing direction, policy and guidance for implementation of various programmes/schemes under the NNM. The Executive Committee shall meet once in a quaters.

7 Financial Implications of NNM

The cost of the proposal of NNM as Government of India share for a period of three years commencing from 2017-18 comes to Rs. 2849.54 crore. The financial implications along with proposed source of funding are given in the table below:

Table-3.6: Financial Implications of National Nutrition Mission at National Level

Year	National Nutrition Mission#	GOI share without EAP*
2017-18	Rs. 3108.43	Rs. 979.16
2018-19	Rs. 3684.70	Rs. 1160.68
2019-20	Rs. 2253.04	Rs. 709.70
Total	Rs. 9046.17	Rs. 2849.54
GOI Share	**Rs. 2849.54**	

Source: Administrative Guidelines of National Nutrition Mission, Government of India

* Cost sharing ratio between the Centre and the States & UTs with legislature will be60:40. For North-Eastern States & Himalayan States it will be 90:10. It will be 100% for Union Territories without legislature.

(i) 50% Externally Aided Project (EAP) funding through IBRD (International Bank for Reconstruction and Development)/ Multi-lateral Development Banks (MDBs).

(ii) 50% funding through Gross Budgetary Support as per applicable cost sharing ratio between the Centre and the States & UTs with legislature will be 60:40. For North-Eastern States & Himalayan States it will be 90:10. It will be 100% for Union Territories without legislature.

Table-3.7: Detail of Cost Sharing Ratio at National Level under NNM

Category	Funds from IBRD/MDB#	Central Government	States/UTs
For activities to be carried out at Central level	50%	50%	00
For States/UTs with legislature	50%	30%	20%
For NER and Himalayan States	50%	45%	5%
For UTs without legislature	50%	50%	00

Source: Administrative Guidelines of National Nutrition Mission, Government of India
Subject to the approval of the fund by the competent authority

8 National Council on India's Nutrition Challenges

In pursuance of Government of India decision for setting up National Nutrition Mission a National Council on India's Nutrition Challenges is constituted for (a) policy direction (b) review; and (c) effective coordination and convergence between ministries which have a sectorial responsibility for the challenges.

Table-3.8 : Composition of the National Council of India's Member

1	Vice Chairperson NITI Ayog	Chairperson
2	Minister, Women and Child Development	Member
3	Minister, Health & Family Welfare	Member
4	Minister, Drinking Water and Sanitation	Member
5	Minister, Rural Development	Member
6	Minister, Tribal Affairs	Member
7	Minister, Panchayati Raj	Member
8	Minister, Consumer Affairs and Food	Member
9	Minister of State Finance	Member
10	Minister/Minister of State, Human Resource Development	Member
11	Minister/Minister of State, Urban Development	Member
12	Minister/Minister of State, Information & Broadcasting	Member
13	Minister/Minister of State, Environment, Forest and Climate Change	Member
14	State Chief Minister or their representative (5 on 2 years rotation basis) i. Bihar ii. Uttar Pradesh iii. Rajasthan iv. Tamil Nadu v. Chhatisgarh	Members
15	Member, Health & Nutrition, NITI Ayog	Member
16	CEO, NITI Ayog	Member
17	Secretary, Health Research &DG, ICMR	Member
18	Secretary	Member

Source: Administrative Guidelines of National Nutrition Mission, Government of India

3.8 Policies and programmes for Child Welfare in Himachal Pradesh

Despite Integrated Child Development Scheme, various other programmes for child development and welfare have also been implemented by government of Himachal Pradesh in the state. These schemes and programmes has been discussed as under:

3.8.1 Beti Hai Anmol

To strengthen the mindset of the community, toward girl child and mother at the time of birth. Beti Hai Anmol scheme has been started i.e. 5th July, 2010. Under this scheme a post birth gram of '10,000/- is deposited in bank/post workplace within the name of the girl child, taking birth in a very BPL family which may be drawn by her once attaining the age of eighteen years. Annual scholarship ranging between '300/- to '1,500/- is additionally provided to those girls once they begin planning to go to school from first to 10+2 standard.[47]

3.8.2 Balwadis

The Department is providing grant to Himachal Pradesh Council for child Welfare and State welfare Board for running one hundred ten Balwadis throughout the State. Under this scheme, pre-school education to the children below the age of 6 years is being provided in these balwadis. Throughout the year 2012-13, budget provision of '155 lakh has been kept. For the year 2013-14, budget provision of '170.00 lakh has been planned.

3.8.3 Mukhyamantri Bal Udhar Yojna

With a view to look after the orphans, semi-orphans and destitute children, the department is providing grant-in-aid for running and maintenance of Bal /Balika Ashrams at Sarahan, Sunni, Rockwood, Durgapur (Shimla), Chilli (Tissa) Kalpa, Bharnal, Kalehi, Mehla, Dehar (Mandi) and Chamba being run by the voluntary organizations. The department is running Bal/ Balika Ashrams at Pragpur (Kangra), TutiKandi, Masli (Shimla), Smoorkalan (Una), Arki, Kalsuien, Sahoo (Chamba) Sundernagar (Mandi) Sujanpur (Hamirpur) and Killar (Chamba). In these ashrams the inmates are provided free boarding and lodging facilities up to the age of 18 years and education upto 10+2 standard. Provision for higher education, professional education, career guidance and job oriented vocational training and rehabilitation has been included in the scheme. Total capacity of these Ashrams/ Shisu girls to accommodate is 1,160 children and present strength is 614. A budget provision of '359.30 lakh has been made for the current financial year for this scheme and '189.70 lakh have been spent upto December, 2015. A Model Home for girls with the cost of '616.82 lakh is being constructed at Mashobra and an observation home with the cost of '204.23 lakh is under construction at Hiranagar (Tutu, Shimla).[48]

3.8.4 Beti Bachao Beti Padhao scheme

This scheme has been launched on 22.1.2015 in one hundred districts of India with the target of preventing gender biased sex selective elimination, making certain survival, protection and education of the woman child. This theme is associate degree initiative to arrest and reverse (improve) the decline in child sex magnitude relation. Within the State this theme is enforced in UNA district wherever child sex magnitude relation was rumored lowest. Through this method, efforts are created to form awareness among lots regarding the adverse effects of declining sex magnitude relation.[49]

3.8.5 Integrated Child Protection Scheme

Integrated Child Protection Scheme is to contribute for the improvement in the well-being of children in difficult circumstances, as well as to the reduction of vulnerability to situations and actions that lead to abuse neglect exploitation, abandonment and separation children from parents. Two shelters have been at Baldeyan (Shimla) and Dharamshala for providing temporary shelter to the children. Further, for implementation of JJ Act in all Districts, Juvenile Justice Boards, Child Welfare Committees and District Level Advisory Boards have been plan in the State. Child Protection Units have been plan in the four districts i.e. Shimla, Mandi, Kangra and Chamba. Childline service bearing phone no. 1098 have been plan in the seven districts i.e. Shimla, Kullu, Kangra, Solan, Mandi, Chamba and Sirmaur under the scheme. To promote adoption in the country State Adoption Agency has been set up. During the current financial year the total allocation of budget from centre is '1,269.67 lakh out of which '816.49 lakh has been utilized upto 31.12.2015.[50]

3.8.6 Supplementary Nutrition Programme (SNP) under ICDS in Himachal Pradesh

The detail of recipes provided to the beneficiaries has been presented in Table 3.9.

Under the programme, cooked food is provided to the children within the age group of six months to six years, pregnant and lactating mothers, BPL adolescent girls and severely malnourished children able to eat food is given to the children who are within the age group of six months in two years. Beneath supplementary nutrition programme, five hundred calories and 12-15 grams of protein is needed to be supplemented to children, 600 calories and 18-20 grams of protein to the pregnant/ wet mothers and adolescent girls and 800 calories and 20-25 grams of protein to the underfed or malnourished children daily. Price or cost of supplementary nutrition is shared by Government of India and authorities within the magnitude relation of 50:50.

Table 3.9 : Detail of Recipes provided under Supplementary Nutrition Programme in Himachal Pradesh

Sr. No.	Beneficiaries	Recipes
1	Children (6 months to 3 years)	Nutrimix-Twice a week as Talk to me Ration (THR) Sweet Dalia Twice a week as THR Khichari-Twice a week as THR
2	Children (3-6 years)	Nutrimix-morning snack six days a week Khichari Twice a week Sweet Dalia Thrice a week Sprouted Gram Once a week
3	Severely Malnourished Children (6 months to 3 years)	Nutrimix –Twice a week as THR Sweet Dalia Twice a week as THR Khichari-Twice a week as THR Nutrimix-THR as part of double diet
4	Severely Malnourished Children (3-6 years)	Nutrimix-Morning snack six days a week Khicari-Twice a week Sweet Dalia Thrice a week Sprouted Gram once a week Nutrimix-THR as part of double diet
5.	Pregnant and Lactating mother	Khichari-Twice a week Sweet Dalia thrice a week Sprouted Gram once a week
6.	BPL adolescent Grls out of school girls School going Girls	Khichari- Twice a week on Wednesday and Saturday as hot Cooked Meal Sweet Dalia 3 days a week as THR Sprouted Gram Once a week Khichari-Twice a week as THR Sweet Dalia 3 Days a week as THR Sprouted Gram Once a week

Source *– Draft 12 five year plan 2012 and Annual Plan 2017-18 Govt. of Himachal Pradesh Shimla, P.125*

Government of India has approved National Nutrition Mission with a three years budget of '9046.17 crore commencing from 2017-18 giving impetus to convergent action towards making India malnutrition free. National Nutrition Mission is to ensure convergence of various programmes across Line Ministries/Departments Accordingly. States need to achieve convergence through close coordination between the departments of Women Child Welfare; Health: Drinking Water and Sanitation; Rural Development; Panchayati Raj; Education and Food; and Food and Nutrition Board. Number of initiatives have been taken at State level to set-in transparency by harnessing technology for efficient delivery and real time monitoring of services, as part of various schemes. The ICDS- Common Application software is the backbone for implementation of NNM. The mobile application facilities the capture of data by frontline functionaries and a six-tier dashboard ensures the monitoring and invention mechanism.

Table-3.10 Funding under National Nutrition Mission to Himachal Pradesh

Year	Total Cost NNM (Rs. in Crore)	Government of India share without EAP (Rs. in Crore)
2017-18	2602.75	819.87
2018-19	3526.08	1110.71
2019-20	2917.34	918.96
Total	**9046.17**	**2849.54**

Source: Directorate of Women and Child Development, Shimla: Department of Social Justice and Empowerment

Government of India has approved National Nutrition Mission with a three years budget of '9046.17 crore commencing from 2017-18 giving impetus to convergent action towards making India malnutrition free. National Nutrition Mission is to ensure convergence of various programmes across Line Ministries/Departments Accordingly. States need to achieve convergence through close coordination between the departments of Women Child Welfare; Health: Drinking Water and Sanitation; Rural Development; Panchayati Raj; Education and Food; and Food and Nutrition Board. Number of initiatives have been taken at State level to do transparency by harnessing technology for efficient delivery and real time monitoring of services, as part of various schemes. The ICDS- Common Application software is the backbone for implementation of NNM. The mobile application facilities the capture of data by frontline functionaries and a six-tier dashboard ensures the monitoring and invention mechanism.

3.9 Machinery for Children Protection & Welfare in Himachal Pradesh District Child Protection Units

In Himachal Pradesh 12 Child Protection Units has been establishes. Different services under Child Protection Units are being implemented by the District Child Protection Units. Following committees has been established to perform the smooth functioning under Integrated Child Protection:

1. State Child Protection Committee (SCPC)
2. District Child Protection Committee (DCPC)
3. Block Level Child Protection Committee (BCPC)
4. Village Level Child Protection Committee (VCPC)
5. State Level Inspection Committee (SLIC)
6. District Level Inspection Committee (DLIC)

Institutional Care-Government Run Homes

In Himachal Pradesh various Institutional Care Government Run Houses has been set up to look after interest of Children as given in Table-3.11

3.9.1 Himachal Pradesh State Child Protection Society

The Directorate of Women and Child Development is implementing through State Child Protection society the Juvenile Justice & care & protection of children Act 2015 in Himachal Pradesh,

Juvenile Justice care and Protection of Children Act 2015

Juvenile justice care & protection of children Modern rules 2016

Table-3.11

Institutional Care-Government Run Homes

Sr. No.	Name & Address of Home	District	Type of Home	Capacity		Actual No. Of Children as on 1.4.2017		No. Of Children with Special Needs (if any)	
				Girls	Boys	Girls	Boys	Girls	Boys
1	Bal Ashram cun Children Home Killar (Pangi)	Chamba	Children Home	0	50	0	32	0	0
2	Gujjar Ashram cum Children Home, Sahoo	Chamba	Children Home	0	25	0	15	0	0
3	Bal Ashrsmcum Children Home Sujanpur	Hamirpur	Children Home	0	50	0	22	0	0
4	Balika Ashram cum Children Home Pragpur	Kangra	Children Home	50	0	27	0	0	0
5	Bal Ashram cum Children Home Sundernagar	Mandi	Children Home	0	50	0	24	0	0
6	Institution for Children with Special Abilities Sundernagar	Mandi	Children Home	0	100	0	105	0	0
7	Bal Ashram Mashobra at Arki	Shimla	Children Home	0	100	0	47	0	0
8	Bal Ashram Masli	Shimla	Children Home	0	100	0	16	0	0
9	Balika Ashram Tutikandi*	Shimla	Children Home	100	0	53	0	0	0
10	Observation cum Special Home Heera Nagar**	Shimla	Observation cum special Home	0	25	0	10	0	0
11	Observation cum Special Home Samoor Kalian	Una	Observation cum special Home	0	25	0	35	0	0
Total				**150**	**525**	**80**	**306**	**0**	**0**

Source: Letter of Ministry of Women and Child Development, Government of India, wide letter number No. 14-9/2009-CW-II Vol. II.

* *Non-recurring grant was approved during 2017-18*

** *Additional home approved during 2017-18*3.

Adoption regulations 2017

Model guidelines for foster care 2016

3.9.2 State Early Childhood Care and Educational Council

In Himachal Pradesh State Early Childhood Care and Educational Council has been set up to look after interests of children its constitution is given below.

Table-3.12 Detail of State Early Childhood Care and Educational Council

S. N.	Department	Designation
1	Minister, Social Justice and Empowerment	Chairperson/ President
2	Additional Chief Secretary (SJ &E)	Member
3	chairperson, SCPCR	Member
4	Additional, Chief Secretary Education	Member
5	Additional Chief Secretary Health & Family Welfare	Member
6	Principal Secretary Finance & Planning	Member
7	Principal Secretary Panchayati Raj	Member
8	Principal Secretary Rural Development	Member
9	HOD (Psychiatry) IGMC Shimla	Member
10	HOD (Pediatrics) IGMC Shimla	Member
11	director Women & Child Development	Member Secretary
12	Associate Professor (Education), State Council of Education Research & Training, Solan	Member
13	General Secretary HP Council for Child Welfare	Member

Source: Department of Social Justice and Empowerment, Himachal Pradesh.

3.9.3 Objectives of Early Childhood Care and Educational Council

The main objective of State ECCE council is to embed the concept and practice for holistic and integrated development of young children in the age group of 0-6 years with requisite quality. This would be achieved by establishing comprehensive ECCE system and development and integrated framework that would contribute to strengthen the foundation of ECE programme in Himachal Pradesh by facilitating and supporting multimodal and multi component interventions; long term data collection and planning and more efficient inter-sectoral service delivery mechanism and platforms.

3.9.4 Himachal Pradesh Commission for Protection of Child Rights

Himachal Pradesh Commission for Protection of Child Rights was set up under Commission of Protection of child Rights 2005vide notification issued by Government of Himachal Pradesh on 27-04-2013.It has six members & chairperson. Powers given to Child commission is equal to civil court for enforcement of child Rights in Himachal Pradesh.

3.9.5 Child Line Services at State Level

In Himachal Pradesh 1098 telephone helpline has been established under Child Line in six districts namely, Shimla, Solan, Kullu (at Manali), Chamba, Mandi and Sirmour.

Conclusion

It can be concluded that at National level constitutional provisions has been made for child welfare. Various legislative provisions have been made & various policies, programmes have been started for child protection and welfare. Government of Himachal Pradesh has been implementing various child developments, child welfare and child protection programmes and schemes in the state with these include Integrated Child Development Services, Supplementary Nutrition Programme, Beti Hai Anmol scheme, Kishori Shakti Yojana, Rajiv Gandhi Scheme for Empowerment of Adolescent Girls-SABLA, Mother Teressa Asahaya Matri Sambal Yojana, Bal Balika Suraksha Yojana, Balwadis, etc. Integrated Child Development Services is an important scheme being implemented by the Government of Himachal Pradesh. It represents one of the world's largest and most unique programmes for early childhood development. It is the foremost symbol of India's commitment to children India's response to the challenge of providing pre-school education on one hand and breaking the vicious cycle of malnutrition, morbidity, and mortality.

References

1 CseindiaportaL, *Child Welfare in India – Programmes & Policy Initiatives.* Retrieved on 11 November 2016 from https://cseindiaportal.wordpress.com: https://cseindiaportal.wordpress. com/2012/11/06/child-welfare-in-india-programmes-policy-initiatives/

2 Gerald P. Mallon and Peg Mccartt Hess (eds.) (2005).*Child Welfare for the Twenty-First Century: A Handbook of Practices, Policies and Programs.* New York: Columbia University Press., p. 1.

3 Government of India (1994): ***National Council For the Handicapped Welfare,*** Ministry of Welfare, Vigyan Bhavan, New Delhi, on 21st September at p. 1.

4 Satpathy, Chinmayee (2012), Children Policies and Programmes in India, Yojana Journal, November 2012, pp 23-27.

5 Kolosov, 'The Rights of the Child', Janusz Symonides (ed), *Human Rights: Concepts and Standards,* Rawat, Jaipur, 2002.

6 M.P. Jain (2009): ***Constitutional Law of India,*** universal publications, New Delhi, at p. 89

7 Sinha, Kounteya (2008, January 24) 'Every Three Seconds One Child Dies in India: UNICEF', New Delhi *The Times of India.*

8 Banu, Zenab, Women Empowerment and Gender Issues, Kanishka Publishers & Distributors, New Delhi, 2001.

9 Government of India (2012), op.cit., pp. 8-9.

10 Roy, Kalpana, Women and Child Developmen, Commonwealth Publishers, New Delhi, 2000, 102-103.

11 Ibid.

12 Pandya, Remeshwari, ed., Women Welfare and Empowerment in India - Vision for 21st Century. New Century Publications, New Delhi, 2008, 110-111.

13 Sachdeva, D.R, Social Welfare Administration in India, KitabMahal, New Delhi, 1995, 91-92.

14 Ibid.

15 Wignaraja, Poona, Women Poverty and Resources, Sage Publications India Pvt. Ltd., New Delhi, 1997, 102-103.

16 Ibid.

17 Joshi, N.C., "Women Welfare-A Priority on the Government's Agenda", Kurukshetra, Vol. 56, No. 11, September 2008.

18 Ibid.

19 Razi, Shahin , "Empowered Women, Empowered Nation", Yojana, Vol. 56, June 2012.

20 Sharma, K.C. 'Variations in the levels of living in Himachal Pradesh - An Empirical investigation", Social Change, Vol. 22, No. 4,December 1992.

21 Ibid.

22 Sinha, Archna, "Empowering Women to Give Greater Control Over Natural Resources", Kurukshetra, Vol. 53, No. 1, November 2004.

23 11th Plan 2007-2012 & Budget Linked Annual Plan, Planning Department, Government of Himachal Pradesh, Shimla, 2008-09.

24 All of them are not totally relevant to children in general & considers women as principal beneficiaries with stress lying on girl child.

25 **Loc.cit.,**p. 9.

26 Child Beggars, (2013) Dalit Freedom Network Australia, Retrieved on 10 August 2013 from

http://www.dalitfreedom.org.au/trafficking/child-beggars.html?fontstyle=f-larger

27 Satpathy Chinmayee, child welfare policies and programmes in India, Yojana journal, November, 2012, pp 25

28 Planning Department (2012) *Ibid.*, p. 131.

29 Department of Women and Child Development, Government of India. 2009 *National Plan of Action – Commitment to the Child*, New Delhi : DWCD, MHRD, GOI.

30 http://vikaspedia.in/education/policies-and-schemes/right-to-education/right-to-education-act

31 http://vikaspedia.in/education/policies-and-schemes/protection-of-children-from-sexual-offences-act

32 Ministry of Women and Child Development, the Gazette of India : Extraordinary, Part II—Sec. 3(i), New Delhi, the 4th January, 2017

33 Ministry of Women and Child Development, The Gazette of India: Extraordinary, Part II—Sec. 3(i), New Delhi, the 4th January, 2017

34 Satpathy Chinmayee, Child welfare policies and programmes in India, Yojana journal, November, 2012,pp 25

35 Committee on the Rights of the Child, General Comment No. 2, The Role of Independent National Human Rights Institutions in the Promotion and Protection of the Rights of the Child, para. 7 (2002).

36 Committee on the Rights of the Child, General Comment No. 2, The Role of Independent National Human Rights Institutions in the Promotion and Protection of the Rights of the Child, para. 7 (2002).

37 *Annual Administrative Report Department of Women and Child Development, Government of India (2016-17)*

38 Ibid.

39 Satpathy Chinmayee, Child welfare policies and programmes in India, Yojana Journal, November, 2012,pp 25

40 Ibid.

41 Roy, Kalpana, Women and Child Development, Commonwealth Publishers, New Delhi, 2000. 93-94.

42 Civil service chronicle, February 2019, p.36

43 Vandana Khullar (March, 1998). "Integrated Child Development Services: A Critique of Evaluation Techniques". *Economic and Political Weekly*. XXXIII(10).

44 Chowdhary, D. Paul, Social Welfare Administration, Atma Ram & Sons, Delhi, 1979.

45 Government of India (December, 2017), POSHAN Abhiyan, Press Information Bureau, Cabinet. from http://www.wcd.nic.in/schemes-listing/2022

46 Government of India (December, 2017), POSHAN Abhiyan, Press Information Bureau, Cabinet. from http://www.wcd.nic.in/schemes-listing/2022

47 Bhardwaj, Ramesh Kumar, "Women Development Programmes" in Mohinder Singh (eds.). Social Policy and Administration, M.D, Publication Pvt. Ltd.,, New Delhi, 1996.

48 Economics and Statistics Department (2016), *Economic Survey 2015-16*. Shimla: Government of Himachal Pradesh. pp. 129-130

49 Government of India (2006), Report of the Working Group on Empowerment of Women for the XI Plan, Ministry of Women and Child Development.

50 Roy, Kalpana, Women and Child Development, Commonwealth Publishers, New Delhi, 2000, 93-94.

4

FUNCTIONING OF INTEGRATED CHILD DEVELOPMENT SCHEMES (ICDS)

The single aim of my life is that every child is: free to be a child, free to grow and develop, free to eat, sleep, see daylight, free to laugh and cry, free to play, free to learn, free to go to school, and above all, free to dream.

Kailash Styarthi

The ICDS Programme is enforced through a network of community- level Anganwadi Centres The ICDS programme approaches a holistic child health comprising health, nutrition, and education elements for pregnant ladies, lectating mothers, and children upto six years. The variety of services targeted at young children and their mothers for growth observations, immunisation, health check-ups, supplementary feeding, nutrition and health education. Through Anganwadi Centres Pre-school education is provided to children between 3 and 6 years of age.[1]In the present chapter an attempt has been made to study working of Integrated Child Development schemes in Himachal Pradesh.[2]

4.1 Working of ICDS at National Level

4.1.1 Child Development

Children between the age group of 0–6 years constitute around 158 million of the population of India (2011 Census). These children are the future human resource of the country. The Ministry of Women and Child Development is administering various schemes for the welfare, development and protection of children.

4.1.2 Coverage under ICDS

During the study an attempt has been made by researcher to analyse progress in the implementation of ICDS Schemes both during X,XI and XII Plans in terms of number of operational projects and Anganwadi Centres (AWCs) and coverage of beneficiaries as indicated in the table below:-

Table-4.1: Trends in Coverage during Tenth Five Year Plan

Year Ending	No. of Operational Projects	No. of Operational AWCs	No. of Supplementary Nutrition Beneficiaries	No. of Pre-School Education Beneficiaries
31.3.2002	4608	5,45,714	375.10 lakh	166.56 lakh
31.3.2003	4903	6,00,391	387.84 lakh	188.02 lakh
31.3.2004	5267	6,49,307	415.08 lakh	204.38 lakh
31.3.2005	5422	7,06,872	484.42 lakh	218.41 lakh
31.3.2006	5659	7,48,229	562.18 lakh	244.92 lakh
31.3.2007	5829	8,44,743	705.43 lakh	300.81 lakh

Source: *Annual Administrative Report Department of Women and Child Development, Government of India (2016-17)*

Table-4.2 Trends in Coverage during Eleventh Five Year Plan

Year Ending	No. of Operational Projects	No. of Operational AWCs	No. of Supplementary Nutrition Beneficiaries	No. of Pre-School Education Beneficiaries
31.3.2008	6070	10,13.337	843.26 lakh	339.11 lakh
31.3.2009	6120	10,44,269	873.43 lakh	340.60 lakh
31.3.2010	6509	11,42,029	884.34 lakh	354.60 lakh
31.3.2011	6722	12,62,267	959.47 lakh	366.23 lakh
31.3.2012	6908	13,04,611	972.49 lakh	358.22 lakh

Source: *Annual Administrative Report Department of Women and Child Development Government of India (2016-17)*

Table-4.3: Trends in Coverage during Twelfth Five Year Plan

Year Ending	No. of Operational Projects	No. of Operational AWCs	No. of Supplementary Nutrition Beneficiaries	No. of Pre-School Education Beneficiaries
31.3.2013	7025	13,38,732	956.12 lakh	353.29 lakh
31.3.2014	7067	13,42,146	1045.09 lakh	370.71 lakh
31.3.2015	7072	13,46,186	1022.33 lakh	365.44 lakh
31.3.2016	7073	13,49,563	1021.31 lakh	350.35 lakh
30.9.2016	7073	13,49,153	1010.56 lakh	345.44 lakh

Source: *Annual Administrative Report Department of Women and Child Development, Government of India (2016-17)*

The above table shows that there was a steady increase in the no of operational Projects, number of operational Aanganwadi workers, number of supplementary nutritional beneficiaries & number of preschool beneficiaries during Tenth, Eleventh & Twelfth Five year plan progressively. Data showed that functioning of ICDS was progressive during Five year Plan period

4.1.3 Financial Progress

Status of implementation of I.C. D.S is analysed in the following Table 4.4

Table-4.4: Status of Implementation of Integrated Child Protection Scheme

Year	No. of States Signed MOUs	Budget Allocation (Rs. in Cr.)		Amount Sanctioned (Rs. in Cr.)	No. of Beneficiaries
		BE	RE		
2009-10	17	60.00	50.00	42.63	36,780
2010-11	34	300.00	100.00	115.13	92,379
2011-12	34	270.00	180.00	177.54	50,118
2012-13	34	400.00	273.20	253.84	75,052
2013-14	35	300.00	270.00	265.78	74,983
2014-15	36	400.00	450.00	448.43	91,769
2015-16	36	402.00	498.57	497.29	78,463
2016-17	36	397.00	597.50	335.58	77,508

Source: *Annual Administrative Report Department of Women and Child Development, Government of India (2016-17)*

It is evident from analysis of above Table that in 2009-2010 Budget allocation was 60 crore and it increased to 397 crore in 2016-2017. While revised estimates were 50 crore and it increased to 597.50 crore It is also interesting to note that in 2016-2017 number of beneficiaries was ,36,780 in 2009-2010 but it increased to 77,508 in 2016-2017. Thus it shows that progression of ICDS is going well in India in past eight years.

4.2 Integrated Child Development Services (ICDS) Programme in Himachal Pradesh

The Integrated Child Development Services (ICDS) programme continues to be the world's most unique early childhood development programme, successfully operated since three decades of its existence.

4.1 Map of Himachal Pradesh

The programme provides package services, comprising supplementary nutrition, immunisation, health check-up, referral services to children below six years of age and expectant and nursing mothers. Non-formal pre-school education is imparted to children of the age group 3-6 years and health and nutrition education to women in the age group of 15-45 years. High priority is accorded to the needs of the most vulnerable younger children under three years of age in the programme through capacity building of caregivers to provide stimulation and quality early childhood care.[3]

The above objectives are sought to be achieved through a package of services comprising:

i. supplementary nutrition,

ii. immunization,

iii. health check-up,

iv. referral services,

v. pre-school non-formal education and

vi. nutrition & health education.

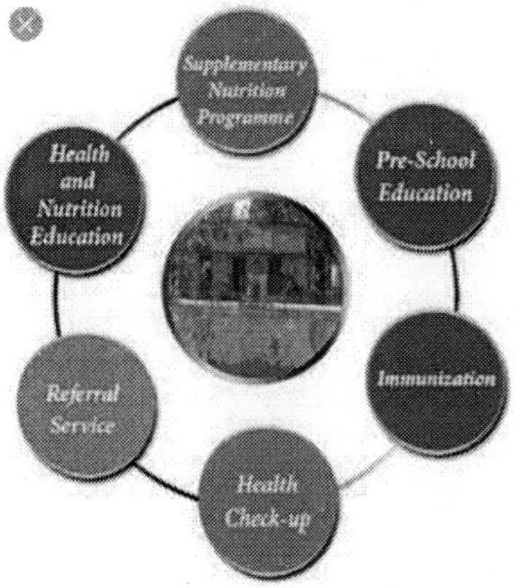

The last three services are associated with health and are provided by Ministry/Department of Health and Family Welfare through NRHM & Health system. The main idea of providing a package of services is predicated totally on the thought that the general impact is bigger if the various services develop in an integrated manner because the effectualness of a specific service depends upon the support it receives from the connected services. For higher governance within the delivery of the theme or scheme, convergence is, therefore, one amongst the key options of the ICDS theme. This convergence is in-built within the theme that provides a platform within the style of Anganwadi Centres for providing all services beneath the theme.[4]

Detail of services, target groups and service provides under ICDS in Himachal Pradesh has been shown in Table 4.5.

Table 4.5: Detail of Services, Target Group and Service Provided under ICDS

Services	Target Group	Service Provided by
Supplementary Nutrition	Children below 6 years Pregnant & Lactating Mothers (P&LM)	Anganwadi Worder and Anganwadi Helper
Immunization*	Children below 6 years Pregnant & Lactating Mothers (P&LM)	ANM/MO
Health Check-up*	Children below 6 years Pregnant & Lactating Mothers (P&LM)	ANM/MO/AWW
Referral Services	Children below 6 years Pregnant & Lactating Mothers (P&LM)	AWW/ANM/MO
Pre-school Education	Children (3 to 6 years)	AWW
Nutrition and Health Education	Women (15-45 years)	AWW/ANM/MO

Source: *Ministry of Women and Child Development (2015). Annual Report 2016-17. New Delhi: Government of India*

*Note: i) *AWW assist ANM in identifying the target group.*

ii) Three of the six services namely Immunization, Health Check-up and Referral Services delivered through Public Health Infrastructure under the Ministry of health and Family Welfare.

Table 4.5 clearly shows that services like supplementary nutrition, immunization, health check-up, referred services, pre-schooling education, nutritional and health education is being provided by the Angnawadi Workers and Anganwadi Helpers in Himachal Pradesh. Services of Immunisation, Health Check-up and Referral Services are made accessible through Public Health Infrastructure under the Ministry of Health & Family Welfare in the state.

Table-4.6: Nutritional Norms in ICDS

Beneficiaries	Calories (cal)	Protein (g)
Children(6 months to 72 months)	500	12-15
Severely malnourished Children (6 months to 72 months)	800	20-25
Pregnant women and Lactating mothers	600	18-20

Source: *Ministry of Women and Child Development (2015). Annual Report 2016-17. New Delhi: Government of India*

It is provided to children below six years of age and expectant/ nursing mothers and BPL adolescent girls in such a way that the nutritional intake is supplemented by 500 calories and 12-15 grams of protein for children 800 calories and 20-25 grams of protein for severely malnourished Children and 600 calories and 18-20 grams of protein for women. This includes supplementary feeding and growth monitoring; and prophylaxis against vitamin A deficiency and control of nutritional anaemia.

All families in the community are surveyed, to identify children below the age of six and pregnant & lactating mothers. By providing supplementary feeding, the Anganwadi attempts to bridge the caloric gap between the national recommended and average intake of children and women in low income and less privileged communities.[5]

Status of ICDS in Himachal Pradesh

Anganwari status can be analysed through following Graph 4.1

District wise Anganwadies Status in Himachal Pradesh:

Graph 4.1

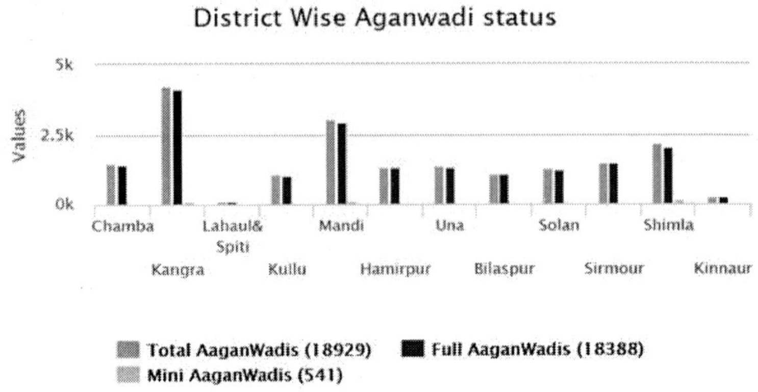

Source :*http:awcmishp.nic.in*

It is pertinent from analysis of the above graph that Kangra, Mandi, and Shimla District have more anganwadis as compared to other Districts of the State.

District wise helper and workers status in Himachal Pradesh:

Graph 4.2

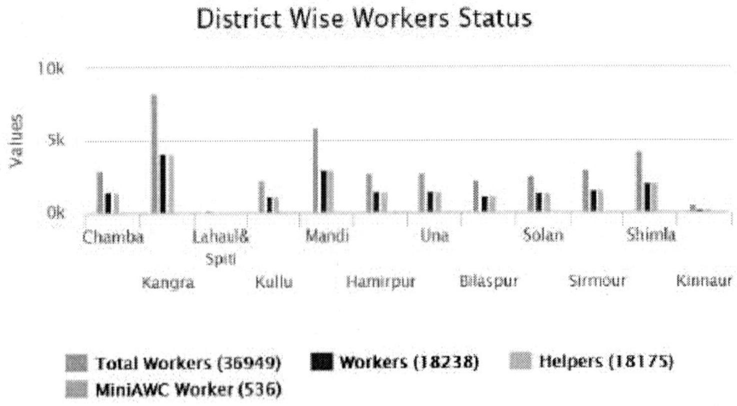

Source: *http:awcmishp.nic.in*

It is pertinent from analysis of above graph that in Kangra, Mandi, and Shimla District have more Anganwadis workers as compared to other Districts of the State. It is because of fact that Anganwadi Centres are also in large number here.

Literacy Status of Anganwadi Workers:

Graph 4.3

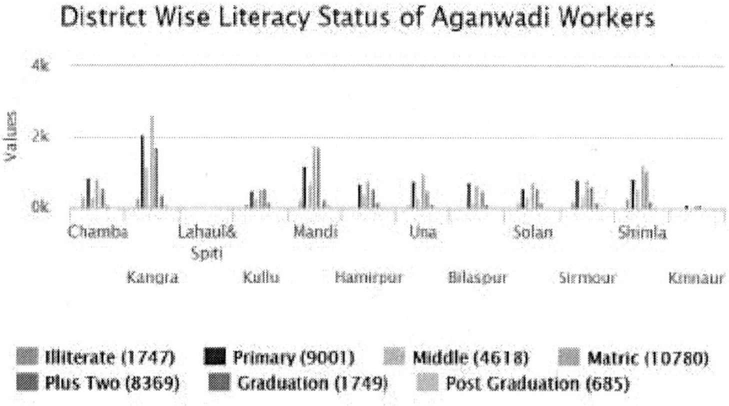

Source: *http:awcmishp.nic.in*

While analysing the literary status of Anganwadi workers it was analysed that majority of Anganwadi workers all over the State had qualification till matriculate

Category wise Status of Anganwadi workers:

Graph 4.4

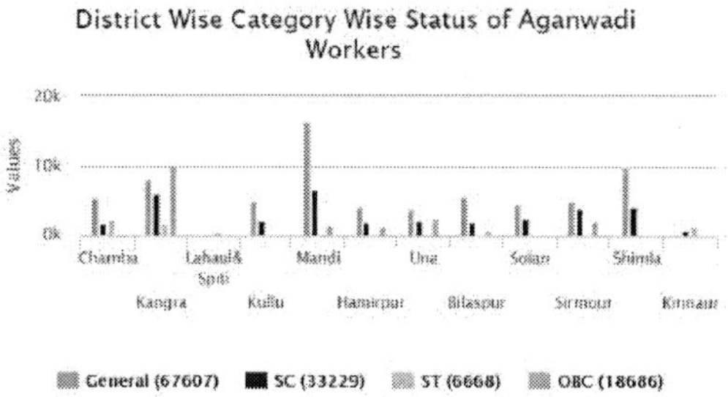

Source: *http:awcmishp.nic.in*

Above Graph reflects that in composition of Anganwadi workers all over the state different categories are reflected thus adequate representation is given to schedule castes, Schedule Tribe & OBC category while making recruitment to Posts of Anganwadi workers in Himachal Pradesh.

While examining the working of ICDS in Himachal Pradesh various Programmes are examined by researcher in the present context as given below.

In order to examine the working status of various programmes run under ICDS in Himachal Pradesh is analysed in following Tables

4.2.1 Supplementary Nutrition Mission in Himachal Pradesh

The government has approved the launch of the National Nutrition Mission (NNM) to counter the problems of under-nutrition, low birth weight and stunting, with a budget of Rs 9,046 crore for a period of three years. The mission, commencing 2017-18, has a target to reduce under-nutrition and low birth weight by 2 per cent each year. This mission will strive to achieve reduction in stunting from 38.4 per cent as per the National Family Health Survey-4 to 25 per cent by 2022.[6]

Under the Nutritional Mission, it has been kept in mind to provide cooked food to the children in the age group of 6 months to 6 years, pregnant and lactating mothers, BPL adolescent girls and severely malnourished children. Ready to eat food is given to the children who are in the age group of 6 months to 2 years. Under supplementary nutrition programme, 500 calories and 12-15 grams of protein is required to be supplemented to children, 600 calories and 18-20 grams of protein to the pregnant/ lactating mothers and adolescent girls and 800 calories and 20-25 grams of protein to the malnourished children daily.7 Cost of supplementary nutrition is shared by Government of India and State Government in the ratio of 50:50. The detail of recipes provided to the beneficiaries has been presented in Table 4.7.

Table 4.7: Detail of Recipes provided under Supplementary Nutrition Programme in Himachal Pradesh

Sr. No.	Beneficiaries	Recipes
1	Children (6 months to 3 years)	Nutrimix-Twice a week as Talk to me Ration (THR) Sweet Dalia Twice a week as THR Khichari-Twice a week as THR
2	Children (3-6 years)	Nutrimix-morning snack six days a week Khichari Twice a week Sweet Dalia Thrice a week Sprouted Gram Once a week
3	Severely Malnourished Children (6 months to 3 years)	Nutrimix -Twice a week as THR Sweet Dalia Twice a week as THR Khichari-Twice a week as THR Nutrimix-THR as part of double diet
4	Severely Malnourished Children (3-6 years)	Nutrimix-Morning snack six days a week Khicari-Twice a week Sweet Dalia Thrice a week Sprouted Gram once a week Nutrimix-THR as part of double diet
5.	Pregnant and Lactating mother	Khichari-Twice a week Sweet Dalia thrice a week Sprouted Gram once a week
6.	BPL adolescent Grls out of school girls	Khichari- Twice a week on Wednesday and Saturday as hot Cooked Meal Sweet Dalia 3 days a week as THR Sprouted Gram Once a week
	School going Girls	Khichari-Twice a week as THR Sweet Dalia 3 Days a week as THR Sprouted Gram Once a week

Source: *Draft 12 five year plan 2012 and Annual Plan 2016-17 Govt. of Himachal Pradesh Shimla, P.125*

Objectives of the Scheme:

1. To sensitize and create awareness among pregnant women and mothers of children up to 2 years of age and their key influencers on key health, nutrition and child care practices in order to strengthen positive practices related to survival, growth and development of children;

2. To create awareness about the benefits available to pregnant woman and Lactating mothers (PW & LM) under PMMVY and JSY;

3. To improve health seeking behaviour amongst the Pregnant Women (PW) and Lactating Mothers (LM);

4. To enhance community participation in promoting good nutrition and health behaviour.

Target beneficiaries

1. Target group: Caregivers viz., mothers, and family members including fathers, grandparents and older siblings
2. Community Representatives: Community leaders, Religious Leaders, PRI Members, SHG Members, VHSNC Members
3. Facilitators/Resource Persons: AWW, ASHA, ANM and ICDS Supervisors

Financial Provision

1. An amount of Rs. 250/- per event has been kept under this activity.
2. States may ensure giving flexibility in utilising this amount by the AWWs.
3. The item-wise expenditure may likely to vary from event to event.
4. Resources may also be mobilised from panchayat /local bodies in meeting expenditures towards specific items as may be required for organising the event.

Detail of nutrition Rate in Himachal Pradesh has been given in Table 4.8.

Table-4.8: Detail of Nutrition Rate in Himachal Pradesh

Sr. No.	Beneficiaries	Cost of Diet	Fuel Cost	Transportation	Total
1	Pregnant Women	Rs. 2.70	Rs.0.25	Rs.0.15	Rs.3.10
2	Lactating Mother	Rs.2.70	Rs.0.25	Rs.0.15	Rs.3.10
3	Adolescent Girls	Rs.2.70	Rs.0.25	Rs.0.15	Rs.3.10
4	Children	Rs.1.60	Rs.0.25	Rs.0.15	Rs.2.00

Source: *Directorate of Women and Child Development, Shimla: Department of Social Justice and Empowerment.*

Growth Monitoring and nutrition observation are two important activities that are undertaken. Children below the age of three years of age are weighed once a month and children 3-6 years of age are weighed quarterly. Weight-for-age growth cards are maintained for all children below six years. This helps to detect growth faltering and helps in evaluating nutritional status. Besides, severely malnourished children are given special supplementary feeding and referred to medical services.

4.2.2 Performance of Supplementary Nutrition in Himachal Pradesh

Year-wise detail of beneficiaries of supplementary nutrition in Himachal Pradesh has been shown in Table 4.9.

Table 4.9: Beneficiaries of Supplementary Nutrition 0-3 Years of Age Children in Himachal Pradesh

District	Years			
	2014-15	2015-16	2016-17	2017-18
Bilaspur	16219	15156	15305	14057
Chamba	25658	25611	26304	23696
Hamirpur	17090	16191	15821	16640
Kangra	54742	56044	54161	51581
Kinnaur	3105	2927	2803	2791
Kullu	16848	16731	16236	15807
Lahoul & Spiti	897	1044	897	1093
Mandi	40915	38925	36762	34743
Shimla	29482	28202	17523	25949
Sirmaur	24317	23303	13255	22704
Solan	22172	21691	10667	19727
Una	20390	20256	19914	19401
Himachal Pradesh	**271835**	**266081**	**261299**	**248245**

Source: *Directorate Women and Child Development Government of Himachal Pradesh, Himland, Shimla.*

Table 4.9 depicts that in the year 2014-15 total beneficiaries of supplementary nutrition in age group 0-3 years was 271835, which decreased to 248245 in the year 2017-18. Hence, the data shows decreasing trend in the number of beneficiaries in Himachal Pradesh. Thus this decreasing trend shows that efforts need to be done in effective way so that problems of malnutrition and stunted growth can be tackled effectively

Year-wise detail of beneficiaries (3-6 year children) of supplementary nutrition in Himachal Pradesh has been shown in Table 4.10.

Table-4.10: Beneficiaries of Supplementation Nutrition to 3-6 Years of Age Children in Himachal Pradesh

District	Years			
	2014-15	**2015-16**	**2016-17**	**2017-18**
Bilaspur	5987	6068	6265	5412
Chamba	9805	9928	9536	8750
Hamirpur	6569	6814	6560	6397
Kangra	21732	21579	21704	20483
Kinnaur	944	913	866	853
Kullu	6582	6489	6467	6275
Lahoul & Spiti	273	267	285	373
Mandi	15243	14589	14925	14657
Shimla	10024	9602	2154	9003
Sirmaur	9688	9128	1486	9094
Solan	8238	8170	1281	7663
Una	7643	7614	7793	7923
Himachal Pradesh	**10272**	**101161**	**100913**	**97183**

Source: *Directorate Women and Child Development Government of Himachal Pradesh, Himland, Shimla.*

Data in Table 4.10 depicts that during 2014-15 the total number of beneficiaries (3-6 years children) was 187120, which decreased to 183430 in the year 2015-16. In the year 2016-17 this number was 187788. It decreased to 178711 in the year 2017-18. Hence, table shows decreasing trend regarding beneficiaries (3-6 years children) of supplementary nutrition in Himachal Pradesh.

Year-wise detail of beneficiaries (pregnant women and lactating mother) of supplementary nutrition in Himachal Pradesh has been shown in Table 4.11.

Figures in Table 4.11 shows that during the year 2014-15 total of 10272 pregnant and lactating mothers were getting supplementary nutrition through ICDS, while in the year 2015-16 this number increased to 101161. After this the number of pregnant and lactating mother shows decreasing trend and it decreased to 97183 in the year 2017-18. Thus decreasing trend shows that less women are coming to take benefit of these schemes.

Table-4.11: Beneficiaries of Supplementation Nutrition to Pregnant and LacCtating Women in Himachal Pradesh

District	Years			
	2014-15	2015-16	2016-17	2017-18
Bilaspur	5987	6068	6265	5412
Chamba	9805	9928	9536	8750
Hamirpur	6569	6814	6560	6397
Kangra	21732	21579	21704	20483
Kinnaur	944	913	866	853
Kullu	6582	6489	6467	6275
Lahoul & Spiti	273	267	285	373
Mandi	15243	14589	14925	14657
Shimla	10024	9602	2154	9003
Sirmaur	9688	9128	1486	9094
Solan	8238	8170	1281	7663
Una	7643	7614	7793	7923
Himachal Pradesh	**10272**	**101161**	**100913**	**97183**

Source: *Directorate Women and Child Development Government of Himachal Pradesh, Himland, Shimla.*

Immunization in Himachal Pradesh

All children below six years of age are immunised against six deadly diseases, namely, tuberculosis, diphtheria, whooping cough, tetanus, polio and measles. Expectant women are immunized against tetanus.[8] These are major preventable causes of child mortality, disability, morbidity and related malnutrition. Immunization of pregnant women against tetanus also reduces maternal and neonatal mortality.[9]

Immunization Programme is one of the key interventions for protection of children from life threatening conditions, which are preventable. It is one of the largest immunization programme in the world and a major public health intervention in the country. Immunization Programme in India was introduced in 1978 as Expanded Programme of Immunization (EPI). The programme gained momentum in 1985 and was expanded as Universal Immunization Programme (UIP) to be implemented in phased manner to cover all districts in the country by 1989-90.

UIP become a part of Child Survival and Safe Motherhood Programme in 1992 Since, 1997, immunization activities have been an important component of National Reproductive and Child

Health Programme and is currently one of the key areas under National Rural Health Mission (NRHM) since 2005.[10]

Through the Universal Immunization Programme, Government of India is providing vaccination to prevent seven vaccine preventable diseases i.e. Diphtheria, Pertussis, Tetanus, Polio, Measles, severe form of Childhood Tuberculosis and Hepatitis B, Hiaemophilus influenza type b (Hib) and Diarrhea

India's UIP provide free vaccines against 11 life threatening diseases- Tuberculosis, Diphtheria, Pertussis, Tetanus, Polio, Hepatitis B, Pneumonia and Meningitis due to Haemophilus Influenzae type b (Hib), Measles, Rubella, Japanese Encephalitis (JE) and Rotavirus diarrhoea. (Rubella, JE and Rotavirus vaccine in select states and districts)

Immunization is one of the most important and cost-effective strategies for the prevention of childhood sicknesses and disabilities and is thus a essential need for all children. The following schedule has been recommended by the Ministry of Health, Govt. of India and is one of the most widely followed by the child health care providers.

Table-4.12: Vaccine schedule administered by ICDS

Vaccine	When to give	Dose	Route	Site
For Pregnant Women				
TT -1	early pregnancy	0.5ml	intra muscular	Upper arm
TT -2	4 weeks after 1st dose of TT*	0.5ml	intra muscular	Upper arm
TT booster	If received 2 TT doses in a pregnancy within the last 3yrs	0.5ml	intra muscular	Upper arm
For Infants				
BCG	At birth or as early as possible till 1 year of age	0.1ml (0.05ml until 1month age)	Intra-dermal	Left Upper Arm
Hepatitis B - Birth dose	At birth or as early as possible within 24 hours	0.5 ml	Intra-muscular	Antero-lateral side of mid-thigh
OPV -0	At birth or as early as possible within first 15 days	2 drops	Oral	Oral
OPV -1,2,3,	6 weeks, 10 weeks & 14 weeks	2 drops	Oral	Oral

DPT- 1,2,3,	6 weeks, 10 weeks & 14 weeks	0.5 ml	Intra-muscular	Antero-lateral side of mid-thigh
Hepatitis B- 1, 2, &3	6 weeks, 10 weeks & 14 weeks	0.5 ml	Intra-muscular	Antero-lateral side of mid-thigh
Pentavalent vaccine - 1, 2 & 3**	6 weeks, 10 weeks & 14 weeks	0.5 ml	Intra-muscular	Antero-lateral side of mid-thigh
Measles	9 completed months - to 12 months. Give up to 5yrs if not received at 9 - 12 months age	0.5 ml	Sub-cutaneous	Right upper arm
Vitamin A (1st dose)	At 9 completed months with measles	1ml (1lakh IU)	Oral	Oral
Japanese Encephalitis (1st Dose)***	At 9 completed months (under consideration)	0.5 ml	Sub-cutaneous	Left Upper Arm
For Children				
DPT booster 1	16- 24 months	0. 5 ml	Intra-muscular	Antero-lateral side of mid-thigh
OPV Booster	16-24 months	2 drops	Oral	Oral
Japanese Encephalitis***(if applicable)	16-24 months	0.5 ml	Sub-cutaneous	Left Upper Arm
Measles - 2nd dose	16 - 24 months age	0.5 ml	Sub-cutaneous	Right upper arm
Vitamin A***(2nd to 9th dose)	18 months (2nd dose). Then, one dose every 6 months upto the age of 5 years.	2 ml (2 lakh IU)	Oral	Oral
DT booster	5- 6 years	0.5 ml	Intra-muscular	Upper arm
TT	10 years &16 years	0.5 ml	Intra-muscular	Upper arm

Source: *District Programme Office, Kangra*

* *Give TT-2 or Booster doses before 36 weeks of pregnancy. However, give these even if more than 36 weeks have passed. Give TT to a women in labour if, she has not previously received TT.*

** *Pentavalent vaccine introduced instead of DPT and Hepatitis B 1,2,3 in select states.*

*** *JE vaccine at select endemic districts*

4.3 Profile of District Kangra

Kangra district derives its name from Kangra town which was called Nagarkot in the ancient times. Kangra proper originally was a part of the ancient Trigartha or Trigarta (Jalandhar) which comprised of the area lying between the rivers "Shatadroo" (probably Satluj) and Ravi. A expanse of land to the east of the Satluj which probably is the area of Sirhind in Punjab also formed a part of Trigartha or Trigarta. Trigartha was comprised of two provinces, via one in the plains with headquarters at Jalandhar and the other in the hills with headquarters at Nagarkot (present Kangra).[11] The present Kangra district came into existent on the 1st September, 1972 consequent upon the reorganization of districts by the Government of Himachal Pradesh. It was the largest district of the composite Punjab in terms of area till it was transferred to Himachal Pradesh on the 1st November, 1966 and had six tehsils namely Nurpur, Kangra, Palampur, Dera Gopipur and Hamirpur. Kullu was also a tehsil of Kangra district upto 1962 and Lahul & Spiti which also formed a part of Kangra was created as a separate district in 1960. On the reorganization of composite Punjab on the 1st November, 1966 the areas constituting Kangra district were transferred to Himachal Pradesh alongwith the districts of Shimla, Kullu and Lahul & Spiti and tehsils of Una and Nalagarh and areas of Dalhousie, Dalhousie CB and Bakloh CB of Gurdaspur.[12]

4.2 Map of Kangra District

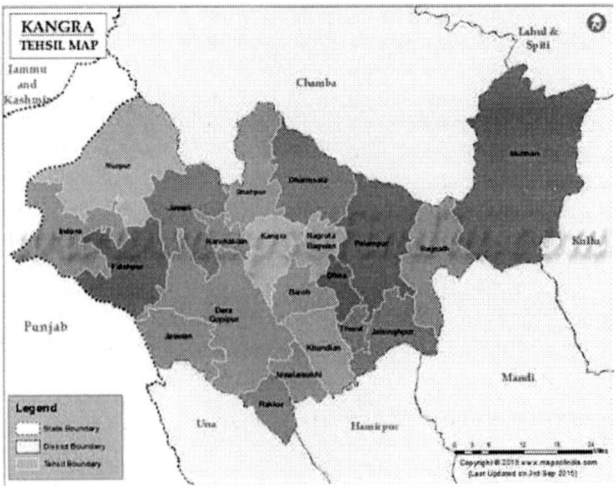

4.3.1 Area and population of district Kangra:

According to census 2011, Kangra had a total population of 1,339,030.out of which 661,254 were males and the remaining 6,77,776 were females.

According to the Surveyor-General of India the area of the district is 5,746 square kilometers. In terms of area, the district constitutes 10.31 per cent of the state area and ranks fourth among the districts. According to the Census of India 2011, the total rural population of the district is 14,23,794 persons with the population density of 248 people per square kilometer. Out of total population of the district, 3,19,385 persons are scheduled castes and 84,564 persons are scheduled tribes. As per the Census of India 2011 the population of the male and female is 7, 05,365 and 7, 18,429 respectively. The sex ratio is 1019 female per 1000 male in the district. Block-wise area, rural population and density of population has been shown in Table 4.13.

Table-4.13: Block-wise Area, Rural Population, Density of Rural Population and Sex Ratio in Kangra District (as per 2011 Census)

Block	Area of Blocks (sq. kms.)	Total Rural Population	%age to total rural population	Density of population (persons per sq. kms.)	Sex ratio (women per 'ooo male)	Literacy rate
Baijnath	1301	90374	6.35	69	993	73.84
Bhawarna	259	91376	6.42	353	1006	79.91
Dehra	236	76469	5.37	324	1185	79.15
Dharamshala	203	68341	4.80	337	971	80.41
Fatehpur	99	63223	4.44	639	1009	79.22
Indora	252	104710	7.35	416	998	81.03
Kangra	183	83005	5.83	454	1019	77.63
Lambagaon	426	104115	7.31	244	1036	76.29
Nagrota Bagwan	713	126804	8.91	178	1064	80.36
Nagrota Surian	416	112689	7.91	271	1045	83.43
Nurpur	309	99101	6.96	321	1041	80.89
Panchrukhi	374	118668	8.33	317	968	80.39
Pragpur	404	105351	7.40	261	927	79.31
Rait	399	109948	7.72	276	985	80.18
Sullah	172	69620	4.89	405	1097	81.20
Total	**5746**	**1423794**	**100.00**	**248**	**1019**	**79.62**

Source: *Block Indicators, District Statistical Office, Dharamshala, Kangra District.*

Table 4.13 shows that area wise, Baijnath (1,301 square kilometer) is the biggest block in the district Kangra. The percentage of rural population is highest in Nagrota Bagwan block (8.91 per cent) and lowest in Fatehpur block (4.44 per cent). Regarding density of population the Table 4.14 shows that the highest density of population (that is, 639 persons per square kilometer) is in Fatehpur block and lowest density of population (that is, 69 persons per square kilometer) is in Baijnath block.

Kangra, being the largest district accounting for more than one fifth of the state population and 10.31 per cent of the total geographical area, plays an significant role in the economy of this hilly state. The economy of district is primarily agrarian with two-thirds of the population directly dependent on agriculture.[13]The district is covered by fertile valleys and agriculture is the main occupation of the rural population. The agro-climatic conditions obtaining in the district are most suitable for the growing of food crops such as Wheat, rice, maize, oil seeds, sugarcane, potatoes and tea. With implementation of various programmes, the government has endeavored to increase the agricultural production by the introduction of improved variety of seeds, increased fertilizers, chemical pesticides, improved agricultural implements, etc.[14]

Beneficiaries of ICDS in District Kangra

Table indicates that in district Kangra in the year 2014-15 total number of beneficiaries in age group 0-3 years was 54,742 which decreased to 51,584 in the year 2017-18. Number of beneficiaries (3-6 years children) was 36,925 in the years of 2014-15 which decreased to 31,775 in the year of 2017-18. Hence, the data show decreasing trend in the number of beneficiaries in Kangra District. Thus this decreasing trend shows that efforts need to be done in effective way so that problems of malnutrition and stunted growth can be tackled effectively.

Year-wise detail of beneficiaries under ICDS district Kangra has been shown in Table 4.14

Table 4.14: Beneficiaries of 0-3 Years, 3-6 years of Age Children, pregnant and lactating mothers and adolescent girls in district Kangra

Years	District kangra				Total
	0-3 years	3 to 6 years	pregnant & lactating mothers	adolescent girls	
2014-15	54742	36925	21732	2265	**115664**
2015-16	56044	36123	21579	2170	**115916**
2016-17	54161	35879	21704	2231	**113975**
2017-18	51584	31775	20483	179	**104021**
Total	216531	140702	85498	6845	**449576**

Source: *Directorate Women and Child Development Government of Himachal Pradesh, Himland, Shimla*

During 2014-15 the total number of pregnant and lactating mothers was 21,732 which shows decreasing trend and it decreased to 20,483 in the year 2017-18. Thus decreasing trend shows that less women are coming to take benefit of these schemes.

During 2014-15 the total numbers of adolescent girls was 2,265 which decreased to 179 in the years of 2017-18. It may be because of new notification adopted by Government of Himachal Pradesh in this regard.

Performance of Supplementary Nutrition under ICDS in Sample Blocks

Detail of beneficiaries (0-3 year children) of supplementary nutrition in sample block of Kangra district has been given in Table 4.15.

Above table indicates that in Dehra block the total number of beneficiaries (0-3 years children) in the year 2014-15 was 5178, which due to some fluctuation decreased to 4766 in the year 2017-18. In Fatehpur block data show decreasing trend. The number of beneficiaries in Fatehpur decreased to 3890 in the year 2017-18 from 4427 in the year 2014-15.In Indora block the

Table-4.15: Beneficiaries of Supplementary Nutrition from 0-3 Years of Age Children in Five Blocks of Kangra District

Year	Blocks				
	Dehra	Fatehpur	Indora	Nurpur	Pragpur
2014-15	5178	4427	4769	4898	4043
2015-16	5297	4267	4785	4840	3915
2016-17	5239	4270	4773	4756	3889
2017-18	4766	3890	5076	4680	3862
Total	**20480**	**16854**	**19403**	**19174**	**15709**

Source: *Directorate Women and Child Development Government of Himachal Pradesh, Himland, Shimla.*

number of beneficiaries between 0-3-years of age children has shown both increasing and decreasing trend. In the year 2014-15 the number was 4769 which increased to 4785 in the year 2015-16. Then it decreased to 4773 during the year 2016-17 and in the year 2017-18 this number again increased to 5076. In Nurpur block the number decreased to 4680 in the year 2017-18 from 4898 in the year 2014-15. In Pragpur block the number of beneficiaries also showed decreasing trend. The number decreased to 3862 in the year 2017-18 from 4043 in the year 2014-15. Overall analysis reflects that Beneficiaries of Supplementary Nutrition from 0-3 Years of Age Children in Five Blocks of Kangra District is also not showing increasing trends

Details of beneficiaries (3-6 year children) of supplementary nutrition in sample block of Kangra district has been given in Table 4.16.

Table 4.16 show that the number of beneficiaries in Dehra block has shown an increasing and decreasing trend. In the year 2014-15 the number was 2042, which decreased to 1852 in 2015-16. In the year 2016-17 the number was 2374. It decreased to 1597 in the year 2017-18.In Fatehpur block the number of beneficiaries decreased to 3996 in the year 2017-18 from 4304 in the year 2014-15. The number of beneficiaries in Nurpur and Pragpur block also show decreasing trend. Beneficiaries (3-6 year

CTable-4.16: Beneficiaries of Supplementary Nutrition from 3-6 Years of Age Children in Five Blocks of Kangra District

Year	Blocks				
	Dehra	Fatehpur	Indora	Nurpur	Pragpur
2014-15	2042	4304	3179	5295	3160
2015-16	1852	4106	3156	5496	2814
2016-17	2374	4112	3564	5185	2429
2017-18	1597	3996	3886	4237	2552
Total	**7865**	**16518**	**13785**	**20213**	**10955**

Source: *Directorate Women and Child Development Government of Himachal Pradesh, Himland, Shimla.*

children) of supplementary nutrition in sample block of Kangra district were also not increasing to required expectations.

Detail of beneficiaries (pregnant and lactating mother) of supplementary nutrition in sample block of Kangra district has been given in Table 4.17.

Table 4.17: Beneficiaries of Supplementary Nutrition from Pregnant and Lactating Mother in Five Blocks of Kangra District

Year	Blocks				
	Dehra	Fatehpur	Indora	Nurpur	Pragpur
2014-15	2168	1607	1743	2010	1616
2015-16	2113	1657	1702	2005	1558
2016-17	2100	1604	1698	2010	1547
2017-18	1800	1605	1786	1918	1641
Total	**8181**	**6473**	**6929**	**7943**	**6362**

Source: *Directorate Women and Child Development Government of Himachal Pradesh, Himland, Shimla.*

Table 4.17 shows that in the year 2014-15 total of 2168 pregnant and lactating mother were getting supplementary nutrition, which decreased to 1800 during the year 2017-18 in Dehra block. In other block the number of pregnant and lactating mother has shown both increasing and decreasing trend. In Fatehpur block the number was 1607 during the year 2014-15 which increased to 1657 in the year 2015-16. Then this number decreased to 1605 in the year 2017-18. In Indora block, the number pregnant and lactating mother beneficiaries in the year 2014-15 was 1743, which decreased to 1698 in the year 2016-17. Then it showed an increasing trend and increased to 1786 during the year 2017-18.In Nurpur block the number of beneficiaries (pregnant and lactating mother) has decreased to 1918 in the year 2017-18 from 2010 in the year 2014-15. While in Pragpur block the number of beneficiaries was decreased to 1547 in the year 2016-17 from 1616 in the year 2014-15. After this it increased to 1641 in the year 2017-18.

Overall analysis shows that there is no steady increase in the number of Beneficiaries of Supplementary Nutrition from Pregnant and Lactating Mothers in last five years in Kangra District & there is need to take efforts in this direction in large scale.

Detail of adolescents girls beneficiaries in age 11-14 and 14-18 under ICDS in five block of distt Kangra have been given in table 4.18

Table 4.18: Beneficiaries adolescent girls age 11-18 years in Five Blocks of Kangra District under ICDS

Year	Blocks				
	Dehra	Fatehpur	Indora	Nurpur	Pragpur
2014-15	145	171	158	172	164
2015-16	116	148	143	166	151
2016-17	110	164	166	175	168
2017-18	6	5	8	3	4
Total	**401**	**488**	**475**	**636**	**487**

Source: *Directorate Women and Child Development Government of Himachal Pradesh, Himland, Shimla.*

Adolescent girls as beneficiaries were although average in 2014-15 till 2016-17 but decreased abruptly in 2017-18. It may be because of new notification adopted by Government of Himachal Pradesh in this regard. According to new notification of March 2018 a new scheme was implemented named as "Scheme for adolescent girls". This scheme was started with an aim of providing basic facilities such as nutritious food, financial help etc. for those adolescent girls who are not going to school. This scheme replaced other scheme which started with an aim of providing basic facilities to all adolescent girls. That is the only one reason for decline in the ratio of adolescent girls who are getting benefits from ICDS[15]. Since all schemes for adolescent girls were closed in 2018 and only schemes for those adolescent girls who are out of school were continued. It may be the reason that numbers of beneficiaries under these schemes were reduced in Himachal Pradesh

Conclusion

The ICDS programme approaches a holistic child health comprising health, nutrition, and education elements for pregnant ladies, wet mothers and children upto six years. The programme is enforced through a network of community- level Anganwadi Centres. The variety of services targeted at young children and their mothers for growth observations, immunisation, health check-ups, supplementary feeding, nutrition and health education Pre-school education is provided to children between 3 and 6 years of age. In the present Chapter working of ICDS in Himachal Pradesh & Kangra District is discussed. Beneficiaries (3-6 year children) of supplementary nutrition in sample block of Kangra district is also not increasing to required expectations. Overall analysis shows there is no steady increase in the number of Beneficiaries of Supplementary Nutrition from Pregnant and Lactating Mother in last Five years in Kangra District in & there is need to take efforts in large direction.

References

1 Chowdhary, D. Paul, Social Welfare Administration, Atma Ram & Sons, Delhi, 1979.

2 Ministry of Women and Child Development. *Integrated Child Development Services (ICDS) Scheme.* Retrieved on 12th August, 2016, Fromhttp://wcd.nic.in: http://icds-wcd.nic.in/icds/icds.aspx

3 Planning Department (2012), *Draft 12th Five Year Plan 2012-17 and Annual Plan 2013-14,* Government of Himachal Pradesh, Shimla, p. 128

4 Ministry of Women and Child Development (2015).*Annual Report 2014-15.* New Delhi: Government of India, p. 21.

5 http://wcd.nic.in/icds.htm

6 Annual Administrative Report Department of Women and Child Development, Government of India (2016-17

7 Goel, S.L., Social Welfare Administration - Organisational Infrastructure & Social Justice & Empowerment, Vol. I & II, Deep & Deep Publications Pvt. Ltd., New Delhi, 2010.

8 Gupta, Sunil, Rural Development Schemes - A Study in Himachal Pradesh, Indus Publishing Company, New Delhi, 2007

9 Tandon. and Gandhi Neeru. Immunization coverage in India for area served by the Integrated Child Development Services Programme. Bull. WHO 1992;70:461-465

10 Annual Administrative Report Department of Women and Child Development, Government of India (2016-17)

11 Kangra, *About* District, retrieved on June 8, 2018 from:https://hpkangra.gov.in/about-district/

12 Planning Department (2009), *op.cit.,* p. 32.

13 *Ibid.*

14 *Directorate Women and Child Development Government of Himachal Pradesh, Himland, Shimla*

5

SOCIO-ECONOMIC PROFILE OF THE RESPONDENTS

Childhood means simplicity. Look at the worlds the child's eye. It is very beautiful.

Kailash Satyarthi

The study of socio-economic characteristics of respondents forms an integral part of a scientific social research. It can prove useful in ascertaining the personalities of respondents and consequently their reaction towards a particular situation. The analysis of socio-economic background of the respondents has its own importance. It will enable the researcher to understand clearly the diverse factors affecting the value orientation of the respondents. To assess the impact and implementation of ICDS programme, a sample of 350 respondents were selected. The sample respondents for the present study were 250 ICDS beneficiaries, 100Anganwadi Workers.

In this chapter, an attempt has been made to analyse the socio-economic background of the sample respondents with the help of some indicators such as, gender, age, marital status, size of family, family status, educational attainment, social classification, income etc. To analyze the socio-economic background of the sample respondents, data has been collected through interview schedules. The present chapter is divided into two sections, that is, Section–I and Section–II
.

In Section–I the profile of ICDS beneficiaries has been discussed, Section–II evaluates the profile of Anganwadi workers.

5.1 Section – I: Profile of Sample ICDS Beneficiaries

The profile of sample ICDS beneficiaries has been analysed under various headings, such as gender of sample respondents, age-wise classification of respondents, educational attainments of respondents, social classification etc.

5.1.1 Age-wise Classification of Sample Respondents

Age is one of the most important aspects in the study of socio-economic profile of respondents. Hence, age-wise classification of sample beneficiaries has been illustrated in Table 5.1.

Table-5.1 Age-Wise Classification of Beneficiaries

Age group	Block					Total
	Dehra	Fatehpur	Indora	Nurpur	Paragpur	
18 – 25 years	12 (24.00)	16 (32.00)	18 (36.00)	4 (8.00)	26 (52.00)	**76 (30.40)**
26 – 35 years	28 (56.00)	32 (64.00)	26 (52.00)	29 (58.00)	20 (40.00)	**135 (54.00)**
36 – 45 years	10 (20.00)	2 (4.00)	6 (12.00)	17 (34.00)	4 (8.00)	**39 (15.60)**
Above 45 years	0 (0.00)	0 (0.00)	0 (0.00)	0 (0.00)	0 (0.00)	**0 (0.00)**
Total	50 (100.00)	50 (100.00)	50 (100.00)	50 (100.00)	50 (100.00)	**250 (100.00)**

Source: *Primary Probe.*

Note: Figures in parentheses represents percentage.

Table 5.1 reveals that out of total respondents, 30.40 per cent of respondents were in the age group of '18-25 years', 54.00 per cent were in '26-35 years' and 15.60 per cent of respondents were in the age group of '36-45 years'. Block-wise data shows that majority of respondents in all the blocks were in the age group of '26-35 years'.

Chart 5.1
Age-wise Classification of Sample Respondents (Beneficiaries)

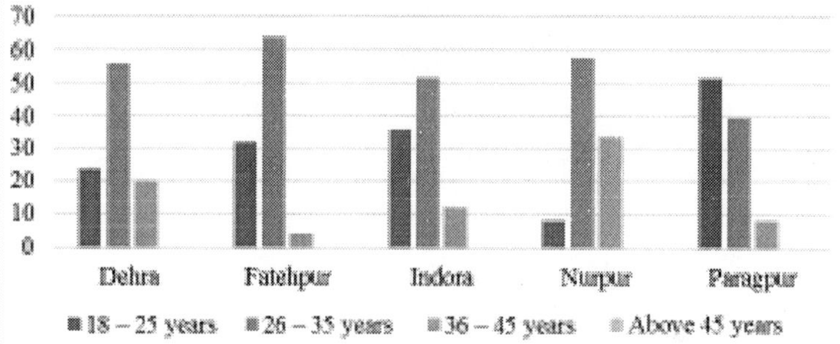

Hence, it can be concluded that majority of respondents (beneficiaries) were young as about 85 per cent of respondents belonged to the age group of '26-35 years' &'18-25 years'.

5.1.2 Type of Beneficiaries

The beneficiaries under ICDS were pregnant or lactating women or mother of 6 months to 3 years old child or mother of 3 years to 6 years old child or mother of adolescent girls. Here, it is important to know the type of beneficiaries included as respondents for the present study. The data related to type of ICDS beneficiaries has been given in Table 5.2.

Figures in Table 5.2 shows that out of total respondents, 28.40 per cent were pregnant women, 26.00 per cent of respondents were lactating women, 18.80 per cent of respondents were mothers of 6 months to 3 years old child, 16.00 per cent of respondents were the mothers of 3 years to 6 years old child and 10.80 per cent were the mothers of adolescent girls who were beneficiaries of ICDS programme.

Table -5.2: Type of ICDS Beneficiaries

Type of Beneficiary	Block					Total
	Dehra	Fatehpur	Indora	Nurpur	Paragpur	
Pregnant Women	12 (24.00)	19 (38.00)	15 (30.00)	10 (20.00)	15 (30.00)	**71 (28.40)**
Lactating Mother	2 (4.00)	17 (34.00)	16 (32.00)	9 (18.00)	21 (42.00)	**65 (26.00)**
Mother of 6 months to 3 years old child	13 (26.00)	7 (14.00)	8 (16.00)	12 (24.00)	7 (14.00)	**47 (18.80)**
Mother of 3 years to 6 years old child	18 (36.00)	6 (12.00)	6 (12.00)	8 (16.00)	2 (4.00)	**40 (16.00)**
Mother of adolescent girls	5 (10.00)	1 (2.00)	5 (10.00)	11 (22.00)	5 (10.00)	**27 (10.80)**
Total	50 (100.00)	50 (100.00)	50 (100.00)	50 (100.00)	50 (100.00)	**250 (100.00)**

Source: *Primary Probe.*

Note: Figures in parentheses represents percentage.

Chart 5.2
Type of Beneficiaries

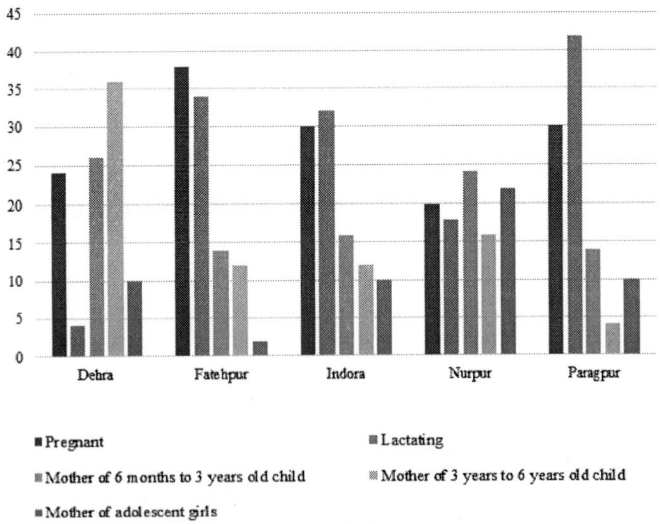

Hence, it is clear from the data that all types of beneficiaries were included in the sample beneficiaries to anayse their opinion regarding the implementation of ICDS services provided to them.

5.1.3 Educational Qualification of Sample Beneficiaries

Education plays an important role in determining one's socio-economic status and outlook towards life. An educated person would certainly be better informed. In any study it is important to know the educational level of the respondents. It gives an idea about the knowledge of respondents with regard to the programme. In this regard the educational level of selected sample beneficiaries has been elicited in Table 5.3.

Table 5.3: Educational Qualification of Sample Beneficiaries

Education	Block					Total
	Dehra	Fatehpur	Indora	Nurpur	Paragpur	
Below Matric	13 (26.00)	3 (6.00)	15 (30.00)	7 (14.00)	15 (30.00)	**53 (21.20)**
Matric	9 (18.00)	10 (20.00)	12 (24.00)	14 (28.00)	10 (20.00)	**55 (22.00)**
10+2	22 (44.00)	34 (68.00)	15 (30.00)	22 (44.00)	21 (42.00)	**114 (45.60)**
Graduation	6 (12.00)	3 (6.00)	8 (16.00)	7 (14.00)	4 (8.00)	**28 (11.20)**
Post-Graduation or above	0 (0.00)	0 (0.00)	0 (0.00)	0 (0.00)	0 (0.00)	**0 (0.00)**
Total	50 (100.00)	50 (100.00)	50 (100.00)	50 (100.00)	50 (100.00)	**250 (100.00)**

Source: *Primary Probe.*

Note: Figures in parentheses represents percentage.

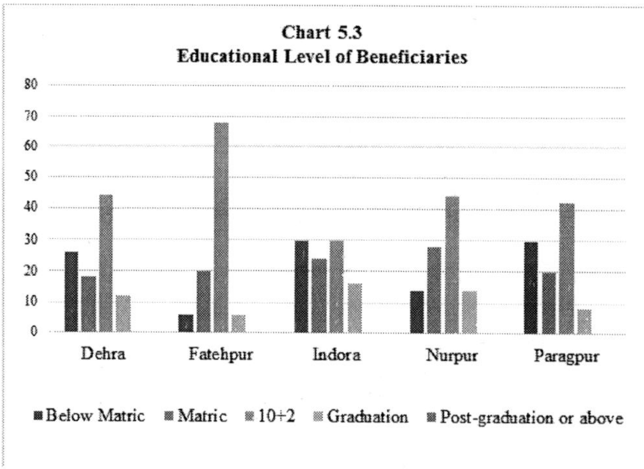

Data in Table 5.3 depict that majority of respondents, that is, 44.00 per cent in Dehra block, 68.00 per cent in Fatehpur block, 30.00 per cent in Indora block, 44.00 per cent in Nurpur Block and 42.00 per cent of respondents in Paragpurblock were educated up to 10+2, while the percentage of those respondents, whose education level was below matric were21.20 per cent in overall. 45.6 percent of the respondents were educated up to 10+2 level. The percentage of matriculate respondents was 22.00 per cent and graduate respondents were 11.20 per cent of the total. The data clearly reveals that the educational level of majority of respondents were found good enough.

5.1.4 Social Category of Sample Beneficiaries

ICDS scheme is providing services to all the people without any discrimination on the basis of caste, creed, religion and sex. Thus it is important to know about the social classification of selected beneficiaries. In this regard the collected data has been shown in Table 5.4.

Table 5.4: Category-wise Classification of Sample Beneficiaries

Category	Block					Total
	Dehra	Fatehpur	Indora	Nurpur	Paragpur	
General	13 (26.00)	25 (50.00)	21 (42.00)	12 (24.00)	24 (48.00)	**95 (38.00)**
Scheduled Caste	9 (18.00)	14 (28.00)	15 (30.00)	15 (30.00)	14 (28.00)	**67 (26.80)**
Scheduled Tribe	2 (4.00)	0 (0.00)	9 (18.00)	10 (20.00)	2 (4.00)	**23 (9.20)**
Other backward classes	26 (52.00)	11 (22.00)	5 (10.00)	13 (26.00)	10 (20.00)	**65 (26.00)**
Total	50 (100.00)	50 (100.00)	50 (100.00)	50 (100.00)	50 (100.00)	**250 (100.00)**

Source: *Primary Probe.*

Note: Figures in parentheses represents percentage.

Chart 5.4
Category-wise classification of sample Beneficiaries

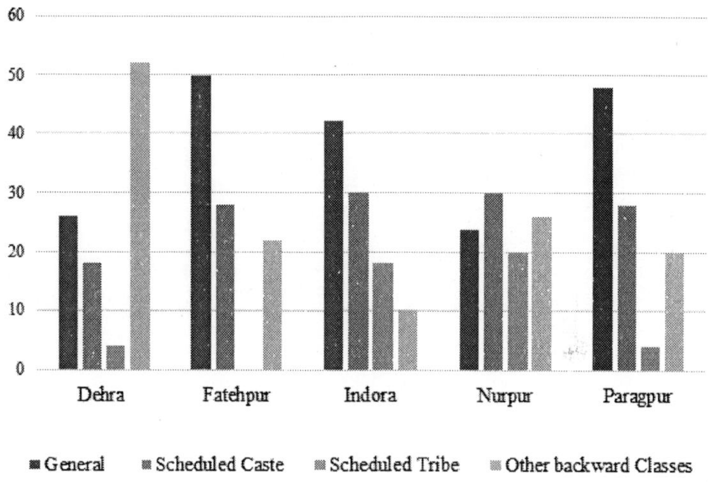

The analysis of social background indicates that out of total respondents, 38.00 per cent belonged to general category, 26.80 per cent belonged to scheduled castes, 9.20 per cent belonged to the scheduled tribes and 26.00 per cent of respondents belonged to other backward classes. Block-wise data reveal that majority of respondents in Dehra block were from other backward classes and in Nurpur from scheduled caste. Whereas, in Fatehpur (50.00 per cent), Indora (42.00 per cent) and in Paragpur (48.00 per cent) block majority of respondents were from general category. Therefore, it is clear that the respondents comprised of all the categories of society.

5.1.5 Income of Sample Beneficiaries

Evaluation of income level of respondents is another important socio-economic aspect. It tells about the well-being of a person and their capacity to have an access to their basic needs. Thus, data regarding the income level of sample beneficiaries has been analysed in Table 5.5.

Table 5.5: Income- wise Distribution of sample Beneficiaries

Income group	Block					Total
	Dehra	Fatehpur	Indora	Nurpur	Paragpur	
UptoRs.10000	30 (60.00)	31 (62.00)	35 (70.00)	26 (52.00)	35 (70.00)	**157 (62.80)**
Rs.10001 – Rs.25000	8 (16.00)	7 (14.00)	8 (16.00)	12 (24.00)	9 (18.00)	**44 (17.60)**
Rs.25001 – Rs.50000	8 (16.00)	8 (16.00)	4 (8.00)	7 (14.00)	4 (8.00)	**31 (12.40)**
Above Rs.50000	4 (8.00)	4 (8.00)	3 (6.00)	5 (10.00)	2 (4.00)	**18 (7.20)**
Total	50 (100.00)	50 (100.00)	50 (100.00)	50 (100.00)	50 (100.00)	**250 (100.00)**

Source: *Primary Probe.*

Note: Figures in parentheses represents percentage.

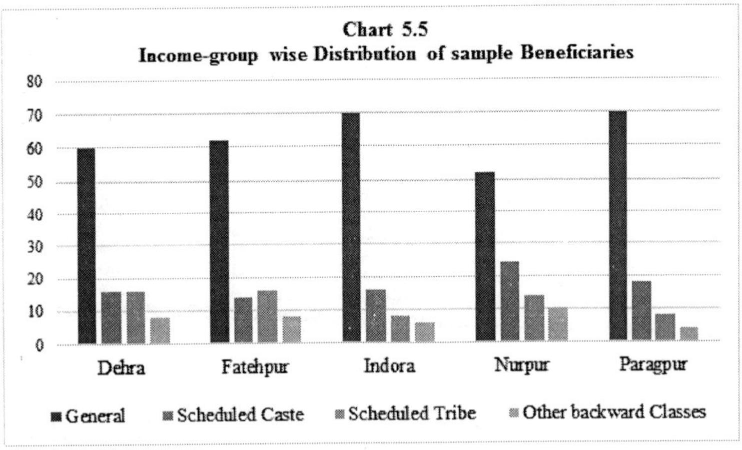

Data related to income groups shows that out of total respondents 62.80 per cent of respondents were in the income group of 'upto `10,000/- per month.17.60 per cent of respondents were in the income group of `10,001 to `25000, 12.40 per cent of respondents were in the income group of `25001 to `50000 and 7.20 per cent of respondents were in the income group of 'above `50,000. Block-wise data show that majority of respondents in all the blocks were from in the income group of upto `10,000, followed by the income group of `10,001 to `25,000.

Hence, it can be concluded that poor people in majority whose income is up to '10,000/- per month are coming forward to take the benefits of ICDS.

5.2 Section–II: Socio-Economic Profile of Sample Anganwadi Workers (AWW) and Helper (AWH)

In this section, an attempt has been made to evaluate the socio-economic profile of sample Anganwadi workers and Helpers on the basis of some indicators, such as age, educational qualification, social category, income etc.

5.2.1 Age-wise Distribution of Sample Anganwadi Workers and Helper

Age plays an important role in the performance of official duties and responsibilities. In case of Anganwadi workers and helpers it is important that these should be young one so that they can perform their field duties effectively. The age-wise distribution of Anganwadi worker and helper has been depicted in Table 5.6.

Table 5.6: Age-Wise Classification of Anganwadi Workers and Helper

Age group	Block					Total
	Dehra	Fatehpur	Indora	Nurpur	Paragpur	
18 – 25 years	0 (0.00)	0 (0.00)	0 (0.00)	1 (5.00)	4 (20.00)	**5 (5.00)**
26 – 35 years	5 (25.00)	7 (35.00)	5 (25.00)	5 (25.00)	5 (25.00)	**27 (27.00)**
36 – 45 years	14 (70.00)	13 (65.00)	14 (70.00)	14 (70.00)	10 (50.00)	**65 (65.00)**
Above 45 years	1 (5.00)	0 (0.00)	1 (5.00)	0 (0.00)	1 (5.00)	**3 (3.00)**
Total	20 (100.00)	20 (100.00)	20 (100.00)	20 (100.00)	20 (100.00)	**100 (100.00)**

Source: *Primary Probe.*

Note: Figures in parentheses represents percentage.

Table 5.6 enumerates that out of total respondents 65.00 per cent were in the age group of 36-45 years, 27.00 per cent of respondents were in the age group of 26-35 years and 5.00 per cent of respondents were in the age group of 18-25 years'.

Chart 5.6

Age-wise Classification of Sample Anganwadi Workers and Helper

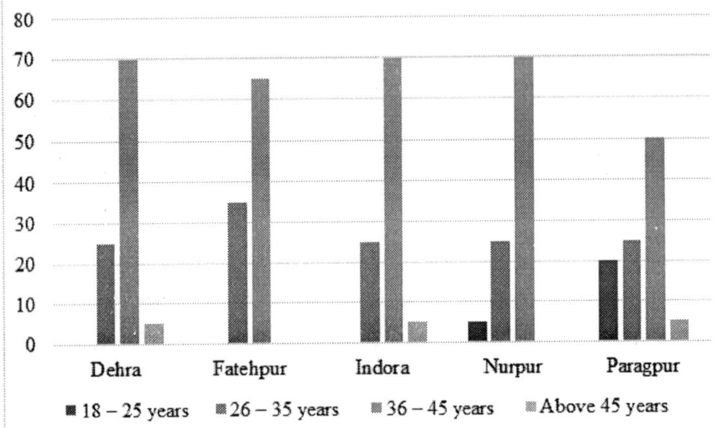

Block wise data reveals that in all the blocks, the majority of sample Anganwadi workers and helpers were in the age group of 36-45 years. Hence, it can be analysed that the Anganwadi workers and helpers were from middle age group.

5.2.2 Work Experience of Sample Anganwadi workers and Helper

Experience plays an important role in the performance of one's duties and fulfillment of the objectives of an organization. Experienced people can be an asset to any organization. In case of ICDS schemes experienced person can handle the technicalities in a better way and contribute to the smooth and effective implementation of the scheme. Data about the work experience of Anganwadi workers and helpers has been presented in Table 5.7.

Table 5.7: Work Experience of Anganwadi Workers and Helper

Experience	Block					Total
	Dehra	Fatehpur	Indora	Nurpur	Paragpur	
1 year	1 (5.00)	0 (0.00)	0 (0.00)	1 (5.00)	0 (0.00)	**2** **(2.00)**
1-5 years	3 (15.00)	4 (20.00)	1 (5.00)	3 (15.00)	2 (10.00)	**13** **(13.00)**
5-10 years	10 (50.00)	13 (65.00)	14 (70.00)	12 (60.00)	10 (50.00)	**59** **(59.00)**
Above 10 years	6 (30.00)	3 (15.00)	5 (25.00)	4 (20.00)	8 (40.00)	**26** **(26.00)**
Total	20 (100.00)	20 (100.00)	20 (100.00)	20 (100.00)	20 (100.00)	**100** **(100.00)**

Source: *Primary Probe.*

Note: Figures in parentheses represents percentage.

Chart 5.7
Work Experience of Sample Anganwadi Workers and Helper

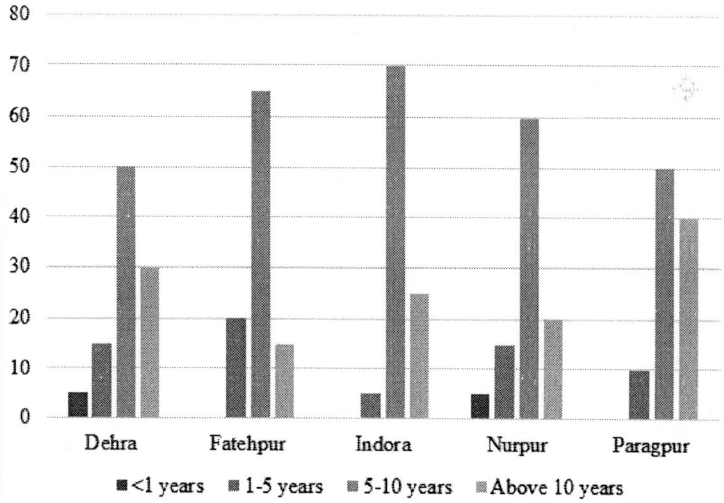

Data about work experience of Anganwadi workers and helpers depicts that in majority of cases these employees have good work experience in the field of ICDS. Out of total respondents, 59.00 per cent of respondents had work experience of '5-10 years' and 26.00 per cent of respondents had work experience of 'above 10 years'.

Block-wise data show that respondents in Dehra and Pragpur block had higher work experience than other blocks. Out of total respondents, 40.00 per cent of respondents in Paragpur block and 30.00 per cent of respondents in Dehra block had the work experience of more than 10 years. Hence, the analysis clearly indicates that the experience level of majority of sample Anganwadi workers and helper was high, which was a good sign as it contribute to implement the ICDS schemes effectively and efficiently.

5.2.3 Educational Qualification of Sample Anganwadi Workers and Helpers

In relation to education qualification, it is said that educated person could be a good source of information. He/She can furnish his/her opinion freely and logically. The minimum educational qualification for Anganwadi workers is matric and that of helper is primary or above. Hence, data has been collected about the educational qualification of sample Anganwadi workers and helpers, and illustrated in Table 5.8.

Figures in Table 5.8 depicts that 45.00 per cent in Dehra, 40.00 per cent in Fatehpur, 30.00 per cent in Indora, 35.00 per cent in Nurpur and 50 per cent in Pargapur were matric pass. Whereas, 25.00 per cent in Dehra, 35.00 per cent in Fatehpur, 35.00 per cent in Indora, 45.00 per cent in Nurpur and 30 per cent in Pargapur were 10+2 pass. The percentage of those who were either graduate or post-graduate was very less. The percentage of post-graduate was 5.00 per cent in all the blocks and those of graduate was 5.00 in three blocks, namely, Fatehpur, Nurpur and Paragpur, and 10.00 per cent in two blocks, namely, Dehra and Indora.

Table 5.8: Educational Qualification of Anganwadi Workers and Helper

Education	Block					Total
	Dehra	Fatehpur	Indora	Nurpur	Paragpur	
Primary / middle	3 (15.00)	3 (15.00)	4 (20.00)	2 (10.00)	2 (10.00)	**14 (14.00)**
Matric	9 (45.00)	8 (40.00)	6 (30.00)	7 (35.00)	10 (50.00)	**40 (40.00)**
10+2	5 (25.00)	7 (35.00)	7 (35.00)	9 (45.00)	6 (30.00)	**34 (34.00)**
Graduation	2 (10.00)	1 (5.00)	2 (10.00)	1 (5.00)	1 (5.00)	**7 (7.00)**
Post-Graduation or above	1 (5.00)	1 (5.00)	1 (5.00)	1 (5.00)	1 (5.00)	**5 (5.00)**
Total	20 (100.00)	20 (100.00)	20 (100.00)	20 (100.00)	20 (100.00)	**100 (100.00)**

Source: *Primary Probe.*

Note: Figures in parentheses represents percentage.

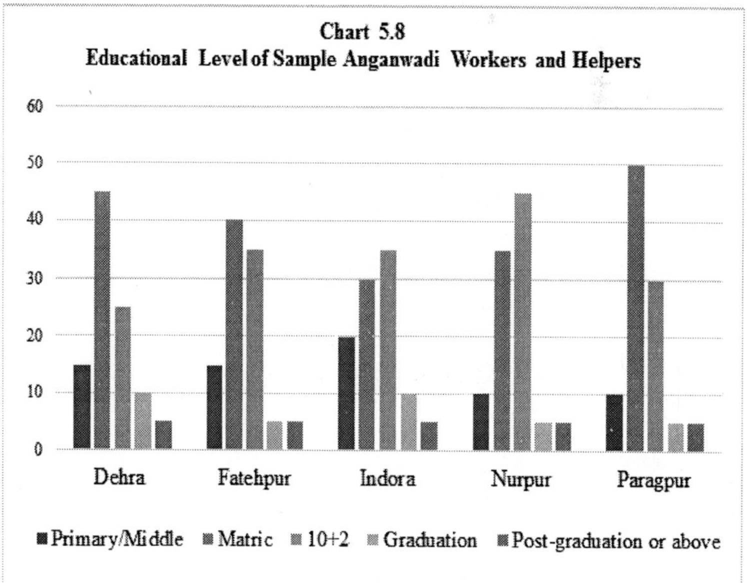

The overall data reveals that out of total respondents in study area, 40.00 per cent were matriculate, 34.00 per cent were 10+2 pass, 7.00 per cent were graduate and 5.00 per cent were post-graduate. Data also shows that 14.00 per cent of respondents were primary/middle pass. It is important to mention that these percentages belonged to Aganwadi helpers. Indora block had the highest percentage (20.00 per cent) of primary/middle pass respondents followed by Dehra and Fatehpur block (15.00 per cent each).

5.2.4 Category of Sample Anganwadi Workers and Helpers

Equal opportunity to all is one of the basic rights in our country. Each and every individual must have equal opportunity to get job without any discrimination on the basis of caste, creed, race etc. Data relating to caste status of Anganwadi Workers and Helpers is analysed in following table-5.9:

Table 5.9: Category-wise Classification of Sample Beneficiaries

Category	Block					Total
	Dehra	Fatehpur	Indora	Nurpur	Paragpur	
General	6 (30.00)	7 (35.00)	8 (40.00)	4 (20.00)	8 (40.00)	**33** **(33.00)**
Scheduled Caste	3 (15.00)	5 (25.00)	7 (35.00)	4 (20.00)	4 (20.00)	**23** **(23.00)**
Scheduled Tribe	0 (0.00)	5 (25.00)	0 (0.00)	4 (20.00)	2 (10.00)	**11** **(11.00)**
Other backward classes	11 (55.00)	3 (15.00)	5 (25.00)	8 (40.00)	6 (30.00)	**33** **(33.00)**
Total	20 (100.00)	20 (100.00)	20 (100.00)	20 (100.00)	20 (100.00)	**100** **(100.00)**

Source: *Primary Probe.*

Note: Figures in parentheses represents percentage.

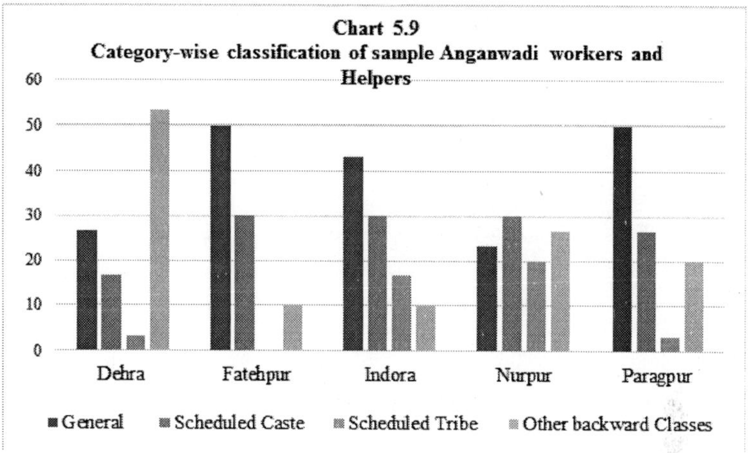

Data in Table 5.9 depict that 33.00 per cent of respondents belonged to general category, 23.00 per cent belonged to scheduled caste, 11.00 per cent to scheduled tribes and 33.00 per cent belonged to other backward classes.

Block-wise data reveal that in 55.00 per cent of cases in Dehra block and 40.00 per cent of cases in Nurpur block belonged to other backward classes. While respondents belonging to general category accounted for 30.00 per cent in Dehra, 35.00 per cent in Fatehpur, 40.00 per cent in Indora, 20.00 per cent in Nurpur and 40.00 per cent in Paragpur block. The highest percentage of scheduled caste was found in Indora block (35.00 per cent) and lowest was in Dehra block (15.00 per cent). Whereas the highest percentage of scheduled tribes was in Fatehpur block (25.00 per cent). In Dehra and Indora block no scheduled tribes were found. Hence, it can be inferred that all the category got opportunity to be the Anganwadi workers and helpers in study area.

5.2.5 Personal Monthly Income of the Anganwadi Workers and Helpers

Economic empowerment is an essential aspect of women empowerment. For the empowerment of women economically, women should have some income generating assets or work or job. In this regard employment as Anganwadi worker provide some income to them, so that they can empower themselves economically. Data about personal income of Anganwadi workers and helpers have been enumerated in Table 5.10.

Table 5.10 :Personal Income wise distribution of sample Anganwadi Workers and Helper

Income group (in months)	Block					Total
	Dehra	Fatehpur	Indora	Nurpur	Paragpur	
UptoRs.5000	20 (100.00)	12 (60.00)	14 (70.00)	17 (85.00)	17 (85.00)	**80 (80.00)**
Rs.5001 – Rs.10000	0 (0.00)	7 (35.00)	6 (30.00)	3 (15.00)	3 (15.00)	**19 (19.00)**
Rs.10001 – Rs.25000	0 (0.00)	1 (5.00)	0 (0.00)	0 (0.00)	0 (0.00)	**1 (1.00)**
Above Rs.25000	0 (0.00)	0 (0.00)	0 (0.00)	0 (0.00)	0 (0.00)	**0 (0.00)**
Total	20 (100.00)	20 (100.00)	20 (100.00)	20 (100.00)	20 (100.00)	**100 (100.00)**

Source: *Primary Probe.*

Note: Figures in parentheses represents percentage.

Data related to monthly personal income in Table 5.10, shows that the income level of majority of sample Anganwadi workers and helpers was found below Rs.5000 pre month.

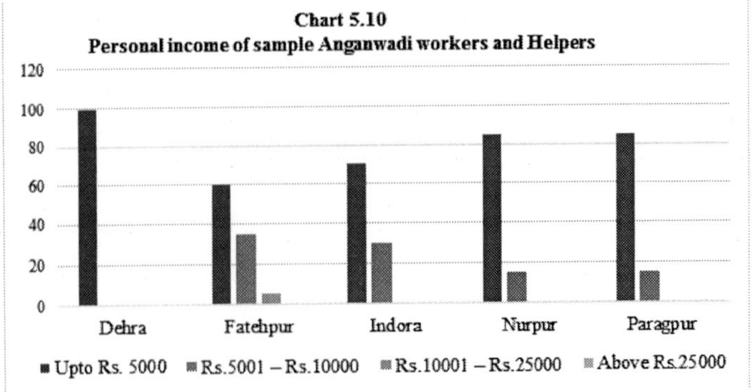

The data depicts that out of total respondents, 80.00 per cent of respondents were in the income group of 'uptoRs.5000' per month 19.00 per cent of respondent were in the income group of 'Rs.5001-Rs.10000' per month and one respondents was in the income group of 'Rs.10001-Rs.25000'. In Dehra block hundred percent of respondents were in the income group of 'uptoRs.5000'. It is clear from the analysis that the only source of Anganwadi workers and helpers was the remuneration given in lieu of their services, that is why the personal income of majority of these workers and helpers was below Rs.5000.

Prime minister announced that salary of Aanganwari workers will be increased that is much more required also taking into consideration their low remuneration.

5.2.6 Family income of Sample Anganwadi Workers and Helpers

Family income gives an impression of one's economic strength and well-being. The data related to the family income of sample Anganwadi workers and helpers has been shown in Table 5.11.

Table 5.11: Family income of Sample Anganwadi Workers and Helpers

Income group	Block					Total
	Dehra	Fatehpur	Indora	Nurpur	Paragpur	
Upto Rs.5000	6 (30.00)	4 (20.00)	9 (45.00)	10 (50.00)	11 (55.00)	**40** **(40.00)**
Rs.5001 – Rs.10000	7 (35.00)	15 (75.00)	8 (40.00)	6 (30.00)	7 (35.00)	**43** **(43.00)**
Rs.10001 – Rs.25000	2 (10.00)	1 (5.00)	2 (10.00)	2 (10.00)	1 (5.00)	**8** **(8.00)**
Above Rs.25000	5 (25.00)	0 (0.00)	1 (5.00)	2 (10.00)	1 (5.00)	**9** **(9.00)**
Total	20 (100.00)	20 (100.00)	20 (100.00)	20 (100.00)	20 (100.00)	**100** **(100.00)**

Source: *Primary Probe.*

Note: Figures in parentheses represents percentage.

Chart 5.11
Family income of sample Anganwadi workers and Helpers

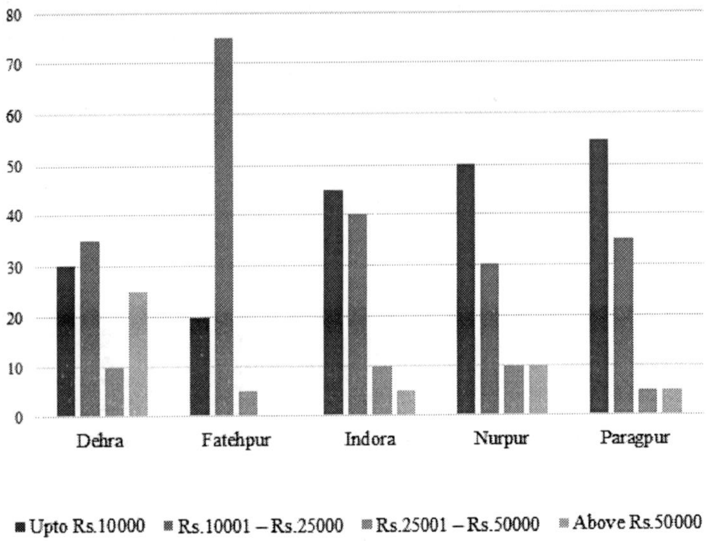

Figures in Table 5.11 show that out of total respondents the family income of 40.00 per cent of respondents fall in the income group of 'uptoRs.10000', while the family income of 43.00 per cent of respondents fall in the income group of 'Rs.10001-Rs.25000', whereas the family income of 8.00 per cent of respondents and 9.00 per cent fall in the income group of 'Rs.25001-Rs.50000' and 'above Rs.50000' respectively. Block-wise data also reveals the same trend. The highest percentage of those respondents, whose family income was between Rs.10001 and Rs.25000 were found in Fatehpur block (that is, 75.00 per cent) and that of uptoRs.10000 were found in Paragpur block (55.00 per cent). It is clear from the data that the family income of sample respondents were also found low.

Conclusion

In this chapter social economic profile of 250 beneficiaries and 100 Anganwadi workers is analysed. An attempt has been made to analyse the socio-economic background of the sample respondents with the help of some indicators such as, gender, age, marital status, size of family, family status, educational attainment, social classification, income etc. It was analysed that Sample was found to be representative in Beneficiaries category and Workers category as well.

6

PERCEPTION OF ANGANWADI WORKERS

> Education is the key to empowerment and sustainability, education is a right which is the key to the rest of the rights of life in society. Education is the key to social justice.
>
> Kailash Satyarthi

In this chapter an attempt has been made to know the opinion of Anganwadi workers/mini Anganwari workers/ helpers regarding working of Anganwadi Centres. Informal discussions with C.D.P.O, A.C.D.P.O/ Supervisors were also conducted to gather information regarding working of ICDS. Their opinion is analysed below:

6.1 Opinion about infrastructure

For the provision of services under ICDS, AWCs are set at the village level. They can only provide these services if these AWCs have their own infrastructure. The data regarding availability of infrastructure facilities has been given in Table 6.1.

Analysis of Table reveals that, Out of total respondents, 75.00 per cent in Dehra block, 80.00 per cent in Fatehpur block, 90.00 per cent in Indora block, 100.00 per cent in Nurpur block and 95.00 of respondents in Paragpur block told that they had their own building of AWCs. While remaining respondents told that the AWCs did not have their own building. These respondents reported that their AWCs were running in rented buildings.

Table 6.1: Availability of Infrastructure

Response	Block					Total
	Dehra	Fatehpur	Indora	Nurpur	Paragpur	
			Own building			
Yes	15 (75.00)	14 (70.00)	16 (80.00)	15 (75.00)	17 (85.00)	**77 (77.00)**
No	5 (25.00)	6 (30.00)	4 (20.00)	5 (25.00)	3 (15.00)	**23 (23.00)**
Total	20 (100.00)	20 (100.00)	20 (100.00)	20 (100.00)	20 (100.00)	**100 (100.00)**
			Drinking water			
Yes	15 (75.00)	14 (70.00)	16 (80.00)	15 (75.00)	17 (85.00)	**77 (77.00)**
No	5 (25.00)	6 (30.00)	4 (20.00)	5 (25.00)	3 (15.00)	**23 (23.00)**
Total	20 (100.00)	20 (100.00)	20 (100.00)	20 (100.00)	20 (100.00)	**100 (100.00)**
			Toilets			
Yes	11 (55.00)	12 (60.00)	14 (70.00)	12 (60.00)	15 (75.00)	**64 (64.00)**
No	9 (45.00)	8 (40.00)	6 (30.00)	8 (40.00)	5 (25.00)	**36 (36.00)**
Total	20 (100.00)	20 (100.00)	20 (100.00)	20 (100.00)	20 (100.00)	**100 (100.00)**
			Electricity			
Yes	17 (85.00)	15 (75.00)	16 (80.00)	14 (70.00)	16 (80.00)	**78 (78.00)**
No	3 (15.00)	5 (25.00)	4 (20.00)	6 (30.00)	4 (20.00)	**22 (22.00)**
Total	20 (100.00)	20 (100.00)	20 (100.00)	20 (100.00)	20 (100.00)	**100 (100.00)**
			Furniture			
Yes	9 (45.00)	8 (40.00)	11 (55.00)	10 (50.00)	9 (45.00)	**47 (47.00)**
No	11 (55.00)	12 (60.00)	9 (45.00)	10 (50.00)	11 (55.00)	**53 (53.00)**
Total	20 (100.00)	20 (100.00)	20 (100.00)	20 (100.00)	20 (100.00)	**100 (100.00)**

Source: *Primary probe.*

Note: Figures in parentheses represent percentage.

With regard to toilets, 64.00 per cent of respondents reported that they had toilet facilities at their AWCs, while 36.00 per cent of respondents were of the opinion that they did not have toilet facilities. The highest percentage of those respondents who reported that they had toilet facilities was found in Pragpur block (75.00 per cent) followed by Indora block (70.00 per cent).

With regard to electricity, data in table shows that in majority of AWCs (78.00 per cent) electricity facility was available, while in 22.00 per cent of AWCs the electricity facility was not available. The data clearly show that electricity facility was not available in all the AWCs of the study area.

In relation to furniture facility, the data show that out of total respondents, 60.00 per cent of respondents in Fatehpur block, 55.00 per cent each in Dehra and Pragpur block, 50.00 per cent in Nurpur block and 45.00 per cent of respondents in Indora block reported that AWCs did not have required furniture, while on the other hand, 45.00 per cent each in Dehra and Pragpur block, 55.00 per cent in Indora block, 50.00 per cent in Nurpur and 40.00 per cent of respondents in Fatehpur block opined that they had required furniture. In overall data, 53.00 per cent of the respondents told that there was scarcity of furniture in the anganwadi centres and in 47.00 per cent of respondents had furniture.

Thus it can be concluded that 23 per cent of official respondents complained that there is no building and water facilities in anganwadi centres. Most of the anganwadi centres were running on rented houses.

Due to unavailability of drinking water the anganwadi workers carry drinking water either from their own house or from public water sources. It was very surprising that when the Swachh Bharat Abhiyanis is being carried out in full swing in the whole country that 36 per cent of the anganwadi centres had no toilets of their own and they send the children to surrounding houses by making request to them. 22 per cent of the anganwadi centres had no electricity connections and 53 per cent of anganwadi centres were not furnished with adequate furniture. Thus without basic facilities the idea of making the anganwadi centers ICT linked and high-tech appears to be distant vision in Kangra district of Himachal Pradesh.

Picture No. 6(a)

Infrastructure of Aganwadi Centres in Noorpoor or Pragpur

6.2 Availability of equipment and Tools

Different types of tools, such as, weighing machine, medical kits, pre-school kit, etc., should be there in the AWCs, so that they could perform their duties and responsibility related to different services in effective way.

The data regarding availability of equipment and tool has been presented in Table 6.2.

Table-6.2: Availability of Equipment and Tools

Equipments	Block					Total
	Dehra	Fatehpur	Indora	Nurpur	Paragpur	
			Pre-school Kit			
Yes	17 (85.00)	16 (80.00)	18 (90.00)	16 (80.00)	18 (90.00)	**85 (85.00)**
No	3 (15.00)	4 (20.00)	2 (10.00)	4 (20.00)	2 (10.00)	**15 (15.00)**
Total	20 (100.00)	20 (100.00)	20 (100.00)	20 (100.00)	20 (100.00)	**100 (100.00)**
			Medicine Kit			
Yes	14 (70.00)	15 (75.00)	15 (75.00)	14 (70.00)	15 (75.00)	**73 (73.00)**
No	6 (30.00)	5 (25.00)	5 (25.00)	6 (30.00)	5 (25.00)	**27 (27.00)**
Total	20 (100.00)	20 (100.00)	20 (100.00)	20 (100.00)	20 (100.00)	**100 (100.00)**
			Growth Chart			
Yes	14 (70.00)	15 (75.00)	17 (85.00)	16 (80.00)	15 (75.00)	**77 (77.00)**
No	6 (30.00)	5 (25.00)	3 (15.00)	4 (20.00)	5 (25.00)	**23 (23.00)**
Total	20 (100.00)	20 (100.00)	20 (100.00)	20 (100.00)	20 (100.00)	**100 (100.00)**
			Weighing Machine			
Yes	16 (80.00)	17 (85.00)	17 (85.00)	15 (75.00)	16 (80.00)	**81 (81.00)**
No	4 (20.00)	3 (15.00)	3 (15.00)	5 (25.00)	4 (20.00)	**19 (19.00)**
Total	20 (100.00)	20 (100.00)	20 (100.00)	20 (100.00)	20 (100.00)	**100 (100.00)**

Source: Primary probe.

Note: Figures in parentheses represent percentage.

15 per cent respondents told that they do not have pre-school kits available at their anganwadi centres. 27 per cent respondents complained regarding non-availability of modern

kit in their anganwadi centres. 23 per cent respondents had reported that growth chart was not available at their anganwadi centres.19 per cent of the respondents told that the weighing machines for children was not available at anganwadi centres.

Data in Table indicates that out of total respondents 85.00 per cent of respondents in Dehra, 80.00 per cent each in Fatehpur and Nurpur block and 90.00 per cent each in Indora and Paragpur block told that they had pre-school kit in their AWCs. While remaining respondents told that they had no pre-school kits. In overall, out of total respondents, 73.00 per cent respondents reported that they had pre-school kits, 23.00 per cent told that they don't have pre-school kits. Hence, it can be concluded that the provision of pre-school education to children depends on the availability of pre-school kit in the AWC, and it was found that pre-school kit was available in majority of AWCs in the study area.

In relation to availability of medicine kit, it was found that medicine kit was available in the AWCs, as hundred per cent of respondents stated that they had medicine kit in their AWCs.

In relation to growth chart, out of total respondents, 70.00 per cent of respondents in Dehra, 75.00 per cent each in Fatehpur and Paragpur block, 85.00 per cent in Indora and 80.00 per cent of respondents in Nurpur block were of the opinion that they had growth chart. While remaining respondents said that they don't have growth chart in their AWCs.

Availability of weighing machine at the AWCs ensures timely and periodic weighing of children and preparation of growth chart. In this regard, hundred per cent of respondents told that they had weighing machine in the AWC. Hence, it can be concluded that the required equipment and tools were available in all the AWCs.

Picture No. 6(b)

Anganwadi workers with growth charts and medicine kit in Pragpur block

6.3 Timely supply of material

Timely supply of materials, such as medicine, nutritious food etc., to the AWCs is important for effective functioning of Aanganwadi Centres. The data in this regard has been analysed in Table 6.3.

Table-6.3: Opinion about Timely supply of Material

Response	Block					Total
	Dehra	Fatehpur	Indora	Nurpur	Paragpur	
Alwayas	18 (90.00)	19 (95.00)	20 (100.00)	20 (100.00)	18 (90.00)	**95 (95.00)**
Sometimes	2 (10.00)	1 (5.00)	0 (0.00)	0 (0.00)	2 (10.00)	**5 (5.00)**
Not at All	0 (0.00)	0 (0.00)	0 (0.00)	0 (0.00)	0 (0.00)	**0 (0.00)**
Total	20 (100.00)	20 (100.00)	20 (100.00)	20 (100.00)	20 (100.00)	**100 (100.00)**

Source: *Primary probe.*

Note: Figures in parentheses represent percentage.

Data in Table reveals that out of total respondents, 90.00 per cent of respondents each in Dehra and Paragpur block, 95.00 per cent in Fatehpur and hundred per cent of respondents each in Indora and Nurpur block, told that supply of necessary materials reach the AWCs well in time. While in overall 5.00 per cent of respondents told that it did not reach in time. It can be inferred that the AWCs in all the blocks get the required material in time.

Picture No. 6(c)

Anganwadi workers with nutritious food in Fatehpur block

Table-6.4: Problems Regarding Supplementary Nutrition

Problems	No. of Respondents
No Separate Kitchen/No Cooking Facilities	21
Irregular Supply of Cooking Material	12
Inadequate Supply of Cooking Material	10
Lack of Storage Facilities	10
Fuel Problem	11
Poor Quality of Food Material	12
Financial constraints	16
Transportation Problem	08
Total	100

Source: *Primary Probe.*

Note: Figures in parentheses represents percentage

It is pertinent from analysis of above Table that 21respondents complained that due to absence of separate Kitchen and no cooking facilities they had to face problems ,10 per cent complained regarding irregular and Inadequate supply of cooking material,11 per cent grumbled due to lack of storage facility and fuel problems.12 per cent complained regarding poor quality of food material , 16 per cent told there was financial constraint in implementation of Programme & 8 per cent complained regarding transportation problems regarding food material.

Picture No. 6(d)

Good Initiatives of AWC in Fatehpur and Nurpur Block

6.4 Adequacy of Training

The opinion of the sample respondents about the adequacy of training has been analyzed in Table 6.5.

Table 6.5: Opinion about Adequacy of Training

Responses	Block					Total
	Dehra	Fatehpur	Indora	Nurpur	Paragpur	
To some Extent	18 (90.00)	20 (100.00)	18 (90.00)	14 (70.00)	17 (85.00)	**87 (87.00)**
To large Extent	2 (10.00)	0 (00.00)	2 (10.00)	6 (30.00)	3 (15.00)	**13 (13.00)**
Not at All	0 (0.00)	0 (0.00)	0 (0.00)	0 (0.00)	0 (0.00)	**0 (0.00)**
Total	20 (100.00)	20 (100.00)	20 (100.00)	20 (100.00)	20 (100.00)	**100 (100.00)**

Source: *Primary probe.*

Note: Figures in parentheses represent percentage.

Data in Table 6.5 depicts that 87 per cent of respondents reported that the training they got was adequate to a some extent only. Only 13 per cent of the respondents reported that the training was adequate to large extent. Though majority of the respondents told that the training was adequate, yet it was observed that some of the AWWs did not know how to fill the register and prepare reports. Hence, on the basis of personal observation it can be concluded that AWWs need more training specific to ICDS programme as well as general and managerial.

It was also observed through interaction that Knowledge of anganwadi workers regarding revised norms for calories and protein for beneficiaries was found to be poor. Thus regular training supportive environment, adequate facilities and infrastructure is required in all the anganwadi centers of the state of Himachal Pradesh.

Picture No. 6(e)

Celebrated special days in Dehra and Pragpur block

6.5 Interaction with supervisor

For the provision of better services under ICDS, supervisor play an important role in guiding, supervising and providing

needed help to anganwadi workers. Therefore, interaction between supervisors of anganwadi workers is of utmost important. Data about the interaction of AWW with supervisor has been analyzed in Table 6.6

Table-6.6: Opinion about Attitude of Supervisor

Response	Block					Total
	Dehra	Fatehpur	Indora	Nurpur	Paragpur	
Very Cooperative	20 (100.00)	20 (100.00)	20 (100.00)	20 (100.00)	20 (100.00)	**100 (100.00)**
Cooperative	0 (0.00)	0 (0.00)	0 (0.00)	0 (0.00)	0 (0.00)	**0 (0.00)**
Not Cooperative	0 (0.00)	0 (0.00)	0 (0.00)	0 (0.00)	0 (0.00)	**0 (0.00)**
Total	20 (100.00)	20 (100.00)	20 (100.00)	20 (100.00)	20 (100.00)	**100 (100.00)**

Source: *Primary probe.*

Note: Figures in parentheses represent percentage.

Table 6.6 depicts that hundred per cent of respondents in all the blocks interacted with the supervisors for guidance and help in the implementation of ICDS programme. AWWs told that they face various technical as well as general problems in understanding various kinds of surveys, maintaining records, filling different kinds of performas etc. For this they frequently interact with the supervisors to solve these problems and attitude of supervisors was very cooperative in this regard.

Picture No. 6(f)

Anganwadi workers Interacting with supervisors in Indora block

6.6 Coordination with Other Institutions

For the proper and effective implementation of ICDS programmes, it is important that the institutions, like, Primary Health centres, gram panchayats, must coordinate and give full cooperation to AWCs. With their coordination and cooperation AWCs cannot fulfill the objectives of ICDS programme. Hence, to know whether these institutions extend their cooperation and coordination to AWCs or not, data has been collected and presented in Table 6.7

Table 6.7: Opinion about Coordination and cooperation from PHCs and Gram Panchayats

Response	Block					Total
	Dehra	Fatehpur	Indora	Nurpur	Paragpur	
Coordination and Cooperation from PHCs						
Always	12 (60.00)	15 (75.00)	16 (80.00)	13 (65.00)	18 (90.00)	**74 (74.00)**
Sometimes	8 (40.00)	5 (25.00)	4 (20.00)	7 (35.00)	2 (10.00)	**26 (26.00)**
Not at all	0 (0.00)	0 (0.00)	0 (0.00)	0 (0.00)	0 (0.00)	**0 (0.00)**
Total	20 (100.00)	20 (100.00)	20 (100.00)	20 (100.00)	20 (100.00)	**100 (100.00)**
Coordination and Cooperation from Gram Panchayats						
Always	8 (40.00)	10 (50.00)	9 (45.00)	12 (60.00)	9 (45.00)	**48 (48.00)**
Sometimes	12 (60.00)	10 (50.00)	11 (55.00)	8 (40.00)	11 (55.00)	**52 (52.00)**
Not at all	0 (0.00)	0 (0.00)	0 (0.00)	0 (0.00)	0 (0.00)	**0 (0.00)**
Total	20 (100.00)	20 (100.00)	20 (100.00)	20 (100.00)	20 (100.00)	**100 (100.00)**

Source: *Primary probe.*

Note: Figures in parentheses represent percentage.

Figures in Table 6.7 show that out of total respondents 90.00 per cent of respondents in Paragpur block, 80.00 per cent in Indora block, 75.00 per cent in Fatehpur block, 65.00 per cent in Nurpur and 50.00 per cent in Dehra block reported that public health centres were cooperative and provides coordination always. While remaining AWWs reported that PHCs did not provides cooperation and coordination to them.

In overall, out of total, 74.00 per cent of respondents were of the opinion that PHCs were cooperative and provide coordination, while 36.00 per cent did not recognize this.

48 percent respondents told that coordination by Gram Panchayat was always given to them while 52 per cent told that coordination & cooperation given by Gram Panchayats were extended sometimes only

Hence, it can be inferred that as far as the coordination and cooperation from PHCs is concerned, it was found that in 74.00 per cent of respondents had perception that PHCs used to extend their cooperation and coordination to them always, while 48.00 per cent of respondents had perception that gram panchayats extend their cooperation and coordination towards AWCs sometimes only. Thus cooperation and coordination from PHCs was always in view of majority respondents, but the cooperation and coordination from gram panchayats sometimes only.

Picture No. 6(g)

Anganwadi workers interating with PHC workers in Dehra Block

6.7 Help from the Officials

It is important that officials must provide help, education and information to the anganwadi workers and helper, so that they can deliver the services in an effective and efficient way. The data in this regard has been shown in Table 6.8.

Table-6.8: Opinion about the Help from Officials

Response	Block					Total
	Dehra	Fatehpur	Indora	Nurpur	Paragpur	
Always	12 (60.00)	10 (50.00)	15 (75.00)	14 (70.00)	14 (70.00)	**65** **(65.00)**
Sometimes	7 (35.00)	10 (50.00)	4 (20.00)	6 (30.00)	5 (25.00)	**32** **(32.00)**
Not at all	1 (5.00)	0 (0.00)	1 (5.00)	0 (0.00)	1 (5.00)	**3** **(3.00)**
Total	20 (100.00)	20 (100.00)	20 (100.00)	20 (100.00)	20 (100.00)	**100** **(100.00)**

Source: *Primary Probe.*

Note: Figures in parentheses represents percentage

Table 6.8 depicts that majority of respondents were of the opinion that officials always provide needed help to the anganwadi workers. Out of total respondents, 60.00 per cent in Dehra block, 50.00 per cent in Fatehpur block, 75.00 per cent in Indora block and 70.00 per cent of respondent each in Nurpur and Paragpur block held view that officials always extend their help to them in time of need.

While 35.00 per cent in Dehra block, 50.00 per cent in Fatehpur block, 20.00 per cent in Indora block 30.00 per cent Nurpur block and 25.00 per cent of respondents in Paragpur block were of the opinion that officials sometimes extend their help. While the percentage of those respondents who opined that officials did not help them was very less. Overall this percentage was just 3.00 per cent.

Picture No. 6(h)

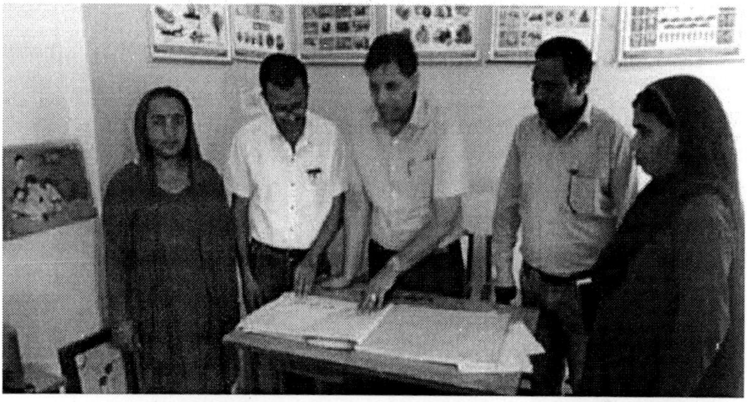

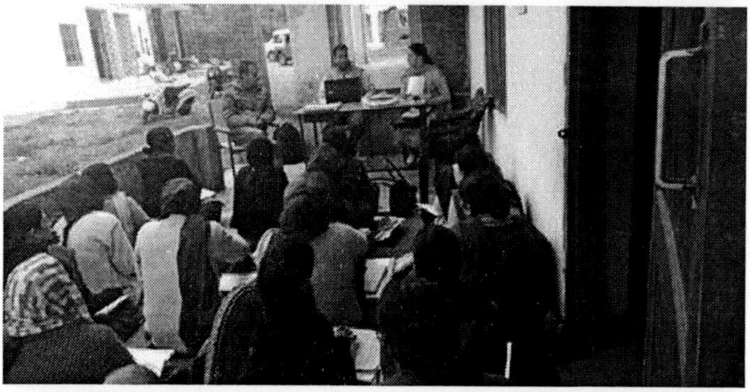

Officials assisting Anganwadi workers at Pragpur

6.8 Behaviour of the Officials

Behaviour of Officials towards subordinate plays an important role in the satisfaction among them. If official's behaviour is cooperative then his/her subordinate work with full zeal. Therefor cooperative behaviour is the need of every organization. So is the case with the functionaries implementing ICDS. To know the behaviour of officials towards anganwadi workers, data has been collected and presented in Table 6.9.

Table-6.9: Opinion about the behaviour of Officials

Behaviour	Block					Total
	Dehra	Fatehpur	Indora	Nurpur	Paragpur	
Very Cooperative	5 (25.00)	6 (30.00)	7 (35.00)	4 (20.00)	8 (40.00)	**30 (30.00)**
Cooperative	10 (50.00)	12 (60.00)	12 (60.00)	13 (65.00)	10 (50.00)	**57 (57.00)**
Cooperative to Some Extent	5 (25.00)	2 (10.00)	1 (5.00)	3 (15.00)	2 (10.00)	**13 (13.00)**
Not Cooperative	0 (0.00)	0 (0.00)	0 (0.00)	0 (0.00)	0 (0.00)	**0 (0.00)**
Total	20 (100.00)	20 (100.00)	20 (100.00)	20 (100.00)	20 (100.00)	**100 (100.00)**

Source: Primary probe.

Note: Figures in parentheses represent percentage.

Data in Table 6.9 show that out of total respondents, 25.00 per cent in Dehra block, 30.00 per cent in Fatehpur block, 35.00 per cent in Indora Block, 20.00 per cent in Nurpur and 40.00 per cent of respondents in Paragpur block were of the opinion that officials were very cooperative. 50.00 per cent in Dehra block, 60.00 per cent each in Fatehpur and Indora block, 65.00 per cent in Nurpur block and 50.00 per cent of respondents in Paragpur block opined that officials were cooperative. While 25.00 per cent of respondents in Dehra block, 10.00 per cent each in Fatehpur and Paragpur block, 5.00 per cent in Indora block and 15.00 per cent of respondents in Nurpur block were of the opinion that officials were cooperative to some extent only.

In overall, out of total respondents, 30.00 per cent of respondents had opinion that behaviour of officials was very cooperative.57.00 per cent of respondents opinion was that behaviour of officials was cooperative only. While 13.00 per cent of respondents had opinion that behaviour of officials was cooperative to some extent only. Hence, it can be concluded that in majority of cases the behaviour of officials towards AWWs and helpers were either very cooperative or cooperative.

Picture No. 6(i)

Research formal meeting with Aganwadi workers at Indora and Dehra

The opinion of the sample Anganwadi workers on the question whether supervisor provide education and information about new schemes under ICDS or not, has been analysed in Table 6.10.

Table-6.10: Education and Information provided by Supervisor

Response	Block					Total
	Dehra	Fatehpur	Indora	Nurpur	Paragpur	
Adequate to some extent	18 (90.00)	17 (85.00)	18 (90.00)	20 (100.00)	19 (95.00)	**92 (92.00)**
Adequate	2 (10.00)	3 (15.00)	2 (10.00)	0 (0.00)	1 (5.00)	**8 (8.00)**
Not Adequate	0 (0.00)	0 (0.00)	0 (0.00)	0 (0.00)	0 (0.00)	**0 (0.00)**
Total	20 (100.00)	20 (100.00)	20 (100.00)	20 (100.00)	20 (100.00)	**100 (100.00)**

Source: *Primary Probe.*

Note: Figures in parentheses represents percentage

Data in Table 6.10 depicts that in majority of cases, that is, 92.00 per cent, supervisors always provided education and information about the new schemes under ICDS that was adequate to some extent only. While 8.00 per cent of respondents opined that supervisors provide adequate education and information.

Hence, it can be inferred that officials and supervisor educate and inform Awws that is adequate to some extent only.

Picture No. 6(j)

Anganwadi centre of Nurpur block with Minister of Social Justice and Empowerment Mrs. Sarveen Chaudhary

आंगनबाड़ी वर्करों को अब
हेल्परों को 2900 मिलेगा मानदेय

राज्य यूनियन ने मानदेय में बढ़ोतरी को बताया संघर्ष की जीत

191. केन्द्र सरकार ने अभी हाल ही में आँगनबाड़ी कार्यकर्ताओं के मासिक मानदेय को 3,000 रुपये से बढ़ाकर 4,500 रुपये कर दिया है। राज्य सरकार द्वारा दिए जाने वाले अतिरिक्त मासिक अँशदान को मिलाकर अब आँगनबाड़ी कार्यकर्ता का मासिक मानदेय 6,300 रुपये होगा। इसी प्रकार से केन्द्र सरकार ने आँगनबाड़ी सहायकों का मासिक मानदेय 1,500 रुपये से बढ़ाकर 2,250 रुपये तथा मिनी आँगनबाड़ी वर्करज़ का मानदेय 2,250 रुपये से बढ़ाकर 3,500 रुपये कर दिया है। राज्य सरकार द्वारा दिये जाने वाले मासिक अँशदान को मिलाकर अब इन्हें क्रमशः 3,200 रुपये एवं 4,600 रुपये मिलेगा।

Media coverage regarding increase salary

6.9 Sufficiency of Salary/Remuneration

Salary is an important hygiene factor in job satisfaction and motivation. If employees get sufficient salary to meet out their daily needs then they will be more satisfied. To know whether the salary given to the AWWs is sufficient or not, opinion of the sample AWWs was collected has been shown in Table below

Table-6.11: Opinion regarding Salary

Salary	Block					Total
	Dehra	Fatehpur	Indora	Nurpur	Paragpur	
Sufficient	0 (0.00)	0 (0.00)	0 (0.00)	0 (0.00)	0 (0.00)	**0** **(0.00)**
Somewhat Sufficient	2 (10.00)	1 (5.00)	3 (15.00)	2 (10.00)	2 (10.00)	**10** **(10.00)**
Not Sufficient	18 (90.00)	19 (95.00)	17 (85.00)	18 (90.00)	18 (90.00)	**90** **(90.00)**
Total	20 (100.00)	20 (100.00)	20 (100.00)	20 (100.00)	20 (100.00)	**100** **(100.00)**

Source: *Primary probe.*

Note: Figures in parentheses represent percentage.

Data in Table 6.11 depicts that out of total respondents majority of respondents in all the blocks had grudges that the salary given to them was not sufficient. Out of total respondents, 90.00 per cent of respondents each in Dehra, Nurpur and Paragpur block, 95.00 per cent of respondents in Fatehpur block and 85.00 per cent of respondents in Indora block opined that the salary was not sufficient. While mere 10.00 per cent of respondents each in Dehra, Nurpur and Paragpur block, 5.00 per cent in Fatehpur block and 15.00 per cent of respondent in Indora block were of the opinion that salary was somewhat sufficient. Hence, it can be concluded that the salary given to AWWs is not sufficient up to their expectation

As per informal discussion with CDPO/ACDPO/ Supervisors it was found that various initiatives has been taken by Government to improve pay anomalies and financial conditions of Anganwari workers. As per new revised Guidelines of government of Himachal Pradesh & the Notification of Government of Himachal Pradesh Dated 29 February, 2016, Honorarium of Aanganwari worker is '3450/ - month, Mini Anganwari worker is '2625/- month & of Aanganwari Helper is '1800/- month. As per announcement of Primeminister of India Aanganwari workers in October 2018 who drew an honorarium of '3000/- will now get '4500/ - and those who used to get '2200/- will get '3,500/-. The honorarium of Anganwadi helpers will be hiked from '1500/ - to '2500/-. Prime Minister of India in October, 2018 announced that Anganwadi workers using techniques such as common application software (ICDS-CAS) would get additional incentive. The incentive ranging from '250/- to '500/ - would be based on performance.

As per order of Ministry of Women & Child Development decided that Anganwadi Workers (Awws)/Anganwadi Helpers under the: Anganwadi Services (Umbrella ICDS Scheme) in the age group of 18-50 years as on 1st June, 2017 would be covered under the Pradhan Mantri Jeevan Jyoti Bima Yojana (PMJJBY) for life cover and those in the age group of 18-59 years as on 1st June, 2017 would be covered under the Pradhan Mantri Suraksha BimaYojana (PMSBY) for accidental cover.

The Government had formulated scheme in 2000-2001 to award Anganwari at National & State level to motivate their exemplary services in ICDS. Earlier award money was '25,000/ - from 2018 this award money was increased to '50.000/- rupees and citation while '10,000/- are given for the State level award.

Thus it can be analysed that government has taken various initiatives for motivation of Aanganwari workers yet their expectations need to be fulfilled.

6.10 Satisfaction with the job

Job satisfaction is the pleasure that one gets from doing his/her job. It is the extent to which a person's hopes, desires, and expectations about the employment he or she is engaged in are fulfilled. Person working in the area of service delivery need to be satisfied with his/her job, so that he/she could deliver his/her best. Aanganwadi workers deliver various kinds of services under ICDS. Hence, their satisfaction with their job is of utmost importance. The data about job satisfaction has been given in Table 6.12

Table 6.12: Opinion about Job Satisfaction

Satisfied	Block					Total
	Dehra	Fatehpur	Indora	Nurpur	Paragpur	
To a great extent	5 (25.00)	4 (20.00)	5 (25.00)	6 (30.00)	4 (20.00)	**24 (24.00)**
To some extent	7 (35.00)	7 (35.00)	7 (35.00)	5 (25.00)	8 (40.00)	**34 (34.00)**
Not at all	8 (40.00)	9 (45.00)	8 (40.00)	9 (45.00)	8 (40.00)	**42 (42.00)**
Total	20 (100.00)	20 (100.00)	20 (100.00)	20 (100.00)	20 (100.00)	**100 (100.00)**

Source: *Primary probe.*

Note: Figures in parentheses represent percentage.

Data in Table 6.12 enumerate that out of total respondents, 24.00 of respondents were satisfied with their job to great extent, 34.00 per cent were satisfied to some extent and 42.00 per cent were not satisfied with their job. Block-wise data reveal that 40.00 per cent of respondents each in Dehra, Indora and Paragpur block and 45.00 per cent of respondents each in Fatehpur and Nurpur block were not satisfied with their job. While 35.00 per cent each in Dehra, Fathepur and Indora block, 25.00 per cent in Nurpur block and 40.00 per cent in Paragpur block were satisfied to some extent. Whereas, 25 per cent each in Dehra and Indora block, 20.00 per cent each in Fatehpur and Paragpur block and 25 per cent of respondent in Indora block were satisfied to great extent. Hence it can be concluded that majority of AWWs were not satisfied with their job.

Recent Government of Himachal Pradesh order to open Pre nursery schools in Government schools has also created tremors of insecurity among aanganwari workers and most of Anganwari workers had gone on strike in Himachal as they were protesting this move of Government of Himachal Pradesh as a threat to their job security and status in coming time ahead.

Conclusion

In this chapter opinion of 100 Anganwadi workers has been analysed 23 per cent of AWW respondents complained that there is no building and water facilities in anganwadi centres. Most of the anganwadi centres were running on rented houses.

Due to unavailability of drinking water the anganwadi workers carry drinking water either from their own house or from public water sources. It was very surprising that when the Swachh Bharat Abhiyan is being carried out in full swing in the whole country, that 36 per cent of the Anganwadi centers had no toilets of their own and they send the children to surrounding houses by making request to them. 22 per cent of the Anganwadi centres had no electricity connections and 53 per cent of Anganwadi centres were not furnished with adequate furniture. Thus without basic facilities the idea of making the Anganwadi centres ICT linked and high-tech appears to be distant vision in Kangra district of Himachal Pradesh. It was observed that some of the AWWs did not know how to fill the register and prepare reports. Hence, on the basis of personal observation it can be concluded that AWWs need more training specific to ICDS programme as well as general and managerial aspects. Availability of weighing machine at the AWCs ensures timely and periodic weighing of children and preparation of growth chart. In this regard, hundred per cent of respondents told that they had weighing machine in the AWC. Hence, it can be concluded that the required equipment and tools were available in all the AWCs. To large extent .Majority of respondents had opinion that there is timely supply of materials in Aanganwadi Centres 32 respondents complained that due to absence of separate Kitchen and no cooking facilities they had to face problems, 29 per cent complained regarding irregular & Inadequate supply of cooking material, 31 per cent grumbled due to lack of storage facility & fuel problems.19 per cent complained regarding poor quality of food material, 33 per cent told there was financial constraint in implementation of Programme.

7

PERCEPTION OF BENEFICIARIES

The Integrated Child Development scheme aims at providing an integrated package of services. These services include supplementary nutrition, immunization, medical check-ups, recommendation services, pre-school non-formal education and nutrition & health awareness. The purpose of providing these services as a package is because each of these issues is dependent on the other. These services are provided through the Anganwadi centres established in rural and urban areas of the state. The present study aimed at evaluation of ICDS in Himachal Pradesh in general and in Kangra district of Himachal Pradesh with particular emphasis.

In this study directed toward the evaluation of the implementation of Integrated Child Development Services, the perception of the beneficiaries who are getting benefit from these centres is important. The involvement and participation of the people concerned in the implementation of ICDS depend upon how they considered the utility and effectiveness of these services. Moreover, it is also important to see whether these services are being provided in accordance with the set procedure or not. Hence, in the present chapter an attempt has been made to analyze the opinion and perception of the respondents (beneficiaries) regarding the Integrated Child Development Services.

The beneficiaries under ICDS are pregnant or lactating women, mother of 6 months to 3 years old child, mother of 3 years to 6 years old child and mother of adolescent girls. In the present study perception of 250 beneficiaries from all these categories were taken to study and analyse their perception regarding services imparted to them through ICDS centres.

7.1 Perception of Beneficiaries

7.1.1 Awareness about the Services under ICDS

Various services are being provided under ICDS in Himachal Pradesh, which includes supplementary nutrition, non-formal pre-schooling, immunization, health check-up, nutrition and health education, referral services etc. Awareness among respondents regarding various services provided by ICDS is analyzed in following table:

Table 7.1: Awareness among Beneficiaries about the Services Provided by ICDS

Block	Response	Supplementary Nutrition	Non-formal Preschool education	Immunization	Health Check-up	Referral Services	Nutrition and Health Education
Dehra	Yes	35 (70.00)	38 (76.00)	40 (80.00)	42 (84.00)	34 (68.00)	33 (66.00)
	No	15 (30.00)	12 (24.00)	10 (20.00)	8 (16.00)	16 (32.00)	17 (34.00)
	Total	50 (100.00)	50 (100.00)	50 (100.00)	50 (100.00)	50 (100.00)	50 (100.00)
Fatehpur	Yes	33 (66.00)	36 (72.00)	39 (78.00)	40 (80.00)	34 (68.00)	35 (70.00)
	No	17 (34.00)	14 (28.00)	11 (22.00)	10 (20.00)	16 (32.00)	15 (30.00)
	Total	50 (100.00)	50 (100.00)	50 (100.00)	50 (100.00)	50 (100.00)	50 (100.00)
Indora	Yes	41 (82.00)	42 (84.00)	40 (80.00)	39 (78.00)	37 (74.00)	35 (70.00)
	No	9 (18.00)	8 (16.00)	10 (20.00)	11 (22.00)	13 (26.00)	15 (30.00)
	Total	50 (100.00)	50 (100.00)	50 (100.00)	50 (100.00)	50 (100.00)	50 (100.00)
Nurpur	Yes	40 (80.00)	38 (76.00)	39 (78.00)	41 (82.00)	35 (70.00)	32 (64.00)
	No	10 (20.00)	12 (24.00)	11 (22.00)	9 (18.00)	15 (30.00)	18 (36.00)
	Total	50 (100.00)	50 (100.00)	50 (100.00)	50 (100.00)	50 (100.00)	50 (100.00)
Paragpur	Yes	39 (78.00)	40 (80.00)	41 (82.00)	42 (84.00)	35 (70.00)	34 (68.00)
	No	11 (22.00)	10 (20.00)	9 (18.00)	8 (16.00)	15 (30.00)	16 (32.00)
	Total	50 (100.00)	50 (100.00)	50 (100.00)	50 (100.00)	50 (100.00)	50 (100.00)
Total	Yes	188 (75.20)	194 (77.60)	199 (79.60)	204 (81.60)	175 (70.00)	169 (67.60)
	No	62 (24.80)	56 (22.40)	51 (20.40)	46 (18.40)	75 (30.00)	81 (32.40)
	Total	**250 (100.00)**	**250 (100.00)**	**250 (100.00)**	**250 (100.00)**	**250 (100.00)**	**250 (100.00)**

Source: Primary probe.

Note: Figures in parentheses represent percentage.

From the Table 7.1 it can be analysed that more than 75 per cent of the respondents were aware about supplementary nutrition, 77.6 per cent respondents were aware about non-formal pre-school education, 79.6 percent respondents were aware about immunization, more than 80 per cent were aware about health check-up, 70 per cent were aware about referral services provided by Anganwadi centers and 67.6 per cent were aware about the nutrition and health education provide by Anganwadi centers. 24.80 per cent of the respondents were not aware about supplementary nutrition, 22.4 per cent were not aware about non-formal pre-school education, 20.4 percent were not aware about immunization, more than 18 per cent were not aware about health check-up, 30 per cent were not aware about referral services and 32.4 per cent of the sample beneficiaries were not aware about the nutrition and health education.

The overall data reveals that out of total respondents, 75.20 per cent of respondents were aware of supplementary nutrition, 77.60 per cent were aware of non-formal pre-schooling, 79.60 per cent were aware about Immunization, 81.60 per cent were of Health check-up, 70.00 per cent were of referral services and 67.60 per cent of respondents were aware about nutrition and health education. Hence, it can be analysed that majority of respondents were aware of services provided under ICDS.

Picture No. 7(a)

Awareness Campaign Organized by Anganwadi Centre at Dehra

7.2 Perceptions regarding Immunization Programme

7.2.1 Opinion About Immunization

Immunization is one of the important activities performed by the Anganwadi Workers. They need to motivate the parents of the children for immunization.

7.2.1.1 Motivating Parents to Immunize their Children

It is important that Anganwadi Workers motivate the parents to immunize their children. The data has been collected from the respondents that whether Anganwadi Workers motivate the parents or not. The collected data has been presented in Table 7.2

Table 7.2 : Motivating Parents to Immunize their Children

Response	Block					Total
	Dehra	Fatehpur	Indora	Nurpur	Paragpur	
Always	14 (28.00)	13 (26.00)	16 (32.00)	13 (26.00)	14 (28.00)	**70 (28.00)**
Sometimes	17 (34.00)	16 (32.00)	15 (30.00)	17 (34.00)	15 (30.00)	**80 (32.00)**
Not at All	19 (38.00)	21 (42.00)	19 (38.00)	20 (40.00)	21 (42.00)	**100 (40.00)**
Total	50 (100.00)	50 (100.00)	50 (100.00)	50 (100.00)	50 (100.00)	**250 (100.00)**

It is evident from the analysis of table number 5.1 that 28 per cent beneficiaries had opinion that Anganwadi Workers always motivate the parents to immunized their children, 32 per cent beneficiaries told that they were sometimes motivated while 40 per cent beneficiaries shared their experiences that Anganwadi Workers not at all motivates them for undergoing immunization of children.

Picture No. 7(b)

Anganwadi workers motivating Parents to Immunize their Children at Nurpur and Fatehpur

7.2.1.2 Information about Immunization Schedule

It is important that the schedule of immunization should be well publicized. It is the duty of AWW to inform the parents of the children about the schedule of immunization. The opinion of beneficiaries regarding immunization schedule is analyzed in follow Table 7.3

Table 7.3: Disseminating Information about Immunization Schedule

Response	Block					Total
	Dehra	Fatehpur	Indora	Nurpur	Paragpur	
Always	41 (82.00)	42 (84.00)	45 (90.00)	46 (92.00)	41 (82.00)	**215 (86.00)**
Sometimes	9 (18.00)	8 (16.00)	5 (10.00)	4 (08.00)	9 (18.00)	**35 (14.00)**
Not at all	0 (0.00)	0 (0.00)	0 (0.00)	0 (0.00)	0 (0.00)	**0 (0.00)**
Total	50 (100.00)	50 (100.00)	50 (100.00)	50 (100.00)	50 (100.00)	**250 (100.00)**

Source: *Primary probe.*

Note: Figures in parentheses represent percentage.

The data in the table number 7.3 reveals that out of total respondents, a massive majority of the respondents 86 per cent respondents opined that the Anganwadi centres always disseminate the information about immunization schedule. Only 14 per cent of the respondents opined that the Anganwadi Workers sometimes disseminate the information regarding immunization schedule. This shows that the Anganwadi Workers are playing their role effectively in Himachal Pradesh.

Thus as the 86 per cent beneficiaries had opinion that information about immunization scheme always given to them by Anganwadi centres. It may be the reason that infant mortality rate has been reduced in Himachal Pradesh.

Picture No. 7(c)

AWW giving information regarding immunization schedule at Indora and Nurpur Block

7.2.1.3 Place of immunization

It is important that immunization of children should be done in a proper place. In this regard collected data has been shown in Table 7.4

Table 7.4: Place of Immunization

Place	Block					Total
	Dehra	Fatehpur	Indora	Nurpur	Paragpur	
AWC	4 (8.00)	3 (6.00)	0 (0.00)	0 (0.00)	1 (2.00)	**8 (3.20)**
Health Sub Centre	42 (84.00)	40 (80.00)	45 (90.00)	40 (80.00)	46 (92.00)	**213 (85.20)**
ANM House	0 (0.00)	0 (0.00)	0 (0.00)	0 (0.00)	0 (0.00)	**0 (0.00)**
Camps	4 (8.00)	7 (14.00)	5 (10.00)	10 (20.00)	3 (6.00)	**29 (11.60)**
Other Public Service units	0 (0.00)	0 (0.00)	0 (0.00)	0 (0.00)	0 (0.00)	**0 (0.00)**
NGO	0 (0.00)	0 (0.00)	0 (0.00)	0 (0.00)	0 (0.00)	**0 (0.00)**
Private clinic	0 (0.00)	0 (0.00)	0 (0.00)	0 (0.00)	0 (0.00)	**0 (0.00)**
Total	50 (100.00)	50 (100.00)	50 (100.00)	50 (100.00)	50 (100.00)	**250 (100.00)**

Source: *Primary probe.*

Note: Figures in parentheses represent percentage.

The data in Table 7.4 depicts that only 3.20 per cent beneficiaries goes to Anganwadi Centres for immunization. 85.20 per cent beneficiaries take the benefit of immunization at Health Sub- Centres. 11.60 per cent goes to camps for immunization. None goes to other public service units, NGOs and private clinic for immunization.

Thus it can be analyzed that majority of 85.20 per cent immunizations is conducted at Health Sub- Centres. It means that more and more beneficiaries are coming to health sub-centers for getting the benefit of immunization.

7.3 Perception regarding Supplementary Nutrition to Pregnant and Lactating Women

Anganwadi centres works as a platform for providing different services to the people under ICDS programme. It is important that all the services under ICDS must be delivered properly. Pregnant and lactating women are also the beneficiaries under ICDS. The evaluation of services to these women has been analyzed as under:

7.3.1 Supplementary Nutrition during pregnancy

Table 7.5: Supplementary Nutrition provided during Pregnancy is sufficient

Responses	Block					Total
	Dehra	Fatehpur	Indora	Nurpur	Paragpur	
To a Large Extent	39 (78.00)	36 (72.00)	37 (74.00)	34 (68.00)	32 (64.00)	**178 (71.02)**
To Some Extent	6 (12.00)	8 (16.00)	6 (12.00)	7 (14.00)	7 (14.00)	**34 (13.06)**
Not at All	5 (10.00)	6 (12.00)	7 (14.00)	9 (18.00)	11 (22.00)	**38 (15.02)**
Total	50 (100.00)	50 (100.00)	50 (100.00)	50 (100.00)	50 (100.00)	**250 (100.00)**

Source: *Primary probe*
Note: Figures in parentheses represent percentage

The data in Table 7.5 shows that out of total 250 respondents, 71.2 per cent respondents opined that the Anganwadi Centres provides supplementary nutrition for pregnant women to a large extent. Only 13.6 per cent respondents opined that the Anganwadi Centers provide supplementary nutrition for pregnant women to some extent and 15.2 per cent of the respondents opined that the Anganwadi Centres provide supplementary nutrition for pregnant women not at all.

Thus it can be concluded that majority of 71.2 per cent respondents had opinion that supplementary nutrition provided to pregnant women to a large extent and were satisfied with it.

Picture No. 7(d)

DPO and AWW distributing supplementary nutrition to lactating and pregnant mother at Pragpur and Indora

7.4 Advice Regarding Delivery Care

Advice regarding delivery care is an important service to be performed by the Anganwadi workers. The data regarding advice regarding delivery care has been enumerated in Table 7.6

Table 7.6: Advice Regarding Delivery Care given by Anganwadi Workers

Responses	Block					Total
	Dehra	Fatehpur	Indora	Nurpur	Paragpur	
Always	40 (80.00)	39 (78.00)	41 (82.00)	38 (76.00)	38 (76.00)	**196 (78.40)**
Sometimes	10 (20.00)	11 (22.00)	9 (18.00)	12 (24.00)	12 (24.00)	**54 (21.60)**
Not at All	0 (00.00)	0 (00.00)	0 (00.00)	0 (00.00)	0 (00.00)	**0 (00.00)**
Total	50 (100.00)	50 (100.00)	50 (100.00)	50 (100.00)	50 (100.00)	**250 (100.00)**

Source: *Primary probe*

Note: Figures in parentheses represent percentage

Data in Table 7.6 reveals that out of total respondents, 78.40 per cent of respondents were of the opinion that Anganwadi workers always provide advice to the pregnant women regarding delivery care, while 21.60 per cent of respondents responded that the Anganwadi workers sometimes provide advice to the pregnant women regarding delivery care.,

Thus majority of 78.40 per cent of respondents were of the opinion that Anganwadi workers always provide advice to the pregnant women regarding delivery care.

Picture No. 7(e)

Anganwadi workers Giving Advice Regarding Delivery Care at Indora

7.5 Advice regarding Nutrition and Health

Nutrition and health is an important aspect for a pregnant and lactating woman. It is important that these women must take care of their nutrition and health. The Anganwadi workers are there to extend every help in educating and advising them in this regard. The data in this regard has been given in Table 7.7

Table 7.7 : Advice Regarding Nutrition and Health

Responses	Block					Total
	Dehra	Fatehpur	Indora	Nurpur	Paragpur	
Always	46 (92.00)	45 (90.00)	43 (86.00)	40 (80.00)	41 (82.00)	**215 (86.00)**
Sometimes	4 (8.00)	5 (10.00)	7 (14.00)	10 (20.00)	9 (18.00)	**35 (14.00)**
Not at All	0 (00.00)	0 (00.00)	0 (00.00)	0 (00.00)	0 (00.00)	**0 (00.00)**
Total	50 (100.00)	50 (100.00)	50 (100.00)	50 (100.00)	50 (100.00)	**250 (100.00)**

Source: *Primary probe.*

Note: Figures in parentheses represent percentage.

The table 7.7 depicts that out of total respondents 86 per cent of the respondents opined that they were always given advice regarding nutrition and health by the Anganwadi workers. Only 14 per cent respondents had opinion that the advice regarding nutrition and health is given sometimes only.

Picture No. 7(f)

_Anganwadi workers giving Advice Regarding Nutrition and Health in Fatehpur

7.6 Family Planning and Birth spacing

Family planning and birth spacing are the needs and necessity of the day. It is important that Anganwadi workers must educate the community, especially, women, about the importance of family planning and birth space. To know whether Anganwadi workers spread education or not, data has been collected and presented in Table 7.8

Table 7.8: Advice for Family Planning and Birth Spacing

Responses	Block					Total
	Dehra	Fatehpur	Indora	Nurpur	Paragpur	
Always	39 (96.00)	36 (92.00)	39 (90.00)	38 (92.00)	34 (88.00)	**186 (74.04)**
Sometimes	9 (18.00)	10 (20.00)	6 (12.00)	8 (16.00)	10 (20.00)	**43 (17.02)**
Not at All	2 (4.00)	4 (8.00)	5 (10.00)	4 (8.00)	6 (12.00)	**21 (8.40)**
Total	50 (100.00)	50 (100.00)	50 (100.00)	50 (100.00)	50 (100.00)	**250 (100.00)**

Source: Primary probe.

Note: Figures in parentheses represent percentage.

The data in the above table reveals that 74.04 per cent of the respondents told that the Anganwadi workers always advise them for family planning and birth place. 17.2 per cent of the respondents told that the Anganwadi workers sometimes advise them for family planning and birth spacing, while only 8.40 per cent of the total respondents opined that the Anganwadi workers advise them for family planning and birth spacing not at all.

Picture No. 7(g)

Anganwadi workers Giving Advice for Family Planning and Birth Spacing at Pragpur

7.7 Supplementary Nutrition During Lactation

Supplementary nutrition is also important during lactation. Lactating women needs to be healthy and need nutritious food. In this regard opinion has been collected and shown in Table 7.9

Table 7.9: Satisfaction with Supplementary Nutrition during Lactation

Responses	Block					Total
	Dehra	Fatehpur	Indora	Nurpur	Paragpur	
To Some Extent	28 (56.00)	30 (60.00)	31 (62.00)	27 (54.00)	31 (62.00)	**147 (58.80)**
To large Extent	16 (32.00)	12 (24.00)	13 (26.00)	16 (32.00)	14 (28.00)	**71 (28.40)**
Not at All	6 (12.00)	8 (16.00)	6 (12.00)	7 3(14.00)	5 (10.00)	**32 (12.80)**
Total	50 (100.00)	50 (100.00)	50 (100.00)	50 (100.00)	50 (100.00)	**250 (100.00)**

Source: *Primary probe.*

Note: Figures in parentheses represent percentage.

It can be analysed from the table 7.9 that 58.8 per cent beneficiaries were satisfied to a some extent with the supplementary nutrition during lactation, while 28.4 per cent beneficiaries were satisfied to large extent with supplementary nutrition during lactation. 12.8 per cent beneficiaries opined that they were not satisfied at all with the supplementary nutrition during lactation. The data shows that there is a need to improve supplementary nutrition during lactation to large masses.

7.8 Post-natal care and breastfeeding

The post natal period is a critical phase in the lives of mothers and newborn babies. Most maternal and infant deaths occur during this time. Therefore, spreading education and awareness about post-natal care is one of the important activities to be performed by the Anganwadi centre. The data in this regard have been illustrated in Table 7.10

Table 7.10: Opinion about Advice for Post-Natal Care and Breastfeeding Practices

Responses	Block					Total
	Dehra	Fatehpur	Indora	Nurpur	Paragpur	
Excellent	11 (22.00)	8 (16.00)	12 (24.00)	10 (20.00)	13 (26.00)	**54 (21.60)**
Good	6 (12.00)	11 (22.00)	16 (32.00)	13 (26.00)	7 (14.00)	**53 (21.20)**
Satisfactory	23 (46.00)	18 (36.00)	11 (22.00)	17 (34.00)	21 (42.00)	**90 (36.00)**
Not Satisfactory	10 (20.00)	13 (26.00)	11 (22.00)	10 (20.00)	9 (18.00)	**53 (21.20)**
Total	50 (100.00)	50 (100.00)	50 (100.00)	50 (100.00)	50 (100.00)	**250 (100.00)**

Source: *Primary probe.*

Note: Figures in parentheses represent percentage.

The data in the Table 7.10 shows that only 21.6 per cent of the beneficiaries rate the advice for post-natal care and breastfeeding practices excellent. 21.2 per cent rate it as good, 36 per cent rate it satisfactory, while 21.2 per cent of the sample beneficiaries rate that it not satisfactory. The results show that the advice given by the Anganwadi workers for post-natal care and breastfeeding practices is not up to the mark.

36 per cent rate Advice for Post-Natal Care and Breastfeeding Practices as satisfactory, while 21.2 per cent of the sample beneficiaries rate that it is not satisfactory. The results show that the advice given by the Anganwadi workers for post-natal care and breastfeeding practices is not up to the mark.

Picture No. 7(h)

_Breast feeding week celebrated at Dehra and Pragpur

7.9 Health Check-up

Health check-up of pregnant and lactating women is important. Anganwadi workers play an important role in this regard. Opinion of respondents regarding health check-up is discussed in Table 7.11

Table 7.11: General Health Check-up Organised by Anganwadi Centres

Responses	Block					Total
	Dehra	Fatehpur	Indora	Nurpur	Paragpur	
Frequently	9 (18.00)	16 (32.00)	10 (20.00)	12 (24.00)	5 (10.00)	**52** **(20.80)**
Sometimes	26 (52.00)	21 (42.00)	28 (56.00)	23 (46.00)	29 (58.00)	**127** **(50.80)**
Not at All	15 (30.00)	13 (26.00)	12 (24.00)	15 (30.00)	16 (32.00)	**71** **(28.40)**
Total	50 (100.00)	50 (100.00)	50 (100.00)	50 (100.00)	50 (100.00)	**250** **(100.00)**

Source: *Primary probe.*

Note: Figures in parentheses represent percentage.

Table 7.11 clearly depicts that 50.8 per cent of the respondents reported that Anganwadi centres sometimes organize the health check-up. 20.80 per cent respondents opined that the Anganwadi centres frequently organize health check-up, while 28.4 per cent of the respondents responded that the Anganwadi centres do not organize health check-up at all.

Thus, 28.4 per cent respondents complained that health checkups are not being organized at all and 50.80 per cent respondents told that health checkups are organized sometimes. Their complaint may be because of financial crunches and infrastructure handicap, that's why health checkups are not organized frequently by Anganwadi centres as required, this may affect the health of mother and children.

Picture No. 7(i)

Health camp organized regarding nutrition health at Fatehpur

7.10 Opinion about Cooked Food

Anganwadi provides cooked food to the children. It is provided to maintain nutrition level among them. It is true that AWCs provides cooked food to the children, but it is important that the quality of cooked food must be good and of rich nutritious value The opinion of sample beneficiaries has been collected whether AWCs providing quality cooked food or not is analyzed in Table 7.12

Table 7.12: Quality of Cooked Food served by the AWCS

Quality	Block					Total
	Dehra	Fatehpur	Indora	Nurpur	Paragpur	
Very Good	25 (50.00)	22 (44.00)	27 (54.00)	24 (48.00)	24 (48.00)	**122 (48.80)**
Good	14 (28.00)	14 (28.00)	12 (24.00)	11 (22.00)	14 (28.00)	**65 (26.00)**
Average	9 (18.00)	13 (26.00)	11 (22.00)	14 (28.00)	12 (24.00)	**59 (23.60)**
Poor	2 (4.00)	1 (2.00)	0 (0.00)	1 (2.00)	0 (0.00)	**4 (1.60)**
Total	50 (100.00)	50 (100.00)	50 (100.00)	50 (100.00)	50 (100.00)	**250 (100.00)**

Source: *Primary probe.*

Note: Figures in parentheses represent percentage.

Table 7.12 depicts that out of total 250 respondents only 48.8 per cent sample beneficiaries rated the quality of cooked food served at Anganwadi centres as average, while 26 per cent beneficiaries rated it good, 23.6 per cent rated it very good and 1.6 per cent rated it as poor. The anasysis shows that there is a need to improve the quality of cooked food, so that the beneficiary children can get quality food.

Picture No. 7(j)

हिम ऊर्जा 60 फीसदी सब्सिडी पर मुहैया करवाएगा सोलर कुकर और सोलर डिश

स्कूल और आंगनबाड़ी में सूर्य की रोशनी से पकेगा मिड डे मील खाना

Media coverage regarding quality of food in Fatehpur

7.10.1 Sufficient Quantity of Food

Along with quality of food the quantity is also important. Food must sufficient enough to fulfill the nutritious need of beneficiaries. If sufficient quantity of food is not given to the beneficiaries then objective of eradicating malnutrition could not be achieved. Opinion regarding quantity of food provided by the Anganwadi centres is analysed in following Table 7.13.

Table 7.13 " Opinion about Quantity of Food

Sufficient Quantity given	Block					Total
	Dehra	Fatehpur	Indora	Nurpur	Paragpur	
To large Extent	16 (32.00)	16 (32.00)	13 (26.00)	10 (20.00)	12 (24.00)	**67 (26.80)**
To some Extent	30 (60.00)	31 (62.00)	35 (70.00)	38 (76.00)	34 (68.00)	**168 (67.20)**
Not at all	4 (8.00)	3 (6.00)	2 (4.00)	2 (4.00)	4 (8.00)	**15 (6.00)**
Total	50 (100.00)	50 (100.00)	50 (100.00)	50 (100.00)	50 (100.00)	**250 (100.00)**

Source: *Primary probe.*

Note: Figures in parentheses represent percentage.

Data in Table 7.13 depicts that more than 67 per cent sample respondents opined that the Anganwadi centres provides sufficient food to some extent only 26.8 per cent responded that the centres provide quantity of food sufficient to large extent, while 6 per cent sample respondents opined that the Anganwadi centres do not provide the sufficient food at all.

Picture No. 7(k)

Quantity of Food checked by Supervisors

7.10.2 Attendance of Children

Attendance of children at the Anganwadi is the duty of Anganwadi workers. To know whether Anganwadi worker used to take attendance of children or not, data has been collected from the sample respondents and presented in Table 7.14

Table 7.14: Opinion about the Attendance of Children taken by the Anganwadi Workers

Response	Block					Total
	Dehra	Fatehpur	Indora	Nurpur	Paragpur	
Yes	34 (68.00)	33 (66.00)	35 (70.00)	38 (76.00)	37 (74.00)	**177 (70.80)**
No	0 (0.00)	2 (4.00)	1 (2.00)	0 (0.00)	2 (4.00)	**5 (2.00)**
Don't Know	16 (32.00)	15 (30.00)	14 (28.00)	12 (24.00)	11 (22.00)	**68 (27.20)**
Total	50 (100.00)	50 (100.00)	50 (100.00)	50 (100.00)	50 (100.00)	**250 (100.00)**

Source: Primary probe.

Note: Figures in parentheses represent percentage.

The above data reveals that more than 70 per cent of the respondents told that the Anganwadi workers take the attendance of the children. 2 per cent told that they do not take the attendance of the children, while more than 27 per cent of the respondents told that they don't know whether the attendance of the children is taken by the Anganwadi workers or not. Regular attendance creates faith among the parents with Angganwadi centres as well as Anganwadi workers.

Thus majority of the respondents shared that attendance of children visiting Anganwadi centres is a regular feature to maintain record and track the number of children visiting to Anganwadi centres.

Picture No. 7(l)

प्रदेश में अब आंगनबाड़ी कार्यकर्ता भी होंगी स्मार्ट

Media coverage relating to Anganwadi centres of Himachal Pradesh

Picture No. 7(m)

आंगनबाड़ी कार्यकर्ताओं को स्मार्ट फोन देगी सरकार

हिमाचल प्रदेश कर्मचारी मंच

फोन के माध्यम से एक क्लिक पर मिलेगी आंगनबाड़ी केंद्र की हर जानकारी, पहले चरण में पांच जिले होंगे शामिल

सुभाष कुमार अग्निहोत्री

फोन से कार्यकर्ता को ये भरनी होंगी जानकारियां

चंबा, ऊना, शिमला, हमीरपुर और सोलन शामिल

रहेगी नजर | आंगनबाड़ी केंद्रों में ऑनलाइन मोबाइल सेवाओं के द्वारा सभी जानकारी रहेगी उपलब्ध, मोबाइल में होगा एप और जीपीएस

आंगनबाड़ी स्कूल में कितने बच्चे आए हैं, मोबाइल से फोटो खींचकर अपलोड होगी अटेंडेंस, रुकेगा फर्जीवाड़ा

16 मास्टर ट्रेनर को दी जा चुकी है ट्रेनिंग

TEACHERS

Children in Anganwadi centres of Pragpur

7.10.3 Health Check-up of the Children at Anganwadi Centres

As the children from the age group of 3 to 6 years are coming to the Anganwadi centres. It is the responsibility of Anganwadi centres to check the health of these children. In this regard health check-up camps are organized by Anganwadi centres and data has been collected from the sample respondents and presented in Table 7.15

Table 7.15: Health Check-up of the Children at Anganwadi Centres are organised

Health Check-up	Block					Total
	Dehra	Fatehpur	Indora	Nurpur	Paragpur	
Frequently	18 (36.00)	19 (38.00)	17 (34.00)	16 (32.00)	16 (32.00)	**86 (34.40)**
Sometimes	22 (44.00)	28 (56.00)	24 (48.00)	31 (62.00)	27 (54.00)	**132 (52.80)**
Never	10 (20.00)	3 (6.00)	9 (18.00)	3 (6.00)	7 (14.00)	**32 (12.80)**
Total	50 (100.00)	50 (100.00)	50 (100.00)	50 (100.00)	50 (100.00)	**250 (100.00)**

Source: Primary probe.

Note: Figures in parentheses represent percentage.

The Table 7.15 depicts that there were 52.8 per cent respondents who responded that the Anganwadi centres sometimes conduct the health check-up of the children at Anganwadi centres. 34.4 per cent of the respondents told that the Anganwadi centres conduct the health check-up of the children frequently, while more than 12 per cent of the respondents told that the Anganwadi centres never conduct the health check-up of children.

Thus majority of 52.8 per cent respondents who responded that the Anganwadi centres sometimes conduct the health check-up of the children at Anganwadi centres.

Picture No. 7(n)

Health camp organized by Anganwadi Centres in Dehra & Fatehpur

7.10.4 Weighing of Children

To find out the effect of nutritious food it is important that the weight of children must increase according to their age. In this regard, it is important that weight of children should be taken time to time to observe their growth and data has been collected from the sample respondents and presented in Table 7.16

Table 7.16 :Weighing of Children at Anganwadi Centres is done

Weighing	Block					Total
	Dehra	Fatehpur	Indora	Nurpur	Paragpur	
Regularly	18 (36.00)	20 (40.00)	22 (44.00)	23 (46.00)	25 (50.00)	**108 (43.20)**
Sometimes	21 (42.00)	21 (42.00)	18 (36.00)	19 (38.00)	19 (38.00)	**98 (39.20)**
Never	11 (22.00)	9 (18.00)	10 (20.00)	8 (16.00)	6 (12.00)	**44 (17.60)**
Total	50 (100.00)	50 (100.00)	50 (100.00)	50 (100.00)	50 (100.00)	**250 (100.00)**

Source: *Primary probe.*

Note: Figures in parentheses represent percentage.

It is evident from the above analysis Table7.16 that only 43.2 per cent of the respondents told that the Anganwadi centres regularly weight the children at Anganwadi centres. More than 39 per cent of the respondents told that Anganwadi centres sometimes weight the children, while 17.6 per cent of the respondents complained that the Anganwadi centres never weight the children at Anganwadi centres.

Picture No. 7(o)

Weighing of children in AWC at Nurpur and Pragpur

7.10.5 Preparation of Growth chart

After measuring the weight of children, it is the duty of AWW and helpers to prepare the growth chart of children. This growth chart helps the AWW to compare the growth of the children and to take necessary steps in case of negative growth. Data in this regard has been collected and illustrated in Table 7.17

Table 7.17: Awareness among Respondents regarding Preparation of Children Growth Chart

Growth Chart	Block					Total
	Dehra	Fatehpur	Indora	Nurpur	Paragpur	
Yes	3 (6.00)	2 (4.00)	2 (4.00)	5 (10.00)	2 (4.00)	**14 (5.60)**
No	5 (10.00)	5 (10.00)	3 (6.00)	2 (4.00)	4 (8.00)	**19 (7.60)**
Don't Know	42 (84.00)	43 (86.00)	45 (90.00)	43 (86.00)	44 (88.00)	**217 (86.80)**
Total	50 (100.00)	50 (100.00)	50 (100.00)	50 (100.00)	50 (100.00)	**250 (100.00)**

Source: *Primary probe.*

Note: Figures in parentheses represent percentage.

Figures in Table 7.17 indicates that only 5.6 per cent of the respondents were aware about the children growth chart. 7.6 per cent of the respondents responded that the Anganwadi workers do not prepare children growth chart, while majority (86.80 per cent) of the beneficiaries were not aware whether growth chart is prepared by the Anganwadi workers. This shows lack of awareness among beneficiaries regarding weighing concerns.

Picture No. 7(p)

Children along with their mothers at AWC at Dehra

7.11 Spreading Awareness about the Schemes for Adolescent Girls

The participation and involvement of people depends on their awareness and knowledge of the schemes. Government has started different schemes for adolescent girls. AWC are responsible for spreading awareness and educating the people about these schemes. Data has been collected from the sample respondents and presented in Table 7.18

Table 7.18: AWC are Spreading Awareness about Schemes for Adolescent Girls

Responses	Block					Total
	Dehra	Fatehpur	Indora	Nurpur	Paragpur	
Always	24 (48.00)	21 (42.00)	20 (40.00)	15 (30.00)	21 (42.00)	**101 (40.40)**
Sometimes	20 (40.00)	24 (48.00)	28 (56.00)	31 (62.00)	27 (54.00)	**130 (52.00)**
Not at All	6 (12.00)	5 (10.00)	2 (4.00)	4 (8.00)	2 (4.00)	**19 (7.60)**
Total	50 (100.00)	50 (100.00)	50 (100.00)	50 (100.00)	50 (100.00)	**250 (100.00)**

Source: *Primary Probe.*

Note: Figures in parentheses represent percentage.

It is evident from Table 7.18 that 52 per cent respondents were of the view that Anganwadi centres sometimes spread awareness about the schemes for adolescent girls. 40.40 per cent of the respondents reported that the Anganwadi workers always spread awareness about these schemes. While 7.60 per cent respondents told that Anganwadi centres not at all spread the awareness about the schemes for adolescent girls.

Thus, majority of 52 per cent respondents were of the view that Anganwadi centres sometimes spread awareness about the schemes for adolescent girls

Picture No. 7(q)

_Adolescent **girls along with children and their mothers at AWC, Indora**

7.11.1 Perception regarding services provided to Adolescent Girls

Different kinds of services are being provided to the adolescent girls by Anganwadi centers. These services include supplementary nutrition, health check-up, nutrition and health education, family life education, training on life skills etc. Data has been collected from the sample respondents and presented in Table 7.19

Responses tabulated in the Table 7.19 regarding different services provided by Anganwadi centres to adolescent girls. With regard to supplementary nutrition, more than 57 per cent respondents opined that the Anganwadi centres sometimes provides supplementary nutrition to the adolescent girls. 24.8 per cent of the respondents told that the Anganwadi centres always provide supplementary nutrition, while 17.6 per cent of the total respondents told that the Anganwadi centres never provide supplementary nutrition to the adolescent girls.

51.6 per cent respondents told that the Anganwadi workers sometimes provided nutrition and health education to the adolescent girls. 24 per cent of the respondents told that the

Table 7.19: Different Services Provided to Adolescent Girls by Anganwadi Centres

Response	Dehra	Fatehpur	Indora	Nurpur	Paragpur	Total
Provision of Supplementary Nutrition						
Always	12 (24.00)	14 (28.00)	13 (26.00)	14 (28.00)	9 (18.00)	**62 (24.80)**
Sometimes	30 (60.00)	24 (48.00)	31 (62.00)	25 (50.00)	34 (68.00)	**144 (57.60)**
Never	8 (16.00)	12 (24.00)	6 (12.00)	11 (22.00)	7 (14.00)	**44 (17.60)**
Total	50 (100.00)	50 (100.00)	50 (100.00)	50 (100.00)	50 (100.00)	**250 (100.00)**
Nutrition and Health Education						
Always	8 (16.00)	12 (24.00)	15 (30.00)	14 (28.00)	11 (22.00)	**60 (24.00)**
Sometimes	24 (48.00)	21 (42.00)	26 (52.00)	25 (50.00)	33 (66.00)	**129 (51.60)**
Never	18 (36.00)	17 (34.00)	9 (18.00)	11 (22.00)	6 (12.00)	**61 (24.40)**
Total	50 (100.00)	50 (100.00)	50 (100.00)	50 (100.00)	50 (100.00)	**250 (100.00)**
Health Check-up						
Always	11 (22.00)	9 (18.00)	8 (16.00)	10 (20.00)	8 (16.00)	**46 (18.40)**
Sometimes	23 (46.00)	24 (48.00)	19 (38.00)	25 (50.00)	22 (44.00)	**113 (45.20)**
Never	16 (32.00)	17 (34.00)	23 (46.00)	15 (30.00)	20 (40.00)	**91 (36.40)**
Total	50 (100.00)	50 (100.00)	50 (100.00)	50 (100.00)	50 (100.00)	**250 (100.00)**
Family Life Education						
Always	9 (18.00)	8 (16.00)	5 (10.00)	7 (14.00)	4 (8.00)	**33 (13.20)**
Sometimes	23 (46.00)	26 (52.00)	34 (68.00)	31 (62.00)	32 (64.00)	**146 (58.40)**
Never	18 (36.00)	16 (32.00)	11 (22.00)	12 (24.00)	14 (28.00)	**71 (28.40)**
Total	50 (100.00)	50 (100.00)	50 (100.00)	50 (100.00)	50 (100.00)	**250 (100.00)**
Training on Life Skills						
Always	1 (2.00)	0 (0.00)	2 (4.00)	0 (0.00)	1 (2.00)	**4 (1.60)**
Sometimes	39 (78.00)	42 (84.00)	38 (76.00)	37 (74.00)	41 (82.00)	**197 (78.80)**
Never	10 (20.00)	8 (16.00)	10 (20.00)	13 (26.00)	8 (16.00)	**49 (19.60)**
Total	50 (100.00)	50 (100.00)	50 (100.00)	50 (100.00)	50 (100.00)	**250 (100.00)**

Source: *Primary probe.*

Note: Figures in parentheses represent percentage.

Anganwadi centres always provides nutrition and health education, where as 24.40 per cent of the respondents told that the Anganwadi centre never provide serves of nutrition and health education to the adolescent girls.

45.2 per cent respondents revealed that the Anganwadi centres sometimes provides health check-up facilities to the adolescent girls. 18.4 per cent respondents told that the Anganwadi centres always provides health check-up facilities; while more than 36 per cent of the total respondents told that the Anganwadi centres never provide health check-up facilities to the adolescent girls.

Picture No. 7(r)

योजना • बोगस एंट्री की भी बनी रहती संभावना, सरकारी आंकड़ा होता है प्रभावित

हाईटेक होंगी आंगनबाड़ी कार्यकर्ता, सरकार देगी टैबले

Naukri.jobsoftoday.in

Adolescent Girls in Anganwadi Centres at Pragpur

More than 13 per cent respondents told that the Anganwadi workers always provide family life education to the adolescent girls. 58.40 per cent of the respondents depicted that the Anganwadi centres sometimes provide family life education, where as 28.4 per cent of the total respondents depicted that the Anganwadi centres never provided family life education to the adolescent girls. Only 1.6 per cent respondents told that the Anganwadi centres always provide training on life skills to the adolescent girls. More than 78 per cent of the respondents told that the Anganwadi centres sometimes provide training on life skills, while 19.6 per cent of the respondents told that the Anganwadi centres never provide training on life skills to the adolescent girls.

Thus it was observed that services are not provided effectively by Anganwadi centres always. It may be because of the fact that Anganwadies are staffed by workers and helpers whose services are not permanent. They belong to poor families and they are not professionally trained and over burdened with multiple activities. Digitalization of Anganwadi centres is the biggest challenge before these centres also.

Picture No. 7(s)

Adolescent girls attending camps for health and hygiene organized by AWC Indora

7.11.2 Awareness about adolescent Girls rights

It is the responsibility of AWCs to spread awareness among the local people about the rights of the girls, age of marriage, hygiene and sanitation. In this regard data has been collected and analysed in Table 7.20

Table 7.20 exhibits the responses of the respondents on spread of awareness by the Anganwadi centres regarding different issues of the girls. The response regarding awareness about rights of the girls spreaded by the Anganwadi centres shows that only 28.4 per cent of the respondents shared that the Anganwadi centres always spread the awareness about the rights of the girls, where as 41.6 per cent told that the Anganwadi centres sometimes spread the awareness in this regard. 30 per cent respondents told that the Anganwadi centres do not spread the awareness regarding rights of the girls at all.

Table-7.20: AWC Spreading Awareness regarding adolescent Girls Rights

Spreading Awareness about	Responses	Block					Total
		Dehra	Fatehpur	Indora	Nurpur	Paragpur	
Rights of the Girls	Always	15 (30.00)	14 (28.00)	18 (36.00)	11 (22.00)	13 (26.00)	**71 (28.40)**
	Sometimes	18 (36.00)	20 (40.00)	19 (38.00)	25 (50.00)	22 (44.00)	**104 (41.60)**
	Not at all	17 (34.00)	16 (32.00)	13 (26.00)	14 (28.00)	15 (30.00)	**75 (30.00)**
	Total	50 (100.00)	50 (100.00)	50 (100.00)	50 (100.00)	50 (100.00)	**250 (100.00**
Age of Marriage	Always	10 (20.00)	12 (24.00)	9 (18.00)	9 (18.00)	10 (20.00)	**50 (20.00)**
	Sometimes	18 (36.00)	20 (40.00)	24 (48.00)	26 (52.00)	27 (54.00)	**115 (46.00)**
	Not at all	22 (44.00)	18 (36.00)	17 (34.00)	15 (30.00)	13 (26.00)	**85 (34.00)**
	Total	50 (100.00)	50 (100.00)	50 (100.00)	50 (100.00)	50 (100.00)	**250 (100.00**
Hygiene & Sanitation	Always	10 (20.00)	12 (24.00)	8 (16.00)	8 (16.00)	9 (18.00)	**47 (18.80)**
	Sometimes	22 (44.00)	21 (42.00)	26 (52.00)	24 (48.00)	22 (44.00)	**115 (46.00)**
	Not at all	18 (36.00)	17 (34.00)	16 (32.00)	18 (36.00)	19 (38.00)	**88 (35.20)**
	Total	50 (100.00)	50 (100.00)	50 (100.00)	50 (100.00)	50 (100.00)	**250 (100.00**
Average Responses	Always	12 (23.33)	13 (25.33)	12 (23.33)	9 (18.67)	11 (21.33)	**56 (22.40)**
	Sometimes	19 (38.67)	20 (40.67)	23 (46.00)	25 (50.00)	24 (47.33)	**111 (44.53)**
	Not at all	19 (38.00)	17 (34.00)	15 (30.67)	16 (31.33)	16 (31.33)	**83 (33.07)**
	Total	50 (100.00)	50 (100.00)	50 (100.00)	50 (100.00)	50 (100.00)	**250 (100.00**

Source: *Primary probe.*

Note: Figures in parentheses represent percentage.

The response regarding awareness about age of marriage of girls spread by the Anganwadi centres shows that 20 per cent of the respondents told that the Anganwadi centres always spread awareness regarding age of marriage, where as 46 percent told that the Anganwadi centres sometimes spread the awareness in this regard. 34 per cent respondents told that the Anganwadi centres do not spread awareness regarding age of marriage of the girls at all.

Regarding awareness about hygiene and sanitation of the girls spread by the Anganwadi centres indicates that only 18.80 per cent of the respondents told that the Anganwadi centres always spread the awareness about hygiene and sanitation of the girls. 46 per cent told that the Anganwadi centres sometimes spread the awareness with this regard, while 35.2 per cent respondents shared that Anganwadi centres do not spread awareness regarding hygiene and sanitation rights of the girls at all.

7.12 Opinion about Supplementary Nutrition

Nutrition health of the beneficiaries of ICDS largely depends on the Anganwadi centres. These Anganwadi centres provides nutritious food to the children and other beneficiaries of the scheme. Along with this, there is a provision for supplementary nutrition to maintain good health of the beneficiaries. Hence data has been collected from the respondents and shown in Table 7.21

Table 7.21: Opinion about the Provision of Supplementary Nutrition

Source: Primary probe.

Response	Block					Total
	Dehra	Fatehpur	Indora	Nurpur	Paragpur	
Yes	30 (60.00)	28 (56.00)	34 (68.00)	32 (64.00)	27 (54.00)	**151 (60.40)**
No	20 (40.00)	22 (44.00)	16 (32.00)	18 (36.00)	23 (46.00)	**99 (39.60)**
Don't Know	0 (0.00)	0 (0.00)	0 (0.00)	0 (0.00)	0 (0.00)	**0 (0.00)**
Total	50 (100.00)	50 (100.00)	50 (100.00)	50 (100.00)	50 (100.00)	**250 (100.00)**

Note: Figures in parentheses represent percentage.

Figures in Table 7.21 show that out of total respondents 60.00 per cent in Dehra, 56.00 per cent in Fatehpur, 68.00 per cent in Indora, 64.00 per cent in Nurpur and 54.00 per cent or respondents in Paragpur block were of the opinion that they were getting supplementary nutrition from the AWCs. While on the other hand, 40.00 per cent in Dehra, 44.00 per cent in Fatehpur, 32.00 per cent in Indora, 36.00 per cent in Nurpur and 46.00 per cent of respondents in Paragpur block reported that AWCs did not provide supplementary nutrition. In overall, data depict that in majority of cases (60.40 per cent) beneficiaries were getting supplementary nutrition from the AWCs.

But those who did not get supplementary nutrition can't be ignored. Hence, they were asked the reason for not getting supplementary nutrition. The collected data has been analysed in Table 7.21 (a).

Table-7.21(a): Opinion about not taking benefit of Supplementary Nutrition Scheme

Reason	Block					Total
	Dehra	Fatehpur	Indora	Nurpur	Paragpur	
Not aware of the service	3 (15.00)	3 (13.64)	1 (6.25)	2 (11.11)	4 (17.39)	**13** **(13.13)**
not aware that I am eligible	0 (0.00)	1 (4.55)	0 (0.00)	0 (0.00)	0 (0.00)	**1** **(1.01)**
Supplementary food not available at AWC	6 (30.00)	5 (22.73)	5 (31.25)	4 (22.22)	7 (30.43)	**27** **(27.27)**
No body is there to go and take the food	2 (10.00)	1 (4.55)	2 (12.50)	1 (5.56)	2 (8.70)	**8** **(8.08)**
AWC is far off	2 (10.00)	2 (9.09)	0 (0.00)	0 (0.00)	0 (0.00)	**4** **(4.04)**
AWW don't tell when the food is distributed	6 (30.00)	10 (45.45)	7 (43.75)	11 (61.11)	9 (39.13)	**43** **(43.43)**
Quality of food is not good	1 (5.00)	0 (0.00)	1 (6.25)	0 (0.00)	1 (4.35)	**3** **(3.03)**
Total	20 (100.00)	22 (100.00)	16 (100.00)	18 (100.00)	23 (100.00)	**99** **(100.00)**

Source: *Primary probe.*

Note: Figures in parentheses represent percentage.

During data analysis it was found that 39.6 per cent respondents do not receive/take supplementary food. In Table

7.21 an attempt has been made to know the reason that why the respondents do not receive the supplementary nutrition. There were total 99 respondents out of 250 who do not receive/take supplementary nutrition. Out of total 99 respondents, 13.13 per cent depicted that they were not aware about the supplementary nutrition available at Anganwadi centres.

1 percent respondents told that unawareness about eligibility was the criteria for not taking benefit of this schemes. 27.27 per cent of the respondents replied that the supplementary nutrition was not available at Anganwadi centres. 8.08 per cent of the respondents told that there was no body at their house to go to the anganwadi centres to receive/take the supplementary nutrition. 4.04 per cent of the respondents told that the anganwadi centres were far off, that was the reason why they had not availed this facility.

43.43 per cent sample respondents revealed that the Anganwadi workers do not inform them about the distribution of supplementary nutrition, where as 3.03 per cent respondents told that the quality of the food available at Anganwadi cantres was not good, that is why they had not taken supplementary nutrition from Anganwadi centres.

7.13 AWW Visit to Beneficiaries' House

To share different kinds of information, tips and guidelines, AWWs should visit the beneficiaries house. Whether AWWs used to visit the beneficiaries house or not? Information regarding this has been analysed in Table 7.22.

It is evident from analysis of Table 7.22, more than 27 per cent beneficiaries opined that the Anganwadi workers always visited their houses. 42 per cent told that the Anganwadi workers sometimes visited their house. Whereas, 30.8 per cent of the respondents told that the Anganwadi workers had not visited their houses at all.

Thus majority of 42 percent respondents told that the Anganwadi workers sometimes visited their house.

Table 7.22: AWW's Visit to Beneficiaries House

Response	Block					Total
	Dehra	Fatehpur	Indora	Nurpur	Paragpur	
Always	15 (30.00)	11 (22.00)	18 (36.00)	11 (22.00)	13 (26.00)	**68** **(27.20)**
Sometimes	18 (36.00)	21 (42.00)	19 (38.00)	25 (50.00)	22 (44.00)	**105** **(42.00)**
Not at all	17 (34.00)	18 (36.00)	13 (26.00)	14 (28.00)	15 (30.00)	**77** **(30.80)**
Total	50 (100.00)	50 (100.00)	50 (100.00)	50 (100.00)	50 (100.00)	**250** **(100.00)**

Source: *Primary probe.*

Note: Figures in parentheses represent percentage.

Picture No. 7(t)

आंगनबाड़ी केंद्रों में दी जा रही हैं सुविधाएं

किशोरी-शक्ति योजना के तहत 30 किशोरियों को व्यवसायिक प्रशिक्षण दिया गया

Anganwadi workers Advising mother at her home regarding post natal care and breast feeding at Fatehpur

7.14 Precaution Related to Disease

There are so many diseases that affect the human beings. These diseases include diarrhea, dysentery, fever, cough/cold, rapid breathing, etc. Children are more prone to these diseases. Hence, it is the duty of the AWWs to advice the local residence about the precautions be taken by them to minimize the attack of these disease. The data related to this have been given in Table 7.23

Table 7.23: Precautions about the Diseases suggested by the Anganwadi Workers

Response	Block					Total
	Dehra	Fatehpur	Indora	Nurpur	Paragpur	
Always	5 (10.00)	8 (16.00)	2 (4.00)	7 (14.00)	1 (2.00)	**23 (9.20)**
Sometimes	45 (90.00)	42 (84.00)	48 (96.00)	43 (86.00)	49 (98.00)	**227 (90.80)**
Not at all	0 (0.00)	0 (0.00)	0 (0.00)	0 (0.00)	0 (0.00)	**0 (0.00)**
Total	50 (100.00)	50 (100.00)	50 (100.00)	50 (100.00)	50 (100.00)	**250 (100.00)**

Source: *Primary probe.*

Note: Figures in parentheses represent percentage.

Data related to precautions suggested by the anganwadi workers shows that out of total respondents, 90.8 per cent told that the anganwadi workers sometimes suggested precautions about the diseases. Whereas 9.2 per cent told that the anganwadi workers always suggested the precautions about the diseases.

Thus the results show that 90.8 per cent respondents told that anganwadi workers sometimes suggested precautions about the diseases.

7.15 Distribution of Iron Supplements

The deficiency of iron among adults and children is a widespread phenomenon. To end this deficiency, iron supplements are distributed among people by AWCs. The data has been collected from the sample respondents that whether these supplements reach the people or not. The collected data has been presented in Table 7.24

Table 7.24: Distribution of Iron Supplements to the People by Anganwadi Workers

Response	Block					Total
	Dehra	Fatehpur	Indora	Nurpur	Paragpur	
Always	2 (4.00)	0 (0.00)	5 (10.00)	8 (16.00)	3 (6.00)	**18 (7.20)**
Sometimes	48 (96.00)	50 (100.00)	45 (90.00)	42 (84.00)	47 (94.00)	**232 (92.80)**
Not at all	0 (0.00)	0 (0.00)	0 (0.00)	0 (0.00)	0 (0.00)	**0 (0.00)**
Total	50 (100.00)	50 (100.00)	50 (100.00)	50 (100.00)	50 (100.00)	**250 (100.00)**

***ource:** Primary probe.*

Note: Figures in parentheses represent percentage.

Table 7.24 depicts that 92.8 per cent of respondents opined that anganwadi workers sometimes distributed the iron supplements, whereas 7.2 per cent respondents opined that the anganwadi workers always distributed the iron supplements.

7.16 Opinion about the Behaviour of official of AWC

The provision and delivery of services under ICDS largely depends on the behaviour of official of AWCs as they directly interact with the women, children and people of the area under their AWCs. Hence, it is important to know the opinion of the beneficiaries about the behaviour of official AWWs of their area. The collected information has been analyzed in Table 7.25.

The data in the Table 7.25 depicts that out of total 250 respondents, 51.6 per cent respondents revealed that the behaviour of officials was very cooperative, whereas 46.4 percent respondents revealed that the behaviour of official was cooperative and mere 2 percent respondents revealed that the behaviour of official was not cooperative. Thus, the results in above analysis show that overall behaviour of the official of the AWCs was cooperative in nature.

Table-7.25: Opinion of Sample Beneficiaries about the Behaviour of official of AWCs

Behaviour	Block					Total
	Dehra	Fatehpur	Indora	Nurpur	Paragpur	
Very Cooperative	21 (42.00)	26 (52.00)	28 (56.00)	30 (60.00)	24 (48.00)	**129 (51.60)**
Cooperative	26 (52.00)	24 (48.00)	22 (44.00)	18 (36.00)	26 (52.00)	**116 (46.40)**
Not cooperative	3 (6.00)	0 (0.00)	0 (0.00)	2 (4.00)	0 (0.00)	**5 (2.00)**
Total	50 (100.00)	50 (100.00)	50 (100.00)	50 (100.00)	50 (100.00)	**250 (100.00)**

Source: *Primary probe.*

Note: Figures in parentheses represent percentage.

7.17 Opinion about the role of ICDS

ICDS aimed at enhancing the nutrition level of children as well as the adolescent girls through different kinds of services. It is important to analyze its role in different aspects. Thus, opinion of the sample beneficiaries has been obtained on the role of ICDs in improving the health of the children, imparting pre-school education, spreading awareness about girls education, girls/women rights, breastfeeding, immunization and inculcating sense of cooperation in the society. The collected data has been analysed in Table 7.26.

Table-7.26: Opinion about Role of ICDS

Block	To a large extent		To a some extent		Not at all		Total	
Role in improving the health of children								
	Frequency	%age	Frequency	%age	Frequency	%age	Frequency	%age
Dehra	24	48.00	16	32.00	10	20.00	50	100.00
Fatehpur	22	44.00	19	38.00	9	18.00	50	100.00
Indora	24	48.00	22	44.00	4	8.00	50	100.00
Nurpur	22	44.00	24	48.00	4	8.00	50	100.00
Paragpur	23	46.00	25	50.00	2	4.00	50	100.00
Total	**115**	**46.00**	**106**	**42.40**	**29**	**11.60**	**250**	**100.00**
Role in Imparting pre-school education								
Dehra	20	40.00	19	38.00	11	22.00	50	100.00
Fatehpur	19	38.00	21	42.00	10	20.00	50	100.00
Indora	20	40.00	22	44.00	8	16.00	50	100.00
Nurpur	19	38.00	24	48.00	7	14.00	50	100.00
Paragpur	22	44.00	20	40.00	8	16.00	50	100.00
Total	**100**	**40.00**	**106**	**42.40**	**44**	**17.60**	**250**	**100.00**
Role in spreading awareness about girl education								
Dehra	18	36.00	20	40.00	12	24.00	50	100.00
Fatehpur	17	34.00	19	38.00	14	28.00	50	100.00
Indora	18	36.00	18	36.00	14	28.00	50	100.00
Nurpur	19	38.00	18	36.00	13	26.00	50	100.00
Paragpur	17	34.00	19	38.00	14	28.00	50	100.00
Total	**89**	**35.60**	**94**	**37.60**	**67**	**26.80**	**250**	**100.00**
Role in Spreading awareness about girls/women rights								
Dehra	15	30.00	19	38.00	16	32.00	50	100.00
Fatehpur	17	34.00	17	34.00	16	32.00	50	100.00
Indora	19	38.00	20	40.00	11	22.00	50	100.00
Nurpur	18	36.00	19	38.00	13	26.00	50	100.00
Paragpur	18	36.00	21	42.00	11	22.00	50	100.00
Total	**87**	**34.80**	**96**	**38.40**	**67**	**26.80**	**250**	**100.00**
Role in inculcating a sense of cooperation in society								
Dehra	11	22.00	18	36.00	21	42.00	50	100.00
Fatehpur	13	26.00	15	30.00	22	44.00	50	100.00
Indora	14	28.00	17	34.00	19	38.00	50	100.00
Nurpur	17	34.00	19	38.00	14	28.00	50	100.00
Paragpur	16	32.00	18	36.00	16	32.00	50	100.00
Total	**71**	**28.40**	**87**	**34.80**	**92**	**36.80**	**250**	**100.00**
Role in spreading awareness about breastfeeding among lactating mothers								
Dehra	35	70.00	14	28.00	1	2.00	50	100.00
Fatehpur	36	72.00	14	28.00	0	0.00	50	100.00
Indora	34	68.00	14	28.00	2	4.00	50	100.00
Nurpur	38	76.00	11	22.00	1	2.00	50	100.00
Paragpur	40	80.00	10	20.00	0	0.00	50	100.00
Total	**183**	**73.20**	**63**	**25.20**	**4**	**1.60**	**250**	**100.00**
Role in spreading awareness about immunization								
Dehra	38	76.00	12	24.00	0	0.00	50	100.00
Fatehpur	40	80.00	10	20.00	0	0.00	50	100.00
Indora	39	78.00	11	22.00	0	0.00	50	100.00
Nurpur	40	80.00	10	20.00	0	0.00	50	100.00
Paragpur	39	78.00	11	22.00	0	0.00	50	100.00
Total	**196**	**78.40**	**54**	**21.60**	**0**	**0.00**	**250**	**100.00**

The Table 7.26 reveals the opinion of the respondents on the role of ICDS on different indicators.46 per cent respondents opined that the Integrated Child Development Services improved the health of children effectively to a large extent. 42.4 per cent opined that the Integrated Child Development Services improved the health of children to some extent. While 11.6 per cent of the respondents opined that the Integrated Child Development Services had not improved the health of children at all.

40 per cent respondents opined that the Integrated Child Development Services improved the pre-school education of children to a large extent. 42.4 per cent opined that the Integrated Child Development Services improved the pre-education of children to some extent only. While 17.6 per cent of the respondents opined that the Integrated Child Development Services had not improved the pre-school education of children at all.

35.6 per cent respondents opined that the Integrated Child Development Services played effective role in spreading awareness about girls education to a large extent. 37.6 per cent opined that the Integrated Child Development Services played role in spreading awareness about girls' education to some extent. While 26.8 per cent of the respondents opined that the Integrated Child Development Services had not played role in spreading awareness about girl's education at all.

With regard to the awareness about girls/women rights 34.8 per cent respondents opined that the Integrated Child Development Services played effective role in spreading awareness about girls/women rights to a large extent. 38.4 per cent opined that the Integrated Child Development Services played effective role in spreading awareness about girls'/women rights to some extent. While 26.8 per cent of the respondents opined that the Integrated Child Development Services had not played effective role in spreading awareness about girls/women rights at all.

28.4 per cent respondents revealed that the Integrated Child Development Services played effective role in inculcating a sense of cooperation in society to a large extent. 34.8 per cent opined that the Integrated Child Development Services played effective role in inculcating a sense of cooperation in society to some extent whereas, 36.8 per cent of the respondents opined that the Integrated Child Development Services had not played effective role in inculcating a sense of cooperation in society at all.

73.2 per cent respondents opined that the Integrated Child Development Services effectively spreading awareness among lactating mothers regarding breastfeeding to a large extent. 25.24 per cent respondents opined that the Integrated Child Development Services effectively spreading awareness among lactating mothers about breastfeeding to some extent. While 1.6 per cent of the respondents opined that the Integrated Child Development Services had not played effective role in spreading awareness among lactating mothers regarding breastfeeding at all.

With regard to the awareness about immunization, 78.4 per cent respondents opined that the Integrated Child Development Services played effective role in spreading awareness about immunization to a large extent, whereas 21.6 per cent opined that the Integrated Child Development Services played effective role in spreading awareness about immunization to some extent.

Overall it was concluded by majority of respondents had feeding that role of ICDS in improving the health of the children, imparting pre-school education, spreading awareness about girl education, girls/women rights, breastfeeding, immunization and inculcating sense of cooperation in the society was effective in study area.

7.18 Opinion about the Working of AWC

All the services under ICDS is provided by the AWCs. The success and failure of the programme depends on the working of AWCs. It is important to know that how people rate the working of AWCs of their area Data in this regard has been shown in Table 7.27.

Table 7.27: Opinion about the Working of Anganwadi Centres

Working	Block					Total
	Dehra	Fatehpur	Indora	Nurpur	Paragpur	
Very good	19 (38.00)	20 (40.00)	21 (42.00)	22 (44.00)	23 (46.00)	**105 (42.00)**
good	23 (46.00)	23 (46.00)	24 (48.00)	21 (42.00)	22 (44.00)	**113 (45.20)**
Average	8 (16.00)	7 (14.00)	5 (10.00)	7 (14.00)	5 (10.00)	**32 (12.80)**
Poor	0 (0.00)	0 (0.00)	0 (0.00)	0 (0.00)	0 (0.00)	**0 (0.00)**
Very Poor	0 (0.00)	0 (0.00)	0 (0.00)	0 (0.00)	0 (0.00)	**0 (0.00)**
Total	50 (100.00)	50 (100.00)	50 (100.00)	50 (100.00)	50 (100.00)	**250 (100.00)**

Source: Primary probe.

Note: Figures in parentheses represent percentage.

Data in the above Table indicates that 42 per cent respondents opined that the Agnanwadi centres were working very good, whereas, 45.2 per cent opined that the centers were working good. 12.8 per cent of the respondents opined that the working of the Anganwadi centres was average. There was no response regarding poor and very poor working of the Anganwadi workers in Himachal Pradesh.

Overall it was analysed that majority of 45.2 per cent opined that the centers were working satisfactory. 12.8 per cent of the respondents opined that the working of the Anganwadi centers was average thus working of Aanganwadi work was satisfactory.

Conclusion

Perception of 250 beneficiaries who were beneficiaries under ICDS programmes were discussed and analysed in present Chapter. 86 per cent of beneficiaries had opinion that information about immunization scheme always given to them by Anganwadi centres. Majority of 85.20 per cent beneficiaries told that an immunization is conducted at Health Sub-Centres Majority of 71.2 per cent respondents had opinion that supplementary nutrition provided to pregnant women was sufficient to a large extent. Majority of 78.40 per cent of respondents were of the opinion that Anganwadi workers always provides advice to the pregnant women regarding delivery care 86 per cent of the respondents opined that they were always given advice regarding nutrition and health by the Anganwadi workers. 91.60 per cent of the respondents told that the Anganwadi workers always advise them for family planning and birth place.58.8 per cent beneficiaries were satisfied to a some extent with the supplementary nutrition during lactation. Majority of 52 per cent respondents were of the view that Anganwadi centres sometimes spread awareness about the schemes for adolescent girls, 90.8 per cent respondents had perception that the Anganwadi workers sometimes suggested precautions about the diseases. 92.8 per cent of respondents opined that anganwadi workers sometimes distributed the iron supplements. Overall it was analysed that majority of 45.2 percent opined that the centres were working satisfactory. Overall during study it was analysed that majority of beneficiaries recognized the services given by AWCs were satisfactory and were not in the category of very good centre.

8

CONCLUSIONS AND SUGGESTIONS

Children are like buds in a garden and should be carefully and lovingly nurtured, as they are the future of the nation and the citizens of tomorrow. Only through right education can a better order of society be built up.

Jawaharlal Nehru

The Constitution of our country gives highest priority to the safety and well-being of children. Children constitute 39 per cent of the population of India (Census 2011). It has been widely accepted by policy makers of our country that investments made for the survival, education, protection and overall well-being of children helps in breaking the inter generational cycle of poverty and ensuring an inclusive growth for the country. In a vast country like India, children face multiple vulnerabilities in terms of accessing quality healthcare, education and child safety and protection services. Moreover, new challenges are emerging every day, such as harassment and exploitation of children, climate change natural and man-made disasters which add to vulnerability of children. The Ministry of Women and Child Development has taken many initiatives to ensure safety and well-being of children.

In quest of the National Policy for Children and India's commitment to provisions enshrined in the Directive Principles of the Constitution, Integrated Child Development Services Programme was introduced in 33 projects on 2nd October 1975 in Himachal Pradesh. During Sixth and Seventh Plan period, more projects were sanctioned to the State. In 1995-96 during universalization phase of the scheme, the Government of India sanctioned 29 new ICDS projects. Four new ICDS projects, namely, Shimla (urban), Haroli, Tauni Devi and Sulah were sanctioned during 2005-06. Thereafter, during 2009-10, two new projects at Dharamshala and Nankhari were sanctioned. Today the scheme is operating in 78 ICDS projects. Out of these 70 projects comes in the arena of Rural Projects, one in Urban Projects and remaining seven in Tribal Projects.

Presently Integrated Child Development Services (ICDS) programme, is being implemented in all Developmental Blocks of the State through 78 ICDS projects. The department is providing supplementary nutrition, nutrition, and health education' immunization, health check-ups referred services and non-formal pre-school education through ICDS in Himachal Pradesh.

ICDS is a Centrally-sponsored Scheme implemented through the State Governments/UT Administrations. Prior to 2005-06, 100 per cent financial assistance for inputs other than supplementary nutrition, which the States were required to provide out of their own resources, was being provided by the Government of India. Since many States were not providing adequately for supplementary nutrition in view of resource constraints, it was decided in 2005-06 to support to States up to 50 per cent of the financial norms or to support 50 per cent of expenditure incurred by them on supplementary nutrition, whichever is less from the financial year 2009-10, Government of India has modified the funding pattern of ICDS between Centre and States. The sharing pattern of supplementary nutrition in respect of North-eastern States between Centre and States has been changed from 50:50 to 90:10 ratios. So far as other States and UTs, the existing sharing pattern of 50:50 continues still now. However, for all other components of ICDS, the ratio has been modified to 90:10 (100 per cent Central Assistance earlier).

The programme make an attempt toward a holistic child health comprising health, nutrition, and education components for pregnant women, lactating mothers, and children less than six years of age. The programme is implemented through a network of community- level Anganwadi Centres. The range of services targeted at young children and their mothers for growth monitoring, immunization, health check-ups and supplementary feeding, as well as nutrition and health education to improve the childcare and feeding practices that mothers adopt. Pre-school education is provided to children between three and six years of age. This research is completed in eight chapter.

First Chapter discusses in detail about demographic profile of Children & throws light on concept of Child welfare status of children in India & evolution of ICDS Programme is discussed in India & Himachal Pradesh. This chapter also discussed in detail the literature relating to topic. Various books, magazine, article etc. were reviewed before study. It also discussed about the importance of study, objective of study, hypothesis, research methodology and chapterization in the end of chapter.

Second Chapter discusses in detail about Organization set up .The analysis of organizational structure clearly reveals that for the achievement of goals and objectives of Integrated Child Development Services a well-organized structure has been established both at the Center & State level. At the central level Ministry of women and Child development is responsible for the implementation of Integrated Child Development Services in the Country. The Department of Women and Child Development was set up in the year 1985 as a part of the Ministry of Human Resource Development to give the much needed impetus to the holistic development of women and children in India. In the year 2006, the Department has been upgraded to a Ministry of Women & Child Development. In Himachal Pradesh Department of Social Justice and Empowerment has the overall responsibility of implementing Integrated Child Development Services. It works for the socio-economic development of the women, child and weaker sections of the society. Himachal Pradesh has shown its concern for the welfare of children through setting a new directorate of Women and Child Development. All the matters concerning socio-economic development and protection are given to this directorate. It implements all the programmes concerning child development and protection and women empowerment. In other words, it has the overall responsibility of implementation and monitoring of ICDS in the state. Then there is ICDS team comprising of Child Development and Project Officer (CDPO), Assistant Child Development and Project Officer (ACDPO), Supervisors, Anganwadi Workers and Angnawadi Helpers who are engaged in providing adequate services to women and children to ensure their physical, mental and social development. These services are being provided through a network of Aanganwadi centres spread throughout the State.

Third Chapter examined Constitutional provisions, legislative measures, Policies & Programmes for Child welfare in India. Constitutional provisions has been made for child welfare ,various legislative provisions has been made & various policies, programmes has been started for child protection and welfare and various laws has been passed for child protection .All these initiatives are discussed in detail in Himachal Pradesh. Government of Himachal Pradesh has been implementing various child development, child welfare and child protection programmes and schemes in the state. These include Integrated Child Development Services, Supplementary Nutrition Programmes, Beti Hai Anmol scheme, Kishori Shakti Yojana, Rajiv Gandhi Scheme for Empowerment of Adolescent Girls-SABLA, Mother Teressa Asahaya Matri Sambal Yojana, Bal Balika Suraksha Yojana, Balwadis, Atal Ashirwad Yojna etc. Integrated Child Development Services is an important scheme being implemented by the Government of Himachal Pradesh. It represents one of the world's largest and most unique programmes for early childhood development.

Fourth Chapter throws light on working of ICDS in Himachal. ICDS approaches a holistic child health comprising health, nutrition, and education elements for pregnant ladies, wet mothers, and children up to six years. The programme is enforced through a network of community-level Anganwadi Centres. The variety of services targeted at young children and their mothers for growth observations, immunisation, health check-ups, supplementary feeding, nutrition and health education Pre-school education is provided to children between 3 and 6 years of age. In the present Chapter working of ICDS in Himachal Pradesh and Kangra District is discussed in detail.

Fifth Chapter assesses the impact and implementation of ICDS programme, a sample of 350 respondents was selected. The sample respondents for the present study were 250 ICDS beneficiaries and 100 Anganwadi Workers. An attempt has been made in the present chapter to analyse the socio-economic background of the sample respondents with the help of some indicators such as, gender, age, marital status, size of family, family status, educational attainment, social classification, income etc.

Sixth Chapter analyses the perception of Anganwadi workers about ICDS .Perception of 100 Anganwadi workers regarding the working of ICDS is discussed in detail in this chapter. Informal interview of officials were also taken in order to gather various information pertaining to ICDS in study area.

Seventh Chapter analyses the perception of beneficiaries of ICDS. Perception of 250 beneficiaries who were beneficiaries under ICDS programmes were discussed and analysed in the present Chapter.

Eight Chapter discusses in detail about findings of study & concludes by giving concrete suggestions for the effective functioning of ICDS in Himachal Pradesh

On the basis of above findings following Hypothesis were proved

Hypotheses

1. Integrated Child Development Services has not been implemented as per its spirit.
2. There is a lack of awareness among the people about the ICDS
3. There is a lack of proper infrastructure& facilities in the anganwadi centres.
4. Proper training is not imparted to anganwadi workers related to the ICDS objectives.
5. Community participation is not effective at ICDS level.
6. There is lack of proper monitoring and supervision of Anganwadi centres.

On the basis of study following findings were drawn

Findings regarding working of Aanganwari Centres

- Decreasing trend in the number of beneficiaries in Supplementary Nutrition Programme for 0-3 Years of Age Children, and also in number of beneficiaries (3-6 years children) of supplementary nutrition programmes run by ICDS in the past five years is not a healthy sign & it shows that more beneficiaries are not interested to come to ICDS for getting benefit of these services.
- Number of Pregnant and lactating mothers as beneficiaries under ICDS programme also shows decreasing trend in Himachal Pradesh. This decreasing trend shows that efforts need to be done to motivate pregnant and lactating mothers in an effective way so that problems of malnutrition and stunted growth can be tackled effectively in Himachal Pradesh.

Findings regarding Aanganwari Workers

- 23 percent of Aanganwadi workers complained that there were no building and water facilities in Anganwadi centres. Most of the Anganwadi centres were running on rented houses.
- Due to unavailability of drinking water the Anganwadi workers carry drinking water either from their own house or from public water sources. It was indeed very surprising that when the Swachh Bharat Abhiyan is being carried out in full swing in the whole country that 36 per cent of the Anganwadi centres had no toilets of their own and they send the children to surrounding houses by making request to them. 22 per cent of the Anganwadi centres had no electricity connections and 53 per cent of Anganwadi centres were not furnished with adequate furniture. Thus without basic facilities the idea of making the Anganwadi centres ICT linked and high-tech appears to be far-fetched vision in Kangra district of Himachal Pradesh.
- Availability of weighing machine at the AWCs ensures timely and periodic weighing of children and preparation of growth chart. In this regard, respondents told that they had weighing machine in the AWC.
- It was also observed through interaction that Knowledge of Anganwadi workers regarding revised norms for calories and protein for beneficiaries was found to be poor. Thus regular training supportive environment, adequate facilities and infrastructure is required in all the Anganwadi centre of Himachal Pradesh.
- It was Analysed through study that 32 per cent Anganwadi workers complained that due to absence of separate Kitchen and cooking facilities they had to face problems, 29 per cent complained regarding irregular & inadequate supply of cooking material, 31

per cent grumbled due to lack of storage facility & fuel problems.19 per cent complained regarding poor quality of food material, 33 per cent told there was financial constraint in implementation of Programme & 26 per cent complained regarding transportation problem

- It was observed that some of the AWWs did not know how to fill the registers and prepare reports. Hence, on the basis of personal observation it can be concluded that AWWs need more general and managerial training specific to ICDS programmes in study area.
- Majority of respondents had perception that cooperation and coordination from PHCs to ICDS was good enough, but the cooperation and coordination from gram panchayats was not encouraging one.
- Majority of respondents were well versed and aware about the services provided through their ICDS.
- .Majority of Aanganwadi workers had perception that their officials and supervisors educate them to some extent only.
- Majority of Aanganwadi workers had perception that they were overburdened with multiple roles and salary given to them is not proportionate to their workload.
- Recent Government of Himachal Pradesh orders to open Pre nursery schools in Government schools which has created tremors of insecurity among Aanganwari workers and most of Anganwari workers had gone on strike in Himachal as most of them had apprehension that this move can threaten their job security. That's why they were protesting this move of Government of Himachal Pradesh as a threat to their job security in coming time ahead.

Findings regarding Beneficiaries

- Majority of 86 per cent beneficiaries had opinion that information about immunization scheme always given to them by Anganwadi centres. It may be the reason that infant mortality rate has been reduced in Himachal Pradesh. Majority of 85.20 per cent beneficiaries shared information that immunizations were conducted at Health Sub-Centers.
- Majority of 71.2 per cent respondents had opinion that supplementary nutrition provided to pregnant women to a large extent and were satisfied with it. Majority of 78.40 per cent of respondents were of the opinion that Anganwadi workers always provide advice to the pregnant women regarding delivery care.
- Majority of 91.60 per cent of the respondents told that the Anganwadi workers always advised them for family planning and birth place.
- Majority of 86 per cent of the respondents opined that they were always given advice regarding nutrition and health by the Anganwadi workers.
- Majority of 58.8 percent beneficiaries were satisfied to some extent only with the supplementary nutrition during lactation, thus need was felt to improve supplementary nutrition during lactation to large masses.
- It was found that 36 per cent beneficiaries rate Advice for Post-Natal Care and Breastfeeding Practices as satisfactory, while 21.2 per cent of the sample beneficiaries had perception that advice for Post-Natal Care and Breastfeeding Practices was not satisfactory.
- Majority of 90.8 per cent respondents had perception that the Anganwadi workers sometimes suggested precautions about the diseases. Majority of 92.8 per

cent of respondents opined that Anganwadi workers sometimes distributed the iron supplements.

- It was found that 28.4 per cent respondents complained that health checkups are not organized at all. Majority of 52.8 per cent respondents had perception that the Anganwadi centres sometimes conduct the health check-up of the children at Anganwadi centres, It may be because of financial constraint and infrastructure handicaps that health checkups are not organized frequently by Anganwadi centres as required, this may affect the health of mother and children.
- Majority of 48.8 per cent sample beneficiaries rated the quality of cooked food served at Anganwadi centres as average. The analysis shows that there is a need to improve the quality of cooked food, so that the beneficiary children can get quality food.
- Majority of 67 per cent sample respondents opined that the Anganwadi centres provide food to some extent only.
- Majority of the beneficiaries respondents shared their perception that attendance of children visiting Anganwadi centres is a regular feature to maintain record and track the number of children visiting to Anganwadi centres.
- 42 per cent beneficiaries respondents opined that the Anganwadi workers sometimes visited their house to give them various important information.
- 39 per cent of the respondents told that Anganwadi centres sometimes weight the children, while 17.6 per cent of the respondents complained that the Anganwadi centres never weight the children at Anganwadi centres.
- Thus it was observed that services were not provided effectively by Anganwadi centres always. It may be

because of the fact that Anganwadies are under staffed by workers and helpers whose services are not even permanent. They belong to poor families. They are not professionally trained and overburdened with multiple activities. Digitalization of Anganwadi centres is the biggest challenge before these centres.

- Majority of beneficiaries had perception that overall behaviour of the Anganwadi workers and helpers was of cooperative in nature.
- Majority of 52 per cent respondents were of the view that Anganwadi centres sometimes spread awareness about the schemes for adolescent girls.
- Overall it was concluded by majority of respondents that role of ICDS in improving the health of the children, imparting pre-school education, spreading awareness about girl education, girls/women rights, breastfeeding, immunization and inculcating sense of cooperation in the society was satisfactory in study area.
- Majority of AWWs were not satisfied with their Salary & service conditions. Recent Government of Himachal Pradesh order to open Pre nursery schools in Government schools has also created tremors of insecurity among Anganwari workers and most of Anganwari workers had gone on strike in Himachal as they were protesting this move of Government of Himachal Pradesh as a threat to their job security and status in coming time ahead.
- Majority of 45.2 per cent beneficiaries had perception that the Aanganwadi centres were working satisfactorily to some extent in Himachal Pradesh. On the basis of above findings following suggestions are given for effective functioning of Aanganwadi Centres in Himachal Pradesh

Suggestions

- Aanganwadi centre should have their own buildings. The buildings for AWCs should be constructed with all required facilities, such as, toilet, drinking water, electricity, sitting facility etc so that they can effectively give their services in their areas.
- Construction of AWC has been notified as a permissible activity under Mahatma Gandhi National Rural Employment Guarantee Act (MNREGA). The construction of AWC buildings can be taken up in convergence with MNREGA. Government of Himachal Pradesh Should give direction to concerned Department to take special initiative on large scale to construct Anganwari centres under MGNREGA initiative in Himachal Pradesh.
- As part of the strengthening and restructuring the ICDS Scheme, the government approved a provision of construction of '200,000/- Anganwadi centre buildings at a cost of '450,000/- per unit during XII Plan period in a phased manner with cost sharing ratio of 75:25 between centre and states (other than the NER, where it will be at 90:10). On similar guidelines of North east states Centre government should give financial assistance to hilly areas of Himachal Pradesh for construction of Aanganwadi Centres.
- Department of Women & child should come forward to procure land for setting up Aanganwadi centres buildings. Rural Development infrastructure fund should also give financial assistance for construction of Aanganwadi centres in Himachal Pradesh.
- As per direction of secretary Ministry of Women & Child to Government of Himachal Pradesh in 2017 as per video conferencing held on 6.6.2017 State government of Himachal Pradesh was also advised to open Anganwadi Centres in those schools where there

are vacant rooms and advised them to contact education Department in this regard also take initiative in this direction till Aanganwadi centres have their own building.

- M. L.A. and M.P. from respective areas from respective M.L.A. fund & M.P. Local area fund should give fund generously for the construction of Aanganwadi centres.
- More & More Aanganwadi Centres should be upgraded as model centres in Himachal Pradesh for providing quality supplementary diets and other services for children, adolescent girls, pregnant and lactating mothers. These Model Aanganwadi Centres should have all basic amenties like Baal Sulabh Sauchalaya, adequate toys to play, material for informal education, proper seating arrangement, clean drinking water and adequate infrastructure.
- Adequate space should be provided to accommodate the enrolled children and the Centres should be located at a convenient and hygiene friendly area of the locality.
- AWC accommodation should be equipped with proper facilities, sanitation facilities, safe drinking water, toilets, sufficient medicines, electricity/power supply, playing instruments/toys, etc. The centres should be protected with boundary walls or barbed wires for the safety concern also.
- Himachal Government should come forward to tap the funds for providing toilet and drinking water facilities in left out AWCs from Swachchh Bharat Mission, Ministries of Panchayati Raj and Drinking Water & Sanitation.
- Environment of Anganwadi Centres should be made friendly and quality services must be provided to beneficiaries.

- Majority of Panchayat leaders are not fully aware of ICDS services. More awareness of all the services needs to be generated among local leaders to provide dynamism to Panchayats & improve their vibrancy & efficiency.
- ICDS functionaries should approach Panchayat representative for any need and assistance & services of ICDS should be utilized to meet the interest of community with assistance & collaboration of Panchayats.
- Involvement of academicians, NGO's CBO's, social workers and retired persons, for organizing awareness camps regarding services provided by ICDS should be encouraged.
- Women, Mahila mandals, Self-help groups should also be encouraged to participate in activities of ICDS.
- More & more women of self help groups of surrounding area should be engaged in making ready to eat food in Aanganwadi centres.
- Ready to eat food in all Aanganwadi centres should be checked regularly by Mahila mandals & self Help groups of surroundings area.
- Anganwadi workers should take interest in all the activities of the project. Honorarium to Anganwadi worekrs under the scheme is not sufficient and should be increased.
- In Budget presented in Himachal Legislative assembly on 9th February 2019 although government has increased the honorarium of Anganwadi workers to Rs.6500 is good initiative taken in this direction.
- All sanctioned Posts of supervisors and CDPOs should be filled up on priority basis so that proper supervision

and checking of Anganwadi centres should be done by them.

- Periodic monitoring of Anganwadi should be evolved so that on Anganwadi effective check and control could be maintained. Gram panchayats should check the working of Anganwadi centres running in their respective gram Panchayat area.
- Training should be given to Anganwadi workers and helper. There is a need to give training to the AWWs in the holistic care of children by qualified trainers from government and non-government organizations. To meet needs of each mother and infant they should receive appropriate advice and motivation during first six to eight weeks to empower mothers and promote their physiological and emotional health. Proper training must be imparted to Anganwadi workers regarding maternal health infant feeding and infant health so that healthy relation between mother and child can be nurtured for the progress of society as well as of the nation.
- Community should be sensitized on reproductive health issues to ensure better coordination from the community.
- Awareness camps should be organized to educate masses about the importance of immunization, health and nutrition.
- Nutrition and health education is very important component of the ICDS in educating and involving communities and hence it should gain a focus for interventions at the AWCs. The AWCs should be supported by supervisors and others in organizing and educating mothers.
- All children in the AWC should be offered a balanced and nutritious diet depending upon how old they are.

All children coming to the AWC should get snacks as well as freshly cooked culturally appropriate hot meals. Regular and proper monitoring of the growth of children is critical for prevention and ensuring early detection of child malnutrition. The weight of children should be recorded every month and height every year. This information along with other developmental milestones should be shared in monthly meetings with parents.

- The AWC should play pivotal role in the implementation of the ICDS. Besides serving as a safe, child-friendly day-long childcare and early childhood education centre, the AWC should also become an active centre for all women-and-child related activities.
- Filling out several registers and forms is one aspect of the workload of Aanganwari workers. If AWCs are to run as fully functional day-care and education centres for children, then there has to be a ban on AWWs being drawn in to perform miscellaneous tasks for other departments.
- The success of ICDS will depend largely on the motivation and competencies of AWWs and other functionaries associated with it. In this case, flexibility should be given to state and local government to evolve method suitable to local needs.
- Broad national guidelines and norms should be sincerely implemented in Himachal Pradesh also for effective functioning of ICDS Centres
- Developing effective national system of information, education and communication on care practices is essential for the effective functioning of ICDS.
- Adequate funds should be made available for the expanded activities of the AWCs envisaged under the ICDS.

- Existing administrative and financial arrangements governing ICDS should be reviewed and changes should be incorporated according to local demands and need in order to make them more efficient.
- Well-defined tangible and easy-to-measure performance indicators should be developed for the different components of ICDS and performance index of ICDS should be mandatory on the basis of these indicators.
- Training of the Anganwari workers should be strictly according to instructions issued by Government of India in 2017. E-training to Anganwari workers should be given from time to time so that they can perform efficiently & effectively with mobile app recently launched for Aanganwari workers of Himachal Pradesh..
- NGOs should also be involved in imparting training to Anganwari workers in Himachal Pradesh as per instructions issued by Niti Ayog in this Direction.
- Regular training should be provided to AWC workers, helpers and their supervisors. They should get refresher training to handle registers and other records independently and efficiently from time to time.
- Regular meetings of State Level Monitoring & Review Committee, District Level Monitoring & Review Committee, Block Level Monitoring Committee and Anganwadi Monitoring & Support Committee should be convened regularly in Himachal Pradesh. While convening these meetings it may be ensured that public representatives attend the meetings.
- National guidelines should be developed by Government of India for the engagement of NGOs and other community-based organizations in the delivery of ICDS.

- It is important that AWCs are seen as belonging to women in the community, and not as Central government-run feeding programme centeres so that more beneficiaries can come forward to take benefit of these centres.
- Adequate number of workers should be engaged in each AWC. AWC workers should not be deployed for other miscellaneous works. Practice of directing Aanganwari workers to attend Government functions just in order to showcase strength of audience need to be discouraged in Himachal Pradesh so that their precious time can be used for community welfare.
- Doctors should visit AWCs regularly. AWCs should keep complete health records of all the children enrolled with them. At present, AWCs are required to maintain around 30 registers which appears to be too many. Review should be carried out to reduce/minimize this number.
- The mothers of the malnourished children should be provided regular special counseling.
- On the spot monitoring and supervision of centers should be done by the Block and District level Officers regularly.
- Government should take initiate to solve insecurity threat among Anganwari workers regarding opening of pre nursery classes in Government schools & should not abruptly closes pre nursely classes in ICDS .
- Food provided at AWCs should be of good quality and nutrition. Enhancement of financial norms may increase the quality of AWC food. Provision of LPG gas for cooking purpose may also be supplied to every AWC on regular basis.
- It was found that different initiative has been taken by Government to improve pay anomalies & financial

conditions of Anganwari workers. As per new revised Guidelines of government of Himachal Pradesh & the Notification of Government of Himachal Pradesh Dated 29 February, 2016, Honorarium of Aanganwari worker is Rs. 3450/ month, Mini Anganwari worker is '2625/- month & of Aanganwari Helper is '1800/ month. As per announcement of Prime minister of India Aanganwari workers in October 2018 who drew an honorarium of '3000/- will now get '4500/- and those who used to get '2200/- will get '3,500/-. The honorarium of Anganwadi helpers will be hiked from '1500/- to '2500/-. Prime Minister of India in October, 2018 announced that Anganwadi workers & helpers using techniques such as common application software (ICDS-CAS) would get additional incentive. The incentive ranging from '250/- to '500/- would be based on performance. As per order of Ministry of Women & Child Development decided that Anganwadi Workers (AWWs)/Anganwadi Helpers under the: Anganwadi Services (Umbrella ICDS Scheme) in the age group of 18-50 years as on 1st June, 2017 would be covered under the Pradhan Mantri Jeevan Jyoti Bima Yojana (PMJJBY) for life cover and those in the age group of 18-59 years as on 1st June, 2017 would be covered under the Pradhan Mantri Suraksha Bima Yojana (PMSBY) for accidental cover. The Government had formulated scheme in 2000-2001 to award Anganwari at National & State level to motivate their exemplary services in ICDS. Earlier award money was '25,000/- from 2018 this award money was increased to '50.000/- rupees and citation at Centre level while '10,000/- are given for the State level award. Thus it can be analysed that government has taken various initiatives for motivation of Aanganwari workers yet their expectations need to be fulfilled thus much more initiatives can be taken in this direction.

- District Administration of Kangra has started an innovative campaign with an aim to provide a better environment for education for the children by developing an ideal system in Anganwadi centres. Under this, all the sub-magistrates, including the senior officials of the district administration, will visit the Anganwadi center at least once a month in their respective sub-divisions. Not only that, he will spend some time there and know their problems and ensure their solution. Officials will also check the quality of meal served to the children by consuming themselves this initiative is healthy and should be continued in all Anganwadi centres of Himachal Pradesh.

- Training in pre-schooling education should be given to AWW so that they could work in better way in imparting pre-school education to the children in their Anganwadi centres.
- So far as early childhood care and pre-school education is concerned, there is a need to improve the skills of the AWWs on the concepts and approaches of the joyful learning (play-way methods). Adequate provisions should be made for procurement of relevant teaching and learning aids. Provisions should also be made for suitable accommodation along with matting and heating provisions at each AWC. There is also a need to develop and strengthen coordination with the local primary schools to seek their support and especially with the primary wing of the ZEO monitoring purposes.

ICDS are playing crucial role in strengthening the foundation of the country, ensuring health and wellbeing of newborn, ensuring nutritional standards and maintaining hygiene and cleanliness. If these suggestions are earnestly implemented ICDS can perform their functions with more vigour & efficiency.

BIBLIOGRAPHY

Books

Ahluwalia, M.S. (1993), History of Himachal Pradesh (2nd ed.), Intellectual Publishing House, New Delhi.

Ahuja, K.K. (1988), Advanced Personnel Management, Kalayani Publishers, New Delhi.

Balokhra, Jag Mohan (2010), The Wonderland Himachal Pradesh: An Encyclopedia on the State of Western Himalayas, H.G. Publications, New Delhi.

Banu, Zenab (2001), *Women Empowerment and Gender Issues*, New Delhi: Kanishka Publishers & Distributors.

Bhardwaj, Ramesh Kumar (1996), "Women Development Programmes" in Mohinder Singh (eds.). Social Policy and Administration, New Delhi: M.D, Publication Pvt. Ltd.

Chandra, Suman K. and Reddy, V. Gang (2007), *Segmented labour Market for Children- Is it a demand side Creation? A case Study of Industry in Makapur.*

Chaudhry, Minakshi (2006) Himachal: A complete Guide to the Land of Gods, Rupa and Company, New Delhi.

Chowdhary, D. Paul (1979), Social Welfare Administration, New Delhi: Atma Ram & Sons.

Dwivedi, Rishi Muni, "Poverty and Development Pogrammes in India", New Century Publications, New Delhi, 2005.

Gokhale, Neela, & Prasad, Vaishali, "Women in 21st Century", Shree Publishers and Distributors, New Delhi, 2007.

Hall, Richard H. (1972), Organization: Structure and Process, Prentice Hall, Inc., Englewood Cliffs, New Jersey.

Jayapalan, N. (1972), *Public Administration*, New Delhi: Atlantic Publishers and Distributors, 2000.

Jayapalan, N. (2000) Public Administration, Atlantic Publishers and Distributors, New Delhi.

Joshi, N.C. (September 2008), "Women Welfare-A Priority on the Government's Agenda", *Kurukshetra*.

Jreat, Manoj (2004), Tourism in Himachal Pradesh, Indus Publishing Company, New Delhi.

Jreat, Manoj (2006), Geography of Himachal Pradesh, Indus Publishing Company, New Delhi.

Katare, P.M., and Barik, B.C., "Development, Deprivation and Human Rights Violation", Rawat Publications, New Delhi, 2002.

Kaul, Jawahar L., "Human Rights: Issue and Perspective", Regency Publishers, New Delhi, 1995.

Khalakdina, M., "Evaluation of Impact of ICDS Services on the beneficiaries in the selected blocks of Himachal Pradesh", unpublished MSC thesis. Department of Child Development, Himachal Pradesh.

Kohli, A.S., "Human Rights and Social Work: Issues, Challenges and Response", Kanishka Publishers, Distributors, New Delhi, 2004.

Krishna, Sumi, ed., 'Women's Livelihood Rights, Recasting citizenship for Development", Sage Publications India Pvt. Ltd, New Delhi, 2007.

Malhotra, Girish (2006) Public Administration, MurariLal and Sons, New Delhi.

Malik, A.S. (2006), "Rural Development Administration in India", in Surat Singh and Mohinder Singh, ed., *Rural Development in the 21st Century: A Multi-Dimensional Study*, New Delhi: Deep and Deep Publications Pvt. Ltd.

Mallon, Gerald P. and Peg Mccartt Hess (eds.) (2005). *Child Welfare for the Twenty-First Century: A Handbook of Practices, Policies and Programs.* New York: Columbia University Press.

Murlkiharan, Rajlakshmi and Kaul, Vanita. (1993), 'Early Childhood Care and Education: Current Status and Problems', in "Human Development and Family Study in India', (Ed) by T.S. Sarswati and Baljeet Kaur, New Delhi: Sage Publicatwn.

Nair, Narayan and Bansal, R.D., "Evaluation of Integrated Child Development Service Scheme" M.D. thesis. Department of Preventive and Social Medicine, Jawaharlal Institute of Post Graduate Medical Education and Research, Pondicheary, New Delhi: NIPCCID,

Pandya, Remeshwari (2008), ed., *Women Welfare and Empowerment in India - Vision for 21st Century*. New Delhi: New Century Publications.

Rai, Rahul, "Human Rights and Fundamental Freedom", Authors Press Publishers, New Delhi, 2004.

Rajan, Nalini, "Democracy and The Limits of Minority Rights", Sage Publications India Pvt. Ltd., New Delhi, 2002.

Reddy, D. Channa (2007) "ChildLabour: A Challenge to the Nation", *Rural Development and Empowerment of Weaker Sections – Practice, Promotion and Programmes*, New Delhi: The Associated Publishers.

Roa, P.S.S., Prasad, K.R. and Indira Bai, K. (1982), "A Study of Leprosy among Urban and Rural School Children" *Leprosy in India*, 54(1).

Robbins, Stephen P., Judge, Timothy A. and Sanghi, Seema (2008), Organizational Behavior, Pearson Prentice Hall, dorling Kindersley (India) Pvt. Ltd.

Roy, Kalpana (2000), Women and Child Development, Commonwealth New Delhi: Publishers.

Sachdeva, D.R (1995), *Social Welfare Administration in India*, New Delhi: Kitab Mahal.

Sears, R.R. (1957) "Identification as a Form of Behavioural Development", Ed. book by D.B.Harris, *The Concept of Development*, University of Minnesota Press.

Sekaran, Uma (2004), Organizational Behaviour: Text and Cases (2nd ed.), Tata McGraw Hill Publishing Company Ltd., New Delhi.

Sekaran, Uma (2004), *Organizational Behaviour: Text and Cases (2nd ed.)* New Delhi: Tata McGraw Hill Publishing Company Ltd.

Sharma, K.C (December 1992). 'Variations in the levels of living in Himachal Pradesh - An Empirical investigation", *Social Change*, 22(4).

Sharma, L.R. (1987), The Economy of Himachal Pradesh: Growth and Structure: A Study in Development Performance, Mittal Publications, New Delhi.

Singh, MianGoverdhan (1999), *Wooden Temples of Himachal Pradesh*, Indus Publishing Company, New Delhi.

Singh, MianGoverdhan (1999), Wooden Temples of Himachal Pradesh, Indus Publishing Company, New Delhi.

Tandon, B.N. (April, 1980), "Evaluation of Health Care Planning with Special Reference to Integrated Child Development Services", *National Conference on Evaluation of Primary Health Care Programme*, New Delhi, ICMR.

Thakur, Laxam S. (1996), The Architectural Heritage of Himachal Pradesh: Origin and Development of Temple Styles, MunshiramManoharlal Publishers, New Delhi.

Tiwari, A.K. (2007), Spatial Dimension of Socio-Economic Development: A Case Study of Himachal Pradesh, Kanishka Publishers and Distributors, New Delhi.

Trivedi, K.D. (1999), Organization and Administrative Theories, Research Publication, Jaipur.

Vivek Adhish, S., Zaheer, M., and Sidhiqui, A. O., (1985) "Acceptability and Impact of Various Components of ICDS Scheme in Different Socio-Economic Groups", NIPCCID, 1995.

Wignaraja, Poona (1997), *Women Poverty and Resources*, New Delhi: Sage Publications India Pvt. Ltd.

Journal and Article

Acharya, Akash and Paul, Mcnamee (September, 2009), "In Name of Child", Economic and Political Weekly, Vol. XLIV, No. 38.

Aguayo, Victor; Singh, Gayatri and Badgaiyan, Nina (April 5, 2014). "Scoring Child Nutrition in India: Measuring the Performance of States", *Economic & Political Weekly*. XLIX (14).

Aradhna (June, 2006), "Checking Child Abuse", Diviner, Vol. 3, No. 1.

Arokiasamy, Perianayagam, Goli, Srinivas (October 20, 2012). "Explaining the Skewed Child Sex Ratio in Rural India Revisiting the Landholding-Patriarchy Hypothesis". *Economic and Political* Weekly. XLVII(42).

Chandra, Suman K. and Reddy, V. Gang (2007), Segmented labour Market for Children- Is it a demand side Creation? A case Study of Industry in Makapur.

Chatterjee, Mirai (August -September 2006), "Decentralized Children Services", Economic and Political Weekly, Vol. 41, No. 34.

Chatterjee, Mirai (August–September 2006), "Decentralized Children Services", *Economic and Political Weekly*, 41(34).

Chinmayee, Satpathy (November, 2012), "Child Welfare Policies And Programmes In India", *Yojana.*

Chowdhury, Renuka (2006). "ICDS: India's Response to Early Child Development", *Yojana.* 50(11).

Gairola, Yogesh and Chauhan, Amita (January - March, 2009), Think India Quarterly, Vol. 12, No. 1.

Gautam, Manjulika (November, 2006), "Chile Development in India", YojnaVol.7

Government of India (2006), *Report of the Working Group on Empowerment of Women for the XI Plan*, Ministry of Women and Child Development.

Government of India (2012), *Children in India 2012- A Statistical Appraisal*, Social Statistics Division, Statistics Office, Ministry of Statistics and Programme Implementation, New Delhi

Gragnolati, Michele; Bredenkamp, Caryn; Gupta, Monica Das; Lee,Yi-Kyoung and Shekar, Meera (March 25, 2006). "ICDS and Persistent Undernutrition Strategies to Enhance the Impact". *Economic and Political Weekly*. XLI(12).

Gupta, Arun and Rohde, Jon E. Infant and Young Child under Nutrition, Economic and Political weekly, Vol. 29, No. 49, Mumbai.

Gupta, Arun and Rohde, Jon E., "Infant and Young Child under Nutrition", *Economic and Political weekly*, 29(49).

Gupta, J.R., Manchanda, V.K., Juyal, R.K., and Joshi, C.B. (1978)."Integrated Child Developn^nt Services Scheme: A Study of its Health Component in a Delhi Anganwari' *Indian Journal of Public Administration*, 25.

Gupta, S.B., Shrivastava, B.C., Bhushan, B.C. and Sharma, P. (1984), "Impact of Child Development Services ", Indian Journal of Medical Research.

Khera, Reetika (October 3, 2015). "Children's Development Baby Steps in Odisha". *Economic and Political Weekly*. 1 (40).

Khullar, Vandana (March, 1998). "Integrated Child Development Services: A Critique of Evaluation Techniques". *Economic and Political Weekly*. XXXIII(10).

Kukum Kumari Sharma (November, 2017) "A Study of the Impact of Socio-economic Status on the Nutritional of Pregnant Women in Patna". *Journal of Community Guidance & Research,* 34(3).

Kumar, Sanjeev and Banerjee, Sainath (January-March, 2015), "Integrated Child Development Services (ICDS) Programme in the Context of Urban Poor and Slum Dwellers in India: Exploring Challenges and Opportunities" in *The Indian Journal of Public Administration,* Vol. LXI, No. 1, New Delhi: Indian Institute of Public Administration.

Lai, Sunder, (1986), "Problem of Malnutrition in Pre-school Children in Rural Areas of Himachal Pradesh, Himachal Health Journal, 1(X39), 1979, pp. 13-15.

Lai, Sunder. (1979), "Child Bangles for Screening of Severely Malnourished Children", *Indian Journal of Preventive Medicine and Social Medicine,* 10(1).

Mehrotra, Santosh (March 2006), "Child Malnurition and Gender Discrimination in South Asia", Economic and Political Weekly, Vol. XLI, No. 10.

Mehrotra, Santosh (March 2006), "Child Malnutrition and Gender Discrimination in South Asia", *Economic and Political Weekly,* XLI (10).

Mishra, Meera (February, 2016), "Reducing malnutrition: Women's health holds the key", *Yojana,* Vol. 60, New Delhi: Ministry of Information and Broadcasting.

Mishra, Rajesh (February, 2017), Determinants of Child Malnutrition in Tribal Areas of Madhya Pradesh, *Economic & Political Weekly.* LII (5).

MoatulaAo, HemkhothangLhungdim (February 8, 2014). "Re-Estimating Malnourishment and Inequality among Children in North-east India". *Economic and Political* Weekly. XLIX (6).

Naik, Dinesh P. and Deore, R.A. (February, 2009), "In the Name of Child", Indian Journal of Psychology and Mental Health, Vol. 3, No. 4.

Nayak, Nandini and Saxena, Naresh C (August 26, 2006). "Implementation of ICDS in Bihar and Jharkhand". *Economic and Political Weekly*.XLI(34).

Ray, Ranjan (February, 2014), "Child Health in India: Some Inconvenient Facts", in *Yojana*, Vol. 58, New Delhi: Ministry of Information and Broadcasting.

Sampagar, Abhilasha, Lakhakar, Bhavana, Bafna, Tanvi and Niranjan, S. Mahantashetti (June, 2018), "A Study to assess the factors associated with development delay and nutritional status among the children with cleft lip and/or cleft palate". *Indian Journal of Child Health.*

Satpathy, C Hinmayee (2012), Children Policies and Programmes in India, *Yojana* Journal.

Sinha, Deepa (August-September, 2006), "Rethinking ICDS: A Right based Perspective", Economic and Political Weekly, Vol. 41, No. 34.

Srinivasan, Sharda and Bedi, S. Arjun (November-December 2009), "Girl Child Protection Scheme in Tamil Nadu", Economics and Political Weekly, Vol. XLIV, No. 48.

Vasudeva, Y.L. and Lai, Sunder (1979), "Health and Nutrition Education at Frontline by Anganwari Workers and ANMs in Integrated Child Development Services Block Kathura", *Haryana Health Journal*, 10(39).

Government Documents

Department of Economics and Statistics (2011), Economic Survey 2010-11, Government of Himachal Pradesh, Shimla.

Department of Economics and Statistics (2012), Economic Survey 2011-12, Government of Himachal Pradesh, Shimla.

Department of Statistics and Economics (2013), Economic Survey 2012-13, Government of Himachal Pradesh, Shimla.

Department of Economics and Statistics (2016), Brief Facts: Himachal Pradesh 2015-16, Government of Himachal Pradesh, Shimla.

Directorate of Census Operations, Census of India 2011: Provisional Population Totals, Paper 1 of 2011 Himachal Pradesh Series-3, Government of Himachal Pradesh, Shimla.

Directorate of Women and Child Development (2014). *Annual Administrative Report 2013-14.* Shimla: Department of Social Justice and Empowerment, Government of Himachal Pradesh.

Directory of ICDS projects in India, Department of Women and Child, evelopment, Ministry of Human Resource Development, Government of India, New Delhi.

Economics and Statistics Department (2013), Economic Survey of Himachal Pradesh 2012-13, Government of Himachal Pradesh, Shimla.

Economics and Statistics Department (2015), *Economic Survey 2014-15*, Government of Himachal Pradesh, Shimla.

Economics and Statistics Department (2016), *Economic Survey 2015-16*, Government of Himachal Pradesh, Shimla.

Government of India (2012), Children in India 2012- A Statistical Appraisal, Social Statistics Division, Statistics Office, Ministry of Statistics and Programme Implementation, New Delhi.

Gupta, Monica Das; Lokshin, Michael; Gragnolati, Michele and Ivaschenko, OleksiyImproving Child Nutrition Outcomes in India: Can the Integrated Child Development Services Program Be More Effective? (June 2005). World Bank Policy Research Paper No. 3647.

Himachal in Figures 2010-11, Department of Economics and Statistics, Government of Himachal Pradesh, Shimla.

International Institute for Population Sciences (IIPS) and Macro International (2007), National Family Health Survey (NFHS-3), 2005–06: India: VolumeI. Mumbai: IIPS

Ministry of Women and Child Development. *Five Year Strategic Plan (2011-2016)*, New Delhi: Government of India.

Ministry of Women and Child Development. *Annual Report 2016-17,* New Delhi: Government of India.

National Council of Applied Economic Research (NCAER) 2001. "Concurrent Evaluation of Integrated Child Development Services, 1998", National Report, volume 1, New Delhi.

National Institute of Public Cooperation and Child Development (NIPCCD) 2006. "National Evaluation of Integrated Child Development Services", New Delhi

Planning Commission (2005), Himachal Pradesh Development Report, Government of India, Academic Foundation, New Delhi.

Planning Commission (2009) Evaluation Report on Integrated Child Development Scheme (ICDS) Jammu and Kashmir, Programme Evaluation Organization, Government of India, New Delhi.

Planning Department (2010), Draft Annual Plan 2010-11, Government of Himachal Pradesh, Shimla.

Planning Department (2012), Draft 12th Five Year Plan 2012-17 and Annual Plan 2013-14, Government of Himachal Pradesh, Shimla.

Programme Evaluation Organization (2011), Evaluation Report on Integrated Child Development Services Volume I & II, Planning Commission, Government of India, New Delhi.

Programme Evaluation Organization (2015), *A Quick Evaluation Study of Anganwadis under ICDS,* NitiAyog, Government of India.

Websites

www.cry.org/resources/.../Children_In_Indias_FiveYear Plans_2013.pdf.

http://www.indiahimachalpradesh.com/ shimla/mashobra-shimla.html

http://himachal.nic.in/economics

http://www.performance.gov.in/

http://en.wikipedia.org/wiki/Mashobra.

http://himachal.nic.in

http://wcd.nic.in/icds.htm

http://www.india.gov.in/knowindia/state_uts.php

http://www.performance.gov.in

http://www.preservearticles.com

http://www.wcd.nic.in/icds.htm

http://hpwcd.blogspot.in

http://www.azadindia.org/social-issues/status-of-children. html

http http://wcd.nic.in/icds.htm

http://himachal.nic.in/economics/REPORTS/sml_block_indicator2010.pdf

http://en.wikipedia.org

http://en.wikipedia.org/wiki/Mashobra.

http://himachal.nic.in

http://www.performance.gov.in/sites/default/files/ document/states/Himachal

http://www.india.gov.in/knowindia/state_uts.php?id=10.

http://www.performance.gov.in/sites

http://www.preservearticles.comwrite-a-short-essay-on-the-social-welfare-in-india.html

https://himachal.nic.in

http://www.wcd.nic.in/icds.htm

http://www.indiahimachalpradesh.com/ shimla/mashobra-shimla.html

http://hpwcd.blogspot.in

http://www.azadindia.org/social-issues/status-of-children.html

http://pib.nic.in/newsite/erelease.aspx.

https://icds-wcd.nic.in.

https://himachal.gov.in.

https://anganwadirecruitment.in/hp-anganwadi-latest-notification.

https://www.hindexam.in/himachal-pradesh-anganwadi-bharti/14800.html

https://icds-wcd.nic.in/icdsimg/snrules2017.pdf

https://www.indiastat.com/social-and-welfare-schemes-data/27/child-schemes.

http://edistrict.hp.gov.in/

https://www.indeed.co.in

https://www.thehindubusinessline.com

https://pib.nic.in/newsite/erelease.aspx

httpshttps://www.wisdomjobs.com/himachal-pradesh-state-council-for-child-welfare://himachalrajbhavan.nic.in/child_welfare.html

http://www.wcd.nic.in/sites/default/files/SANCTIO2018.pdftps://hphamirpur.nic.in

http://www.sociologyguide.com/census/scheduled-tribe-population.php

http://www.tribal.nic.in/index2.asp?sublinkid=522&langid=1